ROUTLEDGE LIBRARY EDITIONS:
CHINA UNDER MAO

I0125092

Volume 6

CHINESE MARXISM IN FLUX
1978–84

CHINESE MARXISM IN FLUX 1978–84

Essays on Epistemology, Ideology and Political Economy

Edited by
BILL BRUGGER

Routledge
Taylor & Francis Group

LONDON AND NEW YORK

First published in 1985 by Croom Helm Ltd

This edition first published in 2019
by Routledge
2 Park Square, Milton Park, Abingdon, Oxon OX14 4RN

and by Routledge
711 Third Avenue, New York, NY 10017

Routledge is an imprint of the Taylor & Francis Group, an informa business

British Library Cataloguing in Publication Data
A catalogue record for this book is available from the British Library

ISBN: 978-1-138-32344-5 (Set)
ISBN: 978-0-429-43659-8 (Set) (ebk)
ISBN: 978-1-138-34101-2 (Volume 6) (hbk)
ISBN: 978-1-138-34104-3 (Volume 6) (pbk)
ISBN: 978-0-429-44043-4 (Volume 6) (ebk)

Publisher's Note
The publisher has gone to great lengths to ensure the quality of this reprint but
points out that some imperfections in the original copies may be apparent.

Disclaimer
The publisher has made every effort to trace copyright holders and would welcome
correspondence from those they have been unable to trace.

Chinese Marxism in Flux 1978-84

Essays on Epistemology, Ideology and Political Economy

Edited by BILL BRUGGER

CROOM HELM
London & Sydney

©1985 Bill Brugger
Croom Helm Ltd, Provident House, Burrell Row,
Beckenham, Kent BR3 1AT
Croom Helm Australia Pty Ltd, First Floor,
139 King Street, Sydney, NSW 2001, Australia

British Library Cataloguing in Publication Data

Chinese Marxism in flux 1978-84: essay on
    epistemology, ideology and political economy.
    1. Communism—China
    I. Brugger, Bill
    335.43'45   HX387
    ISBN 0-7099-3902-7

Printed and bound in Great Britain by
Biddles Ltd, Guildford and King's Lynn

CONTENTS

List of Tables.   vi

Acknowledgements.   vii

Abbreviations.   viii

Introduction.   1

Chapter 1.   Marxist Theory and Socialist   13
             Transition: The Construction of an
             Epistemological Relation -
             Michael Dutton and Paul Healy

Chapter 2.   C.C.P. Ideology Since the Third Plenum -   67
             Michael Sullivan

Chapter 3.   Undeveloped Socialism and Intensive   98
             Development - Bill Brugger

Chapter 4.   Economic Reform, Legitimacy, Efficiency   119
             and Rationality - Kate Hannan

Chapter 5.   The Socialist Transition and the Socialist   142
             Mode of Production - Greg McCarthy

Chapter 6.   The Law of the Value Debate - A Tribute   171
             to the late Sun Yefang - Steve Reglar

Bibliography.   204

Index.   215

LIST OF TABLES

2.1 Class Struggle Before and After the   83
    Transformation of the System of Ownership.

2.2 Policies and Deviations.   88

3.1 Accumulation and Investment by Five Year 109
    Plan.

3.2. Growth in Productivity.   116

3.3 Growth in Productivity by Industry.   116

ACKNOWLEDGEMENTS

The original ideas behind this book took shape at a panel session at the Fourth Conference of the Asian Studies of Australia, Melbourne, 1982. The panel was organised by Colin Mackerras. Colin's advice and inspiration have guided many of the chapters through various revisions. Thanks are due to all the contributors to that panel and to a similar panel at the Fifth Conference in Adelaide, 1984. Versions of Chapters Three and Six and part of Chapter Four were presented at the Conference 'New Directions in the Social Sciences and Humanities in China', Adelaide, 1984. Thanks are due to the participants at that conference. Typing and word processing were undertaken by the secretarial staffs of the Politics Department at Adelaide University, the Politics Discipline at Flinders University and the School of Modern Asian Studies, Griffith University. Particular thanks are due to Pauline Mulberry, Rae Tyler and Anne Gabb. I am grateful also to Elizabeth Neil who solved many technological problems in the course of word processing and to Rhett Marlowe who assisted with editorial work.

Bill Brugger,
The Flinders University of South Australia,

ABBREVIATIONS

ANU.	Australian National University
APC.	Agricultural Producer Co-operative
BR.	Beijing Review (formerly Peking Review)
BFLP.	Beijing Foreign Languages Press (formerly PFLP.)
CC.	Central Committee
CCP.	Chinese Communist Party
CPSU.	Communist Party of the Soviet Union
CW.	Collected Works
FBIS.	Foreign Broadcast Information Service
FFYP.	First Five Year Plan
GMRB.	Guangming Ribao
JPRS.	Joint Publications Research Service
NPC.	National People's Congress
PFLP.	Peking Foreign Languages Press (formerly BFLP)
PLA.	People's Liberation Army
PR.	Peking Review
RMRB.	Renmin Ribao
SCMM.	Selections from China Mainland Magazines, (later SPRCM.)
SCMP.	Survey of China Mainland Press, (later SPRCP.)
SPRCM.	Selections from the People's Republic of China Magazines (formerly SCMM.)
SPRCP.	Survey of the People's Republic of China Press (formerly SCMP.)
SW.	Selected Works
SWB.	Summary of World Broadcasts, (British Broadcasting Corporation), Pt. 3, The Far East
USA.	United States of America
USSR.	Union of the Soviet Socialist Republics

INTRODUCTION

In societies which call themselves 'socialist', Marxism is, on the one hand, a <u>method</u> for understanding and changing social life and, on the other, an <u>ideology</u> which rationalises the interests of those in power. In this, it is no different from any other system of thought. It has, however, long been the central concern of political theory to disentangle the ideological from other elements; and Marxism itself offers a fruitful way of doing just that. This point needs to be stressed because of the renewed tendency in China studies to dismiss all Chinese official thought as ideological rationalisation, and the emphasis in current studies to seek some 'real world' which dispenses with Marxist categories. Whilst rejecting official Chinese statements as 'ideological', 'the real world' analysts paradoxically are only too eager to scan such statements for elements which reinforce their non-Marxist view of the world.

Such real world analysts are caught in the same methodological-ideological bind as official Chinese Marxists. On the one hand, they may offer us insights into social relationships obscured in official rhetoric. Yet, on the other hand, they offer rationalisations of the interests of those who oppose the whole socialist project. Take, for example, those studies which, in rejecting Marxist 'ideology', seek 'reality' in individuals maximising their utilities. Taken as axiomatic is the notion of the atomised individual whose appetites are restrained either by market forces or the external legal system. Analysts of this persuasion take solace in Chinese jokes to the effect that the selfless model, Lei Feng, was really an 'ultra-leftist' because he failed to see the intrinsic value of the individual. They rejoice in the Chinese return to a 'realist' conception of law which allows for the individual to make predictions about the utility-maximising outcomes of behaviour and to a more 'realistic' economic structure which equates material reward more with individual effort. When challenged, they demand that one consult Chinese people themselves about the nature of 'real benefits'. The axiom about the atomised individual is joined to the axiom that people know what is in their best interests, or perhaps that people's opinions are more 'real' than the interplay of social forces.

There is a tendency, therefore, for many Western analysts to use the notion 'the real world' for ideological purposes. The same applies to many analysts in China who use the category 'real' to denounce the 'utopianism' associated with the 'Gang of Four'. Most contributors to this volume agree that the result is an official ideology which is more sterile than that which it superseded and just as, if not more, incoherent. On the other hand, the official denunciation of 'utopianism' has been accompanied by an official denunciation of 'dogmatism'. This has allowed large numbers of non-official Marxist academics to explore the Western Marxist renaissance of the 1960s, the literature critical of

Marxism-Leninism under Stalin and the vigorous debates on development in the Soviet Union of the 1920s. In academic circles, the atmosphere is freer and more exciting than it has been in the Soviet Union for some sixty years. Writers and activists such as Luxemburg, Bukharin, Preobrazhensky and Gramsci are now the subject of lively and open debate. It is even possible to discuss the writings of the early Marx and to speculate on the applicability of the 'Asiatic Mode of Production' to China. It is surely to be hoped that these vigorous debates will spill over into official Party formulations. But there are little signs of this as yet, and the campaign in 1983 against 'spiritual pollution' does not give much cause for hope.

The discussions in this book mostly agree with the comments of Su Shaozhi, the Director of the Institute of Marxism-Leninism and Mao Zedong Thought of the Chinese Academy of Social Sciences,

> Certain aspects of our theoretical work...still revolve around some 'antiques', concerning themselves, as before, with some abstract conclusions which are divorced from real life and thus appear shrivelled and pallid.(1)

But few would agree with Su's instrumentalist position that such should be combated because,

> it provides a sanctuary and hotbed for the 'left' ideology and offers an ideological ground, on the basis of which exponents...can censure the current reforms.(2)

Some contributors to this volume are quite sympathetic to aspects of the 'left' thinking of previous years, even though they would not support its ideological use to preserve the dominance of certain groups. They would not endorse the ideological defence of Marxist studies purely to safeguard economic reforms. On the contrary, they argue that Marxist methodology may be precisely what is needed to evaluate and, in some respects, criticise those reforms. Whilst affirming that Marxism should be rooted in reality, they condemn the use of the 'real' for ideological purposes.

How is it that the concept 'real' has been pressed into the service of ideological rationalisation? At the root of the problem is the inconsistent use of the term 'real' in the Marxist tradition and inconsistent views on how one comes to understand it. There is no unified Marxist epistemology. Empiricist and rationalist strands of thought have co-mingled ever since the time of Marx. In the first chapter, Dutton and Healy try to make sense of these strands, using Althusserian concepts but developing a position which goes beyond

---

1.   Su Shaozhi, Su et.al., 1983, p. 43.
2.   Ibid.

Althusser and is, to a degree, critical of Althusser's rationalism. Their thesis is that there has been a general trend in Marxism-Leninism from a more rationalist position in Marx to a more empiricist position in Stalin. Mao Zedong, they argue, never broke from Stalin's empiricism. Nor indeed does official Marxism after Mao.

Rationalism here is taken as an approach which posits a disjunction between the 'real in thought' and the 'real-concrete' and adopts the former as its object of study; it thus elevates theory to a privileged position. Empiricism, on the other hand, focusses on the latter, taking theory only as generalisations which in principle may always be reduced to perceptions of that 'real-concrete'. Both positions, it is argued, are inescapably dogmatic. Why, Dutton and Healy ask, should ontological privilege be given either to theory or to the real-concrete? In both approaches there is an inevitable tendency towards reductionism. By reductionism, Dutton and Healy mean not simply the tendency to reduce all perceptions to theory or all theory to perceptions but the assignation of ontological priority to what Althusser calls an 'instance' - the economic instance, the political instance or the ideological instance. Mao's empiricism differed from that of Stalin in his tendency to accord ontological privilege to the political rather than the economic, but he was no less reductionist. Stalin tended to a position where the political and the ideological could simply be read off the economic. Mao inverted this, believing more and more that the economic and the ideological could simply be read off the political. He was empiricist in that, in his methodology, there was no notion of 'theoretical practice'. Mao's famous 'leap' from perceptual to rational knowledge was simply no more than the summation and generalisation of previous experience. Laws (guilu) were no more than observed regularities.

The present position in official Chinese Marxism, according to Dutton and Healy, is simply a return to the empiricism of Stalin. The economic is once again privileged and class struggle is collapsed into the economic instance. The empiricism of current official Marxism is much more rigorous than that of Mao, as is manifest in its insistence on adhering to 'objective economic laws' which can be read off by an 'all-knowing subject' located in the labour process. The same methodological errors, however, are still being committed.

Dutton and Healy argue that Mao's approach to Marxist epistemology did not constitute an advance on that of Stalin; he merely reversed the 'privileged site' to which knowledge of society might be reduced. This process of reversal has now occurred once again. If it is not in the field of epistemology, then where does Mao's contribution to Marxist theory lie? Sullivan, in Chapter Two, suggests that it might lie in the conception of socialism as process rather than a system. This is an argument which I have developed elsewhere, noting that the notion of socialism as a system or a discrete mode of production owes much to Stalin's formulation of 1936.(3) Stalin's notion of socialism, 'basically' attained at that time, had more in common with Weber's 'ideal type'. This position was reaffirmed in China at the time of the Eighth Party Congress when the principal contradiction in society (zhuyao maodun) was defined not in terms of class but as that between the 'advanced socialist system' and the 'backward productive forces'. This formulation implied that the basic contradiction (jiben maodun) in society, between the relations of production and the productive forces and between base and superstructure, had been resolved. In the years which followed, Mao was gradually to move away from that position to develop the view that the basic contradiction in society had not been resolved and the principal contradiction was still a matter of class struggle. This led to what I have called elsewhere the 'generative view of class' which was an important element in Mao's thinking which led up to the Cultural Revolution.(4)

The theory of 'continuing the revolution under the dictatorship of the proletariat', which developed and held sway from 1966-1976, was gradually dismantled after the fall of the 'Gang of Four'; and in 1979 attempts were made to return to the line of the Eighth Party Congress. Sullivan points out, however, that the line of the Eighth Party Congress could never be fully rehabilitated. What could be maintained out of the 1956 formulation was the idea of socialism as a 'system'. This led to a functionalist reading of Mao's famous revised edition of the speech 'On the Correct Handling of Contradictions among the People'. The slide into a functionalist totality has occurred several times in the Marxist-Leninist tradition and results from an ambiguity in Marx concerning the nature of the totality which he urged social scientists to focus on.

For Georgy Lukács, it was the concept of totality which defined the Marxist method,

> It is not the primacy of economic motives in historical explanation that constitutes the decisive difference between Marxism and bourgeois thought, but the point of view of the totality...the all pervasive supremacy of the whole over the parts...Proletarian science is revolutionary not just by virtue of its revolutionary ideas...opposed to bourgeois society, but above all because of its method.

---

3.   Brugger, 1981(b).
4.   Brugger, 1978, pp. 20-7.

> The primacy of the category of totality is the bearer of
> the principle of revolution in science.(5)

Lukács went on to argue that, if all the specific propositions of
Marxism were to fall, Marxism would still be useful because of its
totalising method. Such an approach has been criticised by
Althusserians and others on the grounds that Lukács advocated an
'expressive totality', stemming from some ontologically-privileged
principle of organisation (Feuerbachian humanism). They stress, in the
later Marx, what they call a 'decentred totality' where no ontological
privilege may be discerned. They do this, however, within a rationalist
framework which is itself ontologically privileged. But once one
attempts to conceive of a decentred totality within an empiricist
framework, then there is an inevitable slide towards functionalism.
This is precisely what has happened in China where discussions of
relationships within the 'socialist system' resemble Western-style
functional analysis. One may, indeed, recast Chinese comments to the
effect that the Great Leap Forward violated the 'law of planned and
proportionate development' in such a way that the Great Leap is seen
as generating multiple disfunctions. Indeed, Mao Zedong is probably
turning in his grave at the thought that his concept 'non-antagonistic
contradiction' may be treated simply as 'disfunction'.

Though the functionalist reading of socialism as a 'system' has
been retained, there are features of the Eighth Party Congress
Programme which have not. A major problem surrounds the notion that
the socialist system, which supposedly came into being in 1956, was
'advanced'. Looked at from the perspective of the relations of
production, it is argued that it was 'too advanced'; that is to say
changes in the relations of production were promoted at a speed
incommensurate with the development of the productive forces. This
affected profoundly the basic contradiction (between the relations and
forces of production) which supposedly had been resolved. Sullivan
points out that this recent formulation was prefigured by Chen Yun at
the Eighth Party Congress itself. The task in the 1980s, therefore, is
no longer seen as bringing the level of the productive forces up to the
requirements of the 'advanced system'; this had been the source of
disastrous 'leftism' in previous years. Rather, the socialist system
should be modified and for the time being, made more 'backward'. It is
better, therefore, not to talk of a contradiction between an advanced
socialist system and backward productive forces but to posit two
moments of socialism, one undeveloped and one advanced, and each
requiring different configurations of forces and relations of
production. So now we have two 'ideal types' instead of one and twice
the theoretical problems. All the principal contradiction boils down to
now is the contradiction between aspiration and capability, or in the
official jargon 'between the people's demand for the building of an

---

5.   Lukács,(1923), 1971, p. 27; italics in original.

advanced industrial country and the realities of a backward agricultural country' or 'between the people's need for rapid economic and cultural development and the inability of our present economy and culture to meet that need'. Marxist methodology, it seems, has been reduced to arguments about 'relative deprivation'.

The above arguments are elaborated on in Chapter Three which explores the notion of undeveloped socialism. Such a concept, it seems, can only have meaning in terms of a notion of 'advanced socialism'. In contemporary Chinese accounts, this is usually no less than what Marx described as 'the first stage of communism', and differs considerably from the 'advanced socialism' which Soviet ideologists claim, came into existence in the Soviet Union in the 1970s. I argue in Chapter Three that different views exist about the operation of the law of value in each of these two kinds of 'socialism'. These views are diametrically opposed - one holding that the law of value operates more perfectly under advanced socialism than undeveloped socialism and one which holds that it is more perfectly restricted. My main concern, however, is with what Stalin called 'the law of planned and proportionate development'. This is not a law but a formula which, if it is to make any objective sense, requires some order of determination. Chinese planners, it seems, oscillate between two approaches. On the one hand, they resort to the old formula of the 'geneticists' of the Soviet Union who, in the 1920s, argued that the economy was determined by its 'weakest link' (agriculture). Such is the argument that the 'system' of 1956 was 'too advanced'. On the other hand, Chinese planners operate with material balances which are defined only in terms of each other. Here one is presented with a functionalist totality in which the efficient operation of an existing system becomes its own <u>telos</u>. Adherents to the revised genetic view tend to argue that market relations are necessary so long as the agricultural sector is undeveloped; whilst those preoccupied with material balance planning tend to argue that they will always be necessary so long as the information available to the planner is incomplete. The first view has led to a partial restoration of capitalism in agriculture, whilst the second view has led to the adoption of mathematical models which talk about the productivity of <u>all</u> inputs and so contradict the labour theory of value.

To make sense of the notions of undeveloped socialism and advanced socialism, it is argued, one needs a full explication of two other concepts used by socialist political economists in other countries - extensive and intensive development. Such economists use both linear and cyclical models which have to be related to a theory of stages of development. In China, however, discussions of intensive and extensive development tend to be carried on outside any theory of stages. This ahistorical approach is very different from what is normally considered to be Marxist methodology. Systems theory and history have always been uneasy bedfellows.

Systems theory, one must stress, is profoundly unteleological. Though Althusserians would deny it, there is a powerful teleological element in Marxism. Indeed, the claim to legitimacy put forward by Communist Parties has usually been based on such a Party's knowledge of the communist telos. This question of legitimacy is raised by Hannan in Chapter Four. She notes a switch in what Max Weber calls the Party's appeal to substantive rationality (or rationality oriented towards values or teleological considerations). The legitimation crisis faced by the Chinese Communist Party, after years of confusion, has resulted in the abandonment of normative appeals or coercive appeals to carry out class struggle in favour of simple remunerative appeals. Delivering the goods through modernisation has become the new telos, and this provides the basis for a new rationality. Normally, however, when the C.C.P. talks about rationality, it means that which Weber called 'formal' or which Hannan, following Habermas, calls 'purposive'.

The most important end to be pursued, it seems, is economic efficiency. But what is efficiency? Most economists define efficiency in terms of the relationship between inputs and outputs, or more broadly as the economical use of resources. Most sociologists go further than that and interpret efficiency as the attainment of a particular goal with the least possible detriment to other goals. This is not the same as formal rationality. For Weber, formal rationality was the adoption of means appropriate to ends within a set of rules. It is possible, therefore, to have a bureaucratic system which is highly rational but which is also very inefficient and, of course, vice versa. This is surely what Weber had in mind when he commented in 1909 that the rational German bureaucratic machine had achieved much less that the corrupt bureaucracies of France and America.(6) Could it be the case, therefore, that Chinese planners in their single-minded pursuit of efficiency might be contributing to bureaucratic irrationality? Or is it the case that the pursuit of bureaucratic rationality is contributing to new inefficiencies?

In the pursuit of efficiency, Chapter Four argues China's planners failed adequately to change the rules. They failed because the rationality of the system placed a higher premium on stability than on the simple attainment of economic results. At all costs, the instability of some countries in Eastern Europe had to be avoided. Consequently, China's planners were required to pursue the goal of efficiency without being given the means to do so - that is, a reform in the system of administratively-set prices. Thus, the reform proposals of 1978 were watered down and what Hannan calls a 'command economy' persists.

Lack of success in the reform proposals were not simply due to the pursuit of stability. There was a tendency in the bureaucratic system to use bureaucratic means to deal with inefficiencies created

6.   Albrow, p. 64.

8

Introduction

by the bureaucracy itself. The result could only be more bureaucratic problems.The question of bureaucracy is one that Marx dealt with most inadequately. Much could have been made of his suggestive comment in his 'Contribution to the Critique of Hegel's Philosophy of Right' that in a sense, bureaucrats come to own the state.(7) One may not just consign this statement to the category of 'immature thinking' still under the influence of Hegel. It is a thought which raises questions more profound than the much celebrated discussion of the state in 'The Eighteenth Brumaire of Louis Bonaparte'. It is this latter text which many Trotskyists use to criticise the excessive power of the state in the Soviet Union and China. They argue that in a situation where there is a relative balance between class forces, the state rises above civil society and the phenomenon of Bonapartism occurs. The Stalin phenomenon is seen as an example of such Bonapartism, though one is never sure as to the extent Trotskyists might want to apply that epithet to the Chinese version of the 'cult of personality'.

Regrettably, there is no Trotskyist contribution to this volume. Nor is there any representative of that school which talks about a 'state mode of production'. Most contributors, however, are very concerned about the growth of a state apparatus which shows no sign of either 'transcendence' (Aufhebung) or the very different Marxist formulation 'withering away' (Absterben). Any notion of a single transition process between capitalism and communism must address that question. Mao, who did try to see transition as a single process, rarely did; and apart from a few suggestive comments to the effect that rural communes contained 'the sprouts of communism', very few other Chinese Marxists did either. Indeed, as Sullivan notes, most official Chinese accounts, being variations on the model-building approach pioneered by Stalin in 1936, do not see transition as a single process at all. Stalin, it will be remembered, created a socialist mode of production, and the current notion of undeveloped socialism is a similar endeavour. Most of the authors in this volume reject that approach. McCarthy in Chapter Five, by contrast, though highly critical of Stalin and the present Chinese leadership, maintains that what is wrong with Marxism-Leninism is an inadequate theorisation of what, indeed, is a discrete mode of production. A mode of production is, after all, not merely a particular configuration of forces and relations of production but the way the surplus product of society is produced, extracted and distributed.

A few years' ago the Hungarian scholars Konrád and Szelényi, by combining the approaches of Marx, Weber and Polanyi, argued that socialist societies were not half-way stages between capitalism and communism but were governed by principles of integration

---

7.   Marx, (1843), Marx and Engels, CW., III, 1975, p.47.

fundamentally different from either.(8) Capitalism was governed by market integration. Communism was left untheorised but one may assume it was governed by a form of reciprocal integration (exchange of goods and services without the medium of money and market equivalents). Socialism, as it existed, was governed by what Polanyi called redistributive integration, where the surplus was sucked out of the producers by an élite and then redistributed according to that élite's view of rationality. The élite owed its legitimacy to its knowledge of a <u>telos</u> which happened to use Marxist categories. This intellectual élite was on the road to becoming a new class.

McCarthy's contribution to this volume in Chapter Five is set within a more orthodox Marxist framework than the work of Konrád and Szelényi, but his starting point is likewise the way the surplus is produced, extracted and distributed. He suggests that the socialist mode of production has transformed state leaders into a new ruling class, whilst transforming the classes of the old society into a more homogeneous labouring mass. The reforms set in motion since 1978 are not a restoration of capitalism, nor a necessary retreat in order to advance towards communism. They should be seen as the response of the socialist mode to an inability to develop a sufficient agricultural surplus. It is possible, he argues, that the household responsibility system will undermine the dominance of the socialist mode, but there are no signs of that happening as yet.

McCarthy's arguments about a socialist mode of production are rejected by Reglar in Chapter Six who argues that one of the major errors of the late economist Sun Yefang was his acceptance of the idea of a socialist mode of production (albeit vastly different from that of McCarthy). Reglar's assessment of Sun Yefang, however, is largely favourable. As such, Reglar opposes my arguments against the existence of 'objective economic laws', and supports the belief that one may direct planning according to the 'law of value'. Reglar also uses Sun's arguments to oppose what he sees as the 'distributionist' approach of Hannan in Chapter Four. If readers have not been convinced before, there will be no doubt by Chapter Six that this book has been produced in the spirit of 'letting a hundred schools of thought contend'.

There are, however, two aspects which unite most of the contributions to this volume. One, discussed earlier, is the constant stress on the <u>reality</u> of Marxist categories. The second is the importance given to the role of the state in all aspects of Chinese social life. Chapter One talks about the role of an official epistemology. Chapter Two notes the crucial importance of the 'correct ideological line'. Chapter Three discusses the limits imposed by official orthodoxy in political economic debate. Chapter Four argues that the rationality of a bureaucratic machine contradicts its

---

8.   Konrád and Szelényi, 1979.

own desire for efficiency. Chapter Five goes even further and argues that the state is central to the dynamics of a new mode of production and may not be expected to wither away. Chapter Six documents Sun's views on the role of the state in a socialist economy, which are unorthodox both from the Stalinist and the market socialist points of view. Current debates on the role of the state in China are more stimulating than they have been for decades. But the contributors to this book agree that the limits of official ideology are too tightly drawn.

Chapter Four talks about the official desire to harmonise the interests of the state, the economic unit and the individual. In reality, what is addressed is the relationship between the state and the economic unit, and between the economic unit and the individual, but not the relationship between the individual and the state. The relationship between the individual and the state is conventionally considered at a different level - as a legal question. But many citizens are alienated from the state in a way that few legal reforms are going to improve. Legal measures may enhance negative liberty (freedom from interference) but they do little to advance positive liberty (freedom to realise one's potential as the citizen of a new form of polis and as a co-operative producer). The need is to overcome alienation!

Alienation is a Marxist concept which has fared badly in orthodox Marxism-Leninism. Since Stalin's day, it has been considered to be, a residue of the early humanist Marx and tainted with idealism. Yet, since the publication of Marx's Economic and Philosophical Manuscripts some few decades ago, it has engaged the attention of scholars in socialist countries and, in a few cases, has even been discussed in the official Party press. Such was the case in Czechoslovakia in 1968 and for a brief moment, was the case in China in 1983. Between 1978 and 1983, it was estimated that some 600 articles on alienation appeared in Chinese journals and newspapers. It was not until early 1983, however, that the veteran philosopher Zhou Yang's speech on the hundredth anniversary of the death of Marx brought the issue to the fore in the C.C.P. Central Committee newspaper Renmin Ribao. Even then, it was published only after several members of the leadership tried to get the discussion confined to academic journals. In his published speech, Zhou modified, and in some ways reversed, the position he had taken against humanism in 1963. He noted that an official denunciation of Marxist humanism had served to legitimise inhuman activity in the Cultural Revolution. There was a need, he felt, to come to grips with the humanist element in Marxism and to use its central concepts, such as alienation, in an analysis of socialist society,

> Socialist society is immensely superior to capitalist society but that is not to say that there is no alienation at all in socialist society. In the past we did many stupid things in economic construction owing to lack of experience and our failure to understand socialist

construction - that realm of necessity; we were bound to suffer the consequences; this was alienation in the economic field. Because democracy and the legal system were unsound, public servants sometimes made indiscriminate use of the power conferred upon them by the people and became their masters; this was alienation in the political field, or alienation of power. As for alienation in the ideological field, it was typified in the cult of personality. This has certain similarities with the religious alienation denounced by Feuerbach.(9)

For publishing Zhou Yang's views, some senior editorial staff of <u>Renmin Ribao</u> were transferred from their posts, including the deputy editor in chief, Wang Ruoshi, who was himself an authority on alienation. By the autumn of 1983, a full-scale movement was under way to refute the idea that alienation might exist under socialism, the lead being taken by Wang Zhen, the Head of the Central Party School, and Deng Liqun, Director of the Propaganda Department of the Party Central Committee. It culminated with a long speech by the veteran Party historian, Hu Qiaomu, in January 1984.(10)

I have discussed elsewhere the content of the denunciations.(11) They boiled down to the argument that economic alienation could not exist because there was no exploitation, since workers owned the means of production. Bureaucratism, moreover, should not be confused with alienation of power, because to do so would blur the line of demarcation between capitalism and socialism. Finally, one should not talk about ideological alienation as if it were the same as the alienation which Feuerbach noted in the case of religion; in socialist society, apparently, there was no ideological equivalent of religion because religion did not have to fulfil the same instrumental role as opiate.

The speciousness of the above refutation is obvious. What is to the point, however, is that the use of arguments about alienation from what is termed the 'right', hark back to the arguments of the 'left' associated with the late Mao Zedong and the 'Gang of Four'. Mao and the 'Gang's' discussion of 'continuous revolution' rested precisely on the belief that a simple change of legal ownership did not end exploitation and that there was no hard and fast dividing line between socialism and capitalism. Instead of being a model, it will be remembered, socialism was seen as a process which could be reversible. Though Mao and the 'Gang of Four' would denounce any use of the concept 'alienation', they could be seen as arguing much the same sort of thing. This point was

---

9.   RMRB., 16 March 1983, p. 5.
10. Hu Qiaomu, RMRB., 27 January 1984 pp. 1-3.
11. Brugger, 1984(a).

quite apparent to those theorists who denounced the use of the term because it might destabilise the consciousness of the masses.(12)

Though the 'Gang of Four' would probably disagree on the religious aspects of the cult of personality, it would also probably disagree with the arid functionalism from which the instrumentalist view derives. Indeed, even present official ideologists depart from the functionalist view in taking seriously the feudal symbolism which manifested itself in the Cultural Revolution.

In my view, the current official attacks on those who seek to use the early Marx in a critique of socialist society constitute a serious setback in the revival of Marxism in China. It is unlikely, therefore, that the pertinent and insightful use of Rosa Luxemburg's criticisms of Lenin to chart a new method of Party leadership(13) will ever obtain official endorsement. A tendency has developed, once again, to replace the critical dimension of Marxism by the ideological. In this, Marxism may be seen as actually playing a role in furthering ideological alienation. This is the point with which I began this Introduction.

---

12.   Chen Ruisheng and Xu Xiaoying, <u>GMRB</u>., 3 December 1983, p. 3.
13.   Cheng, 1983.

Chapter 1

MARXIST THEORY AND SOCIALIST TRANSITION: THE CONSTRUCTION OF AN EPISTEMOLOGICAL RELATION

Michael Dutton and Paul Healy

This chapter is a work of theory, and as such flies in the face of most of the presently available literature on Chinese Marxism (see endnote 1). For too long, scholars in the field of Asian Studies seem to have emulated rather than studied Mao's epistemology - an epistemology which is firmly empiricist. The insistence upon theory in this chapter has a twofold purpose. First, methodologically, the chapter attempts to establish distance from this empiricist tradition. This is done not by the adoption of a new position within the terrain of epistemology but by a critique of epistemology per se. It is critical of works which rely on epistemology, whether rationalist or empiricist, which assert that the real (either the real-concrete or the real-in-thought) is the object of study. Such works must posit a relationship of distinction/correspondence between the real and thought. They cannot, as Cutler, Hindess, Hirst and Hussain have argued, sustain this assertion, nor can they sustain the conflation of levels of practice to one 'knowing' site.(1) In such reductionist epistemologies one level of practice, be it the economic, political, or theoretical level, becomes the site where all other practices are known. One level is privileged above all others. A subject who has access to this site, therefore, knows all other sites. Second, in examining the work of Marx, Lenin, Stalin, Mao and the post-Mao leadership, this chapter mounts a criticism of the devolution of theory within Marxism. It is critical of readings of Marx which allege that his methodology was empiricist. The effects of such readings are quite dramatic. Theory, its role, its articulation and its usefulness, are no longer questions of Marxist scholarship. The role, articulation and usefulness of theory are obvious and are in fact as 'obvious' as the real nature of the real object of empiricist 'knowledge'. In asserting the anti-empiricist nature of Marx's epistemology we thus agree fully with Althusser.(2) However, as Hindess, Hirst, Cutler and Hussain have argued, Althusser and Marx as well, are guilty of rationalism. While attempting to break with

---

1. See Cutler, Hindess, Hirst and Hussain, 1977, I, pp. 211-5; Hindess, 1977, pp. 4-6; Hindess and Hirst, 1977, pp. 9-19.
2. Althusser, 1979; Althusser and Balibar, 1979.

empiricism, they have not broken with other reductionist epistemologies.(3) It is the twin perils of empiricism and rationalism, indeed the peril of remaining at all within the confines and inconsistencies of epistemology, which has led to massive weaknesses in any of the attempts to theorise socialist transition.

Corrigan, Ramsay and Sayer: Mao's Break with the Bolshevik 'Social Problematic'.

Such weaknesses can be understood only through an examination of Marxist theory, and more specifically through an examination of those bodies of theory which are faced explicitly with the problem of transition (namely, Bolshevism, Chinese Marxism, etc.). Yet scholastic work on China, for the most part, has been unable to see the relationship between the development of this body of theory and the policy direction of the present Chinese leadership. It is refreshing, therefore, to see the publication of a set of texts by Corrigan, Ramsay and Sayer which deal explicitly with this and which treat Chinese Marxism theoretically.(4)   Their texts, in this regard at least, are seminal. They attempt to treat Chinese Marxism, and Mao Zedong Thought in particular, as part of a general corpus of work definable as Marxist theory, not as some Oriental aberration. Unlike most scholars working in the area of Chinese Marxism, Corrigan, Ramsay and Sayer's position does not simply pay lip-service to this claim; they attempt to show its validity. We too assert the necessity of understanding the development of Marxist theory in order to understand the theoretical innovations and problems of Chinese Marxism. Moreover, we believe that scholarship in this area has so far failed in its attempts to work on this problem. In this light, Corrigan, Ramsay and Sayer's work is a major advance.

Corrigan, Ramsay and Sayer state that Mao Zedong Thought must be seen as part of the general corpus of Marxist theoretical work and, therefore, can only be understood in the light of Bolshevism. On these points we agree fully. We differ from them, however, in a number of areas. Their work fails to address one of the basic problems of contemporary Marxism - namely its reductionist epistemology. Moreover, we differ quite dramatically on most of the arguments they present to substantiate their claim that Mao's position is a major innovation in Marxist theory which breaks with the Bolshevik tradition. Mao's work should not be seen as a break with that tradition, for the tradition discussed is not 'unified' enough to warrant the term 'break'.   Further, the use of this term fails to acknowledge

---

3.   Cutler, Hindess, Hirst and Hussain, 1977, I, pp. 107-34; Hindess, 1977, pp. 196-228; Hindess and Hirst, 1977, pp. 1-19, 27-30.
4.   Corrigan, Ramsay and Sayer, 1978; Corrigan, Ramsay and Sayer, 1979.

theoretically the epistemological continuity between the reductionist positions articulated by Stalin and Mao.

Corrigan, Ramsay and Sayer argue that Mao's work breaks (albeit partially) with what they have called the 'Bolshevik problematic'. In this 'problematic', they assert,

> Forces of production were equated with industrial technology per se, and the capitalist industry of the West was viewed as providing the paradigm for their development. This perspective sustained a variety of policies designed to transfer resources from agriculture to heavy industry, the assumption being that subsequently agrarian production could in turn be 'modernised', and its social relations eventually transformed, on a suitably 'advanced' industrial base; it was axiomatic, within this perspective, that mechanisation must precede co-operation.(5)

Thus, the 'Bolshevik problematic' resembles Stalin's theory of the productive forces in that it is almost singularly concerned with modernisation and industrialisation. Mao breaks with this problematic, they assert, by his stress on relations of production and by his emphasising class struggle. They go on to argue,

> Mao's theories and practices of socialist construction implicitly challenge almost the complete canon of Bolshevik strategy, although - and this is far from a simple linguistic matter - he stays frequently in the same problematic in his writings.(6)

In what ways does Mao stay linked to Bolshevism? Corrigan, Ramsay and Sayer assert that Mao Zedong Thought remains linked 'not only at the important level of facilitating crippling separations (between internal and external policy, for example) and sustaining the possible "opening" to bourgeois models of modernisation and rationality', but more importantly Bolshevism permeates 'the core epistemological areas of the C.C.P.'s theory'.(7)

One cannot stress too strongly the importance of epistemology in Corrigan, Ramsey and Sayer's analysis, for it is at this level that they assert Mao breaks with the Bolshevik problematic. 'We begin with Mao's epistemology as basic to his whole perspective, whether on

---

5. Corrigan, Ramsay and Sayer, 1979, p. 62.
6. Ibid., p. 123.
7. Ibid., p. 9.

organisation, on production relations, or on cultural activity'.(8) Thus, it is to epistemology we must turn if we are to validate or invalidate any claims that Mao broke (albeit implicitly and partially) with Bolshevism. It is for this reason that this chapter is centred upon the epistemological. This is not to suggest that we ourselves hold to an epistemological position. Nor it to suggest that we highlight this because we hold to the centrality of the epistemological _per se_. We do not believe that there is a pure epistemological position within Marxism simply awaiting rediscovery. Our centring upon the epistemological is merely to acknowledge that all major Marxist thinkers have held to one epistemological position or another, be that position rationalist or empiricist. The strategy of highlighting the importance of epistemology here is, therefore, similar to the strategy guiding the study undertaken by Corrigan, Ramsay and Sayer. We would argue, however, even given these constraints of working within the epistemological, that Corrigan, Ramsay and Sayer's position is untenable.

The reason for this lies with their concept, 'social problematic'. They write,

> Our usage of the term 'problematic' owes something to the
> Althusserian tradition, in that we employ it to focus
> attention on what we regard as a definite matrix in which
> all variants of Bolshevism, their (important) differences
> notwithstanding, are rooted;   a taken for granted and
> implicit common framework for debate, within whose
> confines their confrontations are articulated.   But we
> qualify this problematic as 'social' - and this point cannot
> be overemphasised - because Bolshevism is not just a set
> of ideas but a body of practices.(9)

For Corrigan, Ramsay and Sayer, a problematic should not be treated 'as merely ideational, rather than social, structures and events'.(10) It is to these social structures and events that we must turn if we are to examine the 'social problematic'. In other words, the object (and subject, for the subject is invested implicitly in the real) of a social problematic is the real.

This has absolutely nothing in common with any Althusserian tradition. For Althusser, a problematic exists entirely in thought, works on a thought object, and is, moreover, entirely a theoretical

---

8.   Corrigan, Ramsay and Sayer, 1978, p. 102.
9.   Ibid., p. 27.
10. Ibid., p. 166.

construction.(11) This is not to suggest that Althusser's notion has no problems; rather it is simply to state that the concepts elucidated in his rationalist position are not readily transferable to an empiricist position. To extract concepts from an epistemological position and utilise them from a different perspective is to make concepts, which are themselves questionable, almost unworkable. A good example of this is Corrigan, Ramsay and Sayer's appropriation of Althusser's notion of problematic. Let us examine this Althusserian concept more thoroughly, for by doing so we will show the untenable nature of Corrigan, Ramsay and Sayer's 'social problematic'. We will show that it simply cannot operate as a device for separating the problematic of Mao and of Bolshevism, and that it cannot even sustain the claim that Bolshevism is unified in a single space known as a 'social problematic'.

For Althusser, as Geras has shown, a problematic designates,

> the theoretical (or ideological) framework which puts into relation with one another the basic concepts, determines the nature of each concept by its place and function in this system of relationships, and thus confers on each concept its particular significance.(12)

It functions, then, as a set of discrete questions; for while a problematic delimits 'all the possible thoughts' of a theoretical complex,(13) it does so without these necessarily being visible. The field of the problematic, then, defines what is visible (and, therefore, what is invisible). It determines the questions which can be asked and the field of answers which must be given. Althusser argues that,

> It is the field of the problematic that defines and structures the invisible as the defined excluded, <u>excluded</u> from the field of visibility and <u>defined</u> as excluded by the existence and peculiar structure of the field of the problematic... (14)

We can see from this that it is just as important, for Althusser, to understand the gaps and silences of a problematic as it is to understand

---

11. See Althusser, 1979; Althusser, 1971; Althusser, 1976; Althusser and Balibar, 1979. For expositions and critical assessment of these works, see Callinicos, 1976; Cutler, Hindess, Hirst and Hussain, 1977-8; Hindess, 1977; Hindess and Hirst, 1975; Hindess and Hirst, 1977; Thompson, 1978; Balibar, 1978; Boyne, 1979; Castells and de Ipola, 1976; Edgeley, 1979; Sayer, 1979; Collier, 1979; Geras, 1977; Glucksmann, 1977; Hirst, 1979(b); Neild and Seed, 1979.
12. Geras, 1977, p. 244.
13. Therborn, 1976, p. 59.
14. Althusser and Balibar, 1979, pp. 25-6.

what is present and continuous. To understand the silences and semi-silences of the problematic, we must probe it theoretically; for the problematic exists entirely in thought and works on a thought object; it is not, therefore, 'open' to 'empirical inspection'. Thus, the problematic (unlike the 'social problematic' of Corrigan, Ramsay and Sayer), posits an object not as a given but as a theoretical construction. Concepts are formed and have their existence within knowledge. They are not reducible to any set of 'given' or 'real' conditions.

The problematic is not, according to Althusser, a device for the interpolation of the real into thought, but rather the mechanism for the production of a knowledge (this knowledge Althusser calls Generalities III) out of a raw material (Generalities I). This raw material, however, is not the real (it is not simply the 'social'), but rather a thought concept of the real - of the social. This raw material is worked upon through a process of <u>theoretical</u> labour (Generalities II), theorised and transformed into knowledge. A problematic, then, as the mechanism of this production, can be seen to be in the category of Generalities II.(15) However, if it is within Generalities II, then it must be entirely in thought and cannot be 'social' - its object is theoretically constructed not empirically given. If a 'social problematic' claims to work on phenomenal forms, on the social - i.e. as a mechanism of mediation between the real and thought - how then can it go beyond those phenomenal forms in the determination of an epistemology? If its object is the real, how can it determine theoretical objects which are not necessarily a simple reflection of the social? In other words, by adopting the notion of a 'social problematic', how can Corrigan, Ramsay and Sayer go beyond phenomenal forms?

The notion of a 'social problematic' should not, however, be simply juxtaposed to the Althusserian notion of problematic. The reason why simple juxtaposition is not possible is that the notion of a 'social problematic' works on and is borne in the silences of the Athusserian notion. The very questions raised by Corrigan, Ramsay and Sayer's 'social problematic' - that is, questions of mediation between the real and thought - cannot simply be dismissed, as Althusser attempts to do, if one holds to an epistemological position. Without descending into infinite regress, it could be argued that a problematic informs Generalities I through mediation with the real. We shall return to the problems of rationalism later. For now, it is enough that we criticise empiricism.

We believe that the position of Corrigan, Ramsay and Sayer is empiricist, and therefore does not, in fact, go beyond phenomenal forms. Rather, they see epistemological positions as nothing more than the effects of these phenomenal forms and, as such, they regard theory

---

15.   Hindess, 1977, p. 244, n. 8.

as simply a mirroring of the social, of the real. In other words, theory becomes nothing but the systematisation of the real. All knowledge exists in the real, simply awaiting extraction. Phenomenal forms in the real do not need theoretical explanation, for their centrality to epistemology is 'visible' through the 'social problematic' which organises them. For example, they take the theory of the productive forces to be central to the Bolshevik problematic. Yet if we examine this concept theoretically, which we will in fact do in the course of this chapter, we may see that this 'theory' is simply an effect of a particular epistemological position and not the epistemological position itself. What we are arguing, then, is that the 'giveness' of their object means that their theoretical position becomes one of extraction. They attempt to extract the essence of the real from the real. Their theoretical position becomes little other than a construction based on empirically-given elements and on empirically-observed correlations between these elements. Knowledge becomes nothing more than the 'good abstraction' of the essence of the real - the separation of the essential from the inessential. In this empiricist conception of knowledge, the whole of knowledge is invested in the real; it is completely inscribed in the structure of the given. We totally reject this empiricist epistemology.

Before continuing, it is necessary to point out that in this chapter, we are attempting to trace the emergence of reductionist epistemologies within Marxism, and the effect of these on the development of socialist strategies of transition. Under this general rubric, we will examine the work of Marx, Lenin, Stalin and Mao, and then attempt to assess how far the present Chinese leadership has broken with the theoretical traditions which have evolved. This work, therefore, traces a path similar to that of Corrigan, Ramsay and Sayer; although, given the difference in our object as we have already outlined, our argumentation and conclusions are substantially different from theirs. In fact, our work constitutes a substantial critique of many of their basic assumptions.

An example of such a critique is the following section on Marx. Here this chapter follows Althusser in asserting the anti-empiricist nature of Marx's work. We attempt to show the fallacy of assertions - a fallacy so heavily defended by Corrigan, Ramsay and Sayer - that Marx was tied to empiricism. We do this by reference to Marx's own works. The aim, however, is not simply to criticise Corrigan, Ramsay and Sayer, but to show that there is no unified epistemological position within the so-called 'Marxist-Leninist tradition'. What we find is a movement from a rationalist epistemology in Marx to an empiricist epistemology in Stalin.

Following the examination of Marx's general theoretical position, this chapter turns to the work of those theorists who are concerned with using this general body of theory for specific sets of calculations in differing conjunctures. It is in this light that Lenin's work is examined. At this point, the chapter turns away from the more abstract philosophical arguments of Marx and attempts to show how these philosophical positions had an effect (or rather a lack of effect) on the elaboration of socialist theories of transition. Lenin's ambiguity on central philosophical questions, coupled with his more than understandable concern for rapid industrialisation and modernisation, it is argued, led theoretically to the erosion of Marx's central epistemological argument. Such then, was the basis for the emergence of the empiricism and positivism of Stalin - a position, we would argue, which was never more than inverted by Mao, and which subsequently it appears, has been 'turned on its head' once more by the present Chinese leadership.

Marx's Position.

Marx defended a distinction between the real object and the object of knowledge, and in so doing broke with empiricist epistemologies. Central to his position was the distinction between ideology and science. Ideology concentrated only on 'phenomenal forms', arising from a perception of how things 'represent themselves'. Ideological knowledge, therefore, was produced on the basis of a correspondence between categories of thought and experience. On the other hand, scientific knowledge was produced on the basis of a distinction between appearance and essence. Marx made this clear in an 1867 letter to Engels,

> There it will be seen how the philistines' and vulgar economists' way of looking at things arises, namely, because it is only the immediate phenomenal form of these relations that is reflected in their brains and not their inner connection. Incidentally, if the latter were the case what need would there be of science?(16)

In Volume III of Capital he made the same point. 'But all science would be superfluous if the outward appearance and the essence of things directly coincided'.(17)   Marx, therefore, argued for going beyond observation - for going beyond 'the visible, merely external movement' to 'the true intrinsic movement', and for him this was the 'work of science'.(18)

This break with empiricism in the production of 'scientific knowledge' and emphasis on the 'scientifically correct method' was clearly evidenced in the 1857 'Introduction'. In dealing with the method of political economy, Marx stated,

---

16.   Marx, (1867), Marx and Engels, 1975, p.179.
17.   Marx, III, 1959, p.817.
18.   Ibid., p. 313.

> It seems to be correct to begin with the real and the concrete, with the real precondition, thus to begin, in economics, with e.g. the population, which is the foundation and the subject of the entire social act of production. However, on closer examination this proves false...Thus, if I were to begin with the population, this would be a chaotic conception (Vorstellung) of the whole, and I would then, by means of further determination, move analytically toward even more simple concepts (Begriff), from the imagined concrete towards even thinner abstractions until I had arrived at the simplest determinations. From there the journey would have to be retraced until I had finally arrived at the population again, but this time not as a chaotic conception of a whole, but as a rich totality of many determinations and relations. The former is the path historically followed by economics at the time of its origins...The latter is obviously the scientifically correct method.(19)

In Marx's epistemology, then, knowledge was not a passive reflection of reality (empiricism); it was a product of activity (of practice) which took place entirely in thought. The work of science, therefore, was to reconstruct the concrete, not by beginning with 'the real and the concrete' but by means of abstract concepts, by means of moving from the abstract to the concrete.

Corrigan, Ramsay and Sayer recognise this position in relation to the 1857 'Introduction', but argue that Marx later rejected this strategy. As evidence of this, they cite his 1880 text, 'Marginal Notes on Adolph Wagner'.(20) In that text Marx wrote,

> This is all 'drivel'. De prime abord I do not start from 'concepts' and hence do not start from the 'concept of value', and therefore do not have to 'divide' the latter in any way. What I start from is the simplest social form in which the labour product is represented in contemporary society, and this is the 'commodity'. I analyse this, and indeed, first in the form in which it appears.(21)

From this, Corrigan, Ramsay and Sayer conclude that the basis of Marx's critique is the empirical - that he begins with the empirical,

---

19. Marx, (1858), 1977, pp. 100-01.
20. Corrigan, Ramsay and Sayer, 1978, p. 16.
21. Marx, (1879-80), 1972, p.50; another translation in Carver (ed.), 1975, p.198.

and that concepts for him are a posteriori constructs, 'end products, not pre-cast tools of analysis'.(22)

Corrigan, Ramsay and Sayer's position, it seems to us, is based on a serious misreading of Marx (see endnote 2). In their discussion of Marx's 'Marginal Notes on Adolph Wagner' they seem to be arguing for a distinction between 'concepts' and 'concrete facts'. But when Marx investigated and discussed the commodity as a 'social form', his starting point was still a concept, the concept of a concrete social entity.(23)   Marx's distinction between starting from 'concepts' and starting from 'social form' stemmed from his concern over the way that Wagner had attempted to define and relate economic concepts, an attempt that Marx dismissed as 'helter-skelter quibbling' over concepts or words.(24)   Thus Marx stated: 'Hence our vir obscurus, who has not even noticed that my analytic method, which does not start from Man but from the economically given period of society, has nothing in common with the German-professorial concept-linking method'.(25) This leads Athar Hussain to conclude,

> 'De prime abord I do not start from "concepts"' does not counterpose thought constructs or 'concepts' to 'real facts', but counterposes the 'concepts' specific to the problematic of Philosophical Anthropology to the concepts of 'Historical Materialism'.   Marx does not start from the concept of 'value', because he had discarded the problematic of Philosophical Anthropology. He starts from the 'concepts' that underlie the statement: 'What I start from is the simplest social form in which the labour-product is represented in contemporary society'.(26)

Corrigan, Ramsay and Sayer's position, therefore, seems untenable. We would argue that there was no change in Marx's position from the 1857 'Introduction' to his 'Marginal Notes on Adolph Wagner'. His 'correct scientific method', his method of analysis, consistently began with concepts, not with the empirical. To argue otherwise, as they do, to see concepts as a posteriori constructs in Marx, leads to a collapse into experiential knowledge and empiricism.   Experiential knowledge becomes equated with scientific knowledge.   Marx certainly rejected this in his elaboration of the 'correct scientific method'. This is clearly evidenced in the 1857 'Introduction' when he stated,

---

22.   Corrigan, Ramsay and Sayer, 1978, pp. 16-7.
23.   Carver (ed.), 1975, pp. 169-70.
24.   Ibid., p. 170.
25.   Marx, (1879-80), 1972, p. 52.
26.   Hussain, 1972, p. 27.   The problematic of philosophical anthropology refers to the Feuerbachian-humanist problematic of the early Marx before the break of 1845-7.   For a brief elucidation of the characteristic features of this problematic, see ibid., p. 24.

The concrete concept is concrete because it is a synthesis of many definitions, thus representing the unity of the diverse aspects. It appears therefore in reasoning as a summing-up, a result, and not as the starting point, although it is the real point of origin, and thus also the point of origin of perception and imagination. The first procedure attenuates meaningful images to abstract definitions, the second leads from abstract definitions by way of reasoning to the reproduction of the concrete situation.(27)

Marx's 'scientific work' did not start with the empirical; rather it began with concepts which were derived from empiricial practices, but not only empirical practices, also ideological practices. Surely Grundrisse, A Contribution to the Critique of Political Economy and Capital all began with an elaboration and critical evaluation of the basic concepts and propositions of bourgeois political economy. Marx nowhere just observed the world and gathered 'facts'. Always he worked on previously developed ideological concepts and theories. The 1857 'Introduction' to Grundrisse is just one testimony to this.

Marx, therefore, outlined a theoretical process which was carried out in thought within a determinate problematic. Having dismissed the real as the site of knowledge-production, he distinguished a terrain of practice other than the real, but did so without denying the latter's existence. Having stripped the real of the ontological privilege that was attributed to it in most historical accounts, Marx was able to state that 'the totality as it appears in the head, as a totality of thoughts, is a product of the thinking head'.(28) In saying this, however, Marx did not deny the real, for he claimed that it 'retains its autonomous existence outside the head just as before'.(29) In his view of the production of 'scientific knowledge', Marx, quite clearly then, had broken with empiricist epistemologies which conflate the real object and the thought object.

There are, however, problems with Marx's conception of knowledge- production; he remained within the field of epistemology by adopting a rationalist position. The epistemology he advanced, albeit not as a general philosophical doctrine but for a definite knowledge - political economy, was the same as that advanced by Althusser, namely the 'appropriation of the concrete in thought'. His 'correct scientific method' conceived the world as a rational order that was capable of representation through concepts. General concepts were formed through abstraction from the real-concrete and were

---

27. Marx, (1857), Marx, 1970, p. 206.
28. Marx, (1858), 1977, p. 101.
29. Ibid.

developed and worked upon in thought to produce the thought-concrete. A correspondence between knowledge and its object, that is between two ontologically distinct realms, namely 'thought' and 'the concrete' was produced.

A number of difficulties emerge from this.   For Marx (and Althusser), the entire process of knowledge-production took place in thought. This being the case, the obvious questions to ask are: what is the relationship between the real and thought, and between knowledge of the real and the real?   Framed in this way, such questions would appear to be constructed in terms of a 'problem of knowledge', that is, the questions designate their own answers. Concepts of the real must have some correspondence with the real, as must knowledge of the real. This is because the concept appropriates the concrete reality in thought and, therefore, must reflect it. Hence, we appear to arrive at Lenin's 'reflection theory' which has for so long underpinned most of the empiricist misreadings of Marxism.   However, if we follow the work of Macherey and Balibar in literature and of Lecourt in philosophy, then perceptions, images, representations and concepts (the results of previous practices) are fractured reflections of the real, fractured not identical, not mimesis (one-to-one correspondence). Lecourt asserts that there is not one but two propositions in Lenin's epistemological theory of reflection as outlined in 'Materialism and Empirio-Criticism'.   The first proposition of the reflection theory is that thought does reflect an existant reality; and the second is that reflection should not be seen as mirroring. The reflection Lenin talked about, according to Lecourt, is a reflection without a mirror.(30) This is because, as Macherey points out, quoting Lenin initially,

> 'We can hardly call a "mirror" that which does not give a precise reflection of the world'. Thus the mirror is only superficially a mirror, or at least it reflects in its own special way...In effect, the relationship between the mirror and what it reflects (the historical reality) is partial, the mirror selects, it does not reflect everything. The selection itself is not fortuitous, it is symptomatic; it can tell us about the nature of the mirror.(31)

The partial nature of the reflection means that knowledge of the real cannot be found in the relationship between the reflected real and the real, but must be located in the theoretical process (i.e.   entirely in thought) which works on this partial reflection to make a knowledge of the real.   We can say, therefore, that knowledge of the real is theoretical.

---

30.   Lecourt, cited in Macherey and Balibar, 1978, p.5.
31.   Macherey, 1978, p. 120.

However, if the reflection is partial, then what is the basis of this partiality? If the partiality is symptomatic and tells us about the mirror, then this partiality must be produced (perhaps unconsciously). If it is produced (even unconsciously) then it must be, according to Althusser, the product of a particular problematic (in that is it not simply 'given' to thought but is first produced through theoretical labour). It is, therefore, the problematic which determines the partiality of the reflection (through the production of that partiality). It can, therefore, be said to belong to Generalities II. However, Generalities II only work on concepts not on a given. Consequently, if we are correct, there is a contradiction between the assertion that Generalities work entirely in thought and in the articulation of the reflection theory. There appears at this point to be a theoretical slippage in the work of Marx and Althusser, for neither really addressed themselves to the question of abstraction from the real, to the question of the process of mediation between the real and thought. Indeed, it is a question that cannot be answered in the rationalist position they adopt except by admitting that there is a real empiricist process of knowledge that takes place in ideology and, therefore, precedes the work of science. As such, empiricism, as a category, is displaced only in the production of scientific knowledge; it is not displaced totally. Dangers emerge in this position, not only in terms of a highly questionable distinction between science and ideology,(32) but also in seeing the ideological mis-reading of the process of mediation between the real and thought as the problem-area in the production of scientific knowledge. On what basis is rationalism given its scientific status and empiricism condemned to be forever ideological? Silences at this point, we believe, allow for the 'resurrection' of empiricism. They allow Corrigan, Ramsay and Sayer, for example, to claim that the problem of Althusserianism is theoreticism and, therefore, to argue that by making the notion of a problematic 'social' (i.e. as a device of mediation between the real and thought), they are making it more scientific.

The question of the relationship between knowledge and the real is just as problematic. The correspondence produced between these two realms is possible for Marx because, despite their different processes of formation, both are synthetic.(33) Thus, Marx was not committed to the Hegelian conception that the 'process of evolution of the concrete world itself' is conceived as a result inseparable from its genesis. Rather, Marx took a very different direction,

> It would be inexpedient and wrong therefore to present the
> economic categories successively in the order in which
> they have played the dominant role in history. On the
> contrary, their order of succession is determined by their

---

32. Hindess, 1977, pp. 199-211; Hirst, 1979(a).
33. Cutler, Hindess, Hirst and Hussain, 1977, I, p. 111.

> mutual relation in modern bourgeois society and this is quite the reverse of what appears to be natural to them or in accordance with the sequence of historical development. The point at issue is not the role that various economic relations have played in the succession of various social formations appearing in the course of history; even less is it their sequence 'as concepts' (Proudhon) (a nebulous notion of the historical process), but their position within modern bourgeois society.(34)

The understanding of the real-concrete is obtained not from the genesis of its result, but rather from its contemporary structure. The concrete is conceived as a 'synthesis of many determinations', as a social totality with an effectivity internal to it - that which Althusser calls the 'society effect' which makes the result exist as a society.(35) The central issue for Marx (and Althusser too) was the effectivity of a structure. For Marx, effects were not outside a structure; rather a structure was immanent in its effects. In short, a structure which is merely an articulated, hierarchical, systematic combination of its peculiar elements, is nothing outside its effects. As Cutler, Hindess, Hirst and Hussain point out, if the concrete were not synthetic, if it were not formed into an ordered whole, then it would not be accessible to representation in a rational totality of concepts.(36) Knowledge too, as we have already argued, is seen as a synthetic process by Marx (see note 28 above). The production of the thought concrete produces a correspondence between the two realms of concrete and thought. Thus, one synthetic combination of elements corresponds to and represents another.(37)   Relations between concepts in thought represent the real relations existing in the concrete. Both thought and the concrete possess a rational order; and further the order of the two series correspond.

By breaking (partially) with empiricism but holding to a rationalist conception of knowledge-production and thus remaining within the field of epistemology, Marx's position betrays its inherent dogmatism. The same applies to Althusser's position, indeed to any epistemologically-based argument. All epistemologies posit both a distinction and a correspondence between the two realms of being (the concrete) and knowledge (thought) - distinction because the two realms are ontologically separate and the existence of being is not dependent on the existence of knowledge; correspondence because knowledge is assumed to correspond to or designate being, and further, knowledge and being must exist in forms appropriate to one another if this correspondence is possible. This correspondence is effected through

---

34.   Marx. (1857), Marx, 1970, p. 213.
35.   Althusser and Balibar, 1979, p. 65.
36.   Cutler, Hindess, Hirst and Hussain, 1977, I, p. 111.
37.   Ibid.

the experience of the subject in empiricist doctrines, and through the operation and order of, and relations between, concepts in rationalist epistemologies. Valid knowledge must conform to epistemological specifications, but these specifications themselves presuppose a prior 'knowledge' of the nature of being and knowledge and of the adequacy of knowledge to being. For example, in empiricist epistemologies how is the validity of the agency of human experience to be established except by reference to experience itself? All epistemologies are inescapably dogmatic.(38)

We would also argue that all epistemologies involve further problems, namely tendencies toward reductionism. This is because all epistemologies posit a uniquely privileged level of discourse which provides the means of designating existing objects. Discourses not compatible with this privileged level are rejected as unscientific, for it is against this privileged level that all other forms of discourse are measured. In empiricist epistemologies the privileged level is a site or sites in the real. For rationalism, the privileged level is theory (theoreticism). Thus, any epistemology, while not necessarily determining a particular site of knowledge-production, allows for a collapse to one 'knowing site' - either the level of theory or a particular site in the real (the political, economic or ideological instances of the social formation). Access to this one 'knowing site' enables one to know all other sites. It is this reductionist tendency of all epistemological positions that has led to serious problems in terms of theories and strategies of socialist transition - problems which have plagued Marxism. In the work of Marx and Lenin these reductionist tendencies were ambiguous and limited. However, with the emergence of Stalin and the resurrection of the theoretical position of Bogdanov, they became dominant. It is to these ambiguities and limitations in Lenin's work that we must now turn in order to understand the emergence of the position of Stalin and Bogdanov.

Lenin's Position.

Lenin, like Marx, attempted to differentiate the real object from the thought object and to posit the existence of a site of theoretical practice which was separate from other practices. For Lenin, thought was not regarded as being the act of an individual subject, 'without motion, like a genius',(39) but rather as a process - a process of theoretical production,

---

38.   For a critique of the dogmatism and inescapable circularity of epistemological positions and for an alternative to the epistemological exercise, see Cutler, Hindess, Hirst and Hussain, esp. I; Hindess, 1977; Hindess and Hirst, 1977.

39.   Lenin, (1914), CW., XXXVIII, 1972, p. 195.

> Cognition is the eternal, endless approximation of thought
> to the object. The <u>reflection</u> of nature in man's thought
> must be understood not 'lifelessly', not 'abstractly', <u>not</u>
> <u>devoid of movement</u>, <u>not without contradictions</u>, but in the
> eternal <u>process</u> of movement, the arising of contradictions
> and their solution.(40)

The process of knowledge, therefore, is not an empty abstraction but
rather 'of living <u>Gang, Bewegung</u> (progress, the movement) , deeper and
deeper, of our knowledge about things'.(41) For Lenin, then, knowledge
was derived from a theoretical practice - a process which worked on
concepts.

Thought, as Lenin pointed out in relation to Spinoza, is not the
product of a 'free, independent conscious subject', but rather an
attribute of substance.(42) It was for this reason that Lenin asserted
the materiality of thought concepts: '<u>Begriff</u> (the concept) is still not
the highest concept: still higher is the <u>idea</u> = the unity of <u>Begriff</u> and
Reality'.(43)   Lenin here asserted the materialist basis of thought.
Thought can not be understood as being independent of the real
because, as we have seen, he regarded it as a part of substance.

This is not to suggest that Lenin saw the real and thought as
one;   rather he saw thought as tied to the real through the
epistemological category of reflection. He said,

> Knowledge is the reflection of nature by man. But this is
> not a simple, not an immediate, not a complete reflection,
> but the process of a series of abstractions, the formation
> and development of concepts, laws, etc., and these
> concepts, laws, etc. (thought, science = 'the logical idea')
> <u>embrace</u> conditionally, approximately, the universal law-
> governed character of eternally moving and developing
> nature...Man cannot comprehend = reflect = mirror nature
> <u>as a whole</u>, in its completeness, its 'immediate totality', he
> can only <u>eternally</u> come closer to this, creating
> abstractions, concepts, laws, a scientific picture of the
> world, etc., etc.(44)

Hence reflection, as we have argued earlier, was not a mirroring; its
gaze was partial and only came closer to a true gaze through the
production of concepts, through a theoretical practice.   Macherey,
Balibar and Lecourt, it will be remembered, pointed out that it was a

---

40.   Ibid.
41.   Ibid., p. 91.
42.   Ibid., p. 168.
43.   Ibid., p. 170.
44.   Ibid., p. 182.

reflection without a mirror.(45) As Lenin said, 'a mirror which does not reflect things correctly could hardly be called a mirror'.(46) Thought and the real, for Lenin, were irreducible; they were separate sites of practice and should not be confused. Here then, we can see that on the question of epistemology at least, Lenin attempted to maintain a fidelity to Marx's position, a fidelity, we might add, which was soon to disappear with the emergence of Stalin and the consecration of empiricism as the universal epistemological position of Marxism-Leninism.

While it would be absurd to argue that such empiricist tendencies began with Stalin, there is certainly a case to be made to the effect that such tendencies, which were ambiguous and limited in Marx and Lenin, were finally consecrated under Stalin. What we can show is that, in the case of Lenin, certain fundamental theoretical weaknesses and ambiguities led to the assertion that empiricism was Marxist-Leninist epistemology. One of the most important weaknessess in Lenin's work was his failure to criticise adequately the philosophical position of the left Bolshevik A.A. Bogdanov.

Bogdanov and Stalin: Thoroughgoing Empiricism.

This weakness was central to Bolshevik practice, for it was in the work of Bogdanov that the question of the relationship between philosophy and technological development was to be 'settled'. Bogdanov's first major assertion in this settlement was that, through certain privileged forms of experience, being and consciousness became identical,

> Social life in all its manifestations is a consciously psychical life... Sociality is inseparable from consciousness. Social being and social consciousness are, in the exact meaning of these terms, identical.(47)

This identity of being and consciousness, which Bogdanov asserted, was achieved through the ontological privileging of what he called 'living experience'. This 'living experience' was not simply any type of human experience but rather socially-organised experience based on a

---

45. Lecourt, cited in Macherey and Balibar, 1978; for more on the reflection theory in literature, see Macherey, 1978, esp. pp. 105-35.
46. Lenin, (1908), <u>CW</u>., XV, 1963, p. 202.
47. Bogdanov, cited in Lenin, (1908) <u>CW</u>., XIV, 1962, p. 322.

tectological conception of labour organisation.(48)

Such socially-organised experience, which acts as the nodal point in the unification of being and consciousness, was ontologically privileged in that, if subjects had access to this site, then they would be (ontologically) 'knowing'. This site, was the nodal point not only in the conflation of real and thought but ipso facto led to the construction of a knowing subject. Knowledge, then, no longer functioned, as it did with Marx and Lenin, as a process without a subject, but rather the reverse, as the full expression of the subject's experiential assertions and sensations.(49)

According to Bogdanov, it was the working class which had access to this ontologically privileged site, for it was that class which had experienced the most developed organisational and technical forms of production. Working class experience, for Bogdanov, was the highest form of socially-organised experience, because his tectological conception of the labour process meant that those with experience in modern scientific industry were, as a result, those with the highest form of political and scientific consciousness. Thus, it was the 'experience of labour' which was a scientific experience. As Bogdanov saw it,

> In machine production the fundamental divergences in the nature of labour begin to disappear. The 'working hands' are no longer merely hands, the worker is not a passive mechanical performer. He is subordinated, but he also rules his 'iron slave' - the machine. The more complicated and perfect the machine, the more his labour is reduced to observation and control. The worker must know all the aspects and conditions of the work of his machine, and interfere in its motion only when necessary; while, at the inevitable moments of caprice or derangement on the part of the machine, he must be capable of quick perception, initiative, and resolution. All these are fundamental and typical traits of organisational work, and for them one must possess knowledge, intelligence, the capacity for exerted attention, which are the traits of the organiser. But there still remains the physical effort; together with the brains, the hands also have to work.
> At the same time sharp distinctions between the workers also begin to disappear; specialisation is transferred from them to the machines, the work at different machines is in its essential 'organisational' contents almost the same. Thus there is room for contact

---

48.   Tectology is defined as the universal science of labour organisation; it is a biological metaphor.
49.   See Lenin's criticism of this, Lenin, (1908), CW., XIV, 1962, p. 59.

and mutual understanding in work done in common, an opportunity to assist each other with counsel and action. Here is the origin of that fellowship in collaboration which is the basis upon which the proletariat constructs all its organisation.

This form of labour is characterised by the fact that organisational work is closely connected with execution.Here the organiser and the executor are not individual persons, but collectivities.(50)

It was this position which was to emerge again under Stalin in the late 1920s; for while Bogdanov's political career came to an end as a result of Lenin's criticisms, these criticisms were by no means adequate seriously to erode the theoretical position Bogdanov argued from. While Bogdanov was personally vilified, his theoretical position was covertly rehabilitated under Stalin.

In a position strikingly similar to Bogdanov's, Stalin argued that the development of 'consciousness' was always preceded by the development of the 'material side' and that 'consciousness' would then 'change accordingly'.(51) In other words, material conditions (one's relation to the means of production) determined 'consciousness'. This was clearly evidenced even in Stalin's early writings. In 'Anarchism or Socialism?', for example, he stated that,

There was a time when men fought nature collectively, on the basis of primitive communism; at that time their property was communist property and, therefore, at that time they drew scarcely any distinction between 'mine' and 'thine', their consciousness was communistic. There came a time when the distinction between 'mine' and 'thine' penetrated the process of production; at that time property, too, assumed a private, individualist character and, therefore, the consciousness of men became imbued with the sense of private property. Then came the time, the present time, when production is again assuming a social character and, consequently, property too will soon assume a social character - and this is precisely why the consciousness of men is gradually becoming imbued with socialism.(52)

Stalin's position, particularly close to Bogdanov's, was a long way theoretically from Lenin who clearly did not see 'material conditions' (i.e. the production process) as the site for the production of 'consciousness', through some sort of spontaneous process of 'self-realisation'.

---

50. Bogdanov, 1923, pp. 357-8.
51. Stalin, (1906-7), Works, I, 1952, p. 319.
52. Ibid., p. 317.

Lenin made this perfectly clear in 'What Is To Be Done?' (a position, we argue, he never abandoned).   In that text Lenin emphatically stated,

> It is often said that the working class spontaneously gravitates towards socialism. This is perfectly true in the sense that socialist theory reveals the causes of the misery of the working class more profoundly and more correctly than any other theory, and for that reason the workers are able to assimilate it so easily, provided, however, this theory does not itself yield to spontaneity, provided it subordinates spontaneity to itself.(53)

The provisions Lenin placed upon the development of socialism within the working class are important in that they show us that, for Lenin, the economic position of certain agents in the production process made agents more receptive to socialist theory. But it was still through theory (which emanated from discursive practice and not from some economic instance) that the conditions for the politicisation of the workers were produced and developed. In other words, the working class was not spontaneously socialist simply because of its members being workers; workers were politicised through revolutionary theory, through theory which had a separate site of production from the economic. With such a clear difference between Lenin and the social spontaneism of Bogdanov and Stalin, how was it that the latter was to prevail after Lenin's death? (see endnote 3)

Lecourt has convincingly demonstrated at least part of the reason why Lenin failed. Lecourt says that 'in the central matter of labour and its organisation he (Lenin) shared with a whole generation of Bolsheviks some of the ideological presuppositions that Bogdanov systematised in his metaphysical theory'.(54) These presuppositions were the positivist and technicist tendencies in his thought with regard to the organisation of the labour process. While we would not disagree with Lecourt that Lenin failed to break with these tendencies, we would dispute the assertion that these tendencies were Bolshevik in origin.

Marx's own work gave more than a hint of this tendency. For example, in a discussion of joint stock companies in Volume III of Capital Marx noted that,

> In stock companies the function is divorced from capital ownership, hence also labour is entirely divorced from ownership of the means of production and surplus-labour. This result of the ultimate development of capitalist

---

53.   Lenin, (1902), CW., V, 1961, p. 386.
54.   Lecourt, 1977, p. 141.

production is a necessary transitional phase towards the reconversion of capital into the property of producers, although no longer as the private property of the individual producers, but rather as the property of associated producers, as outright social property. On the other hand, the stock company is a transition toward the conversion of all functions in the reproduction process which still remain linked with capitalist property, into mere functions of associated producers, into social functions.(55)

Marx here asserted that ownership and the relations of production were largely divorced one from another. One effect of this analysis was to deny that capitalist ownership did, by definition, specify the relations of production as capitalist. Rather it worked on the assumption that stock companies were determined as being capitalist by virtue of the fact that they were the private property of individual producers. They were not analysed as being capitalist because they were inscribed by a production process which was firmly capitalist; rather, the question was seen as being one of legal ownership. The danger of a position which left the determination of the nature of the labour process to the question of ownership and did not examine relations of production is readily apparent when we look at technicist tendencies in Marx's work. In <u>Grundrisse</u> Marx argued that,

> To the degree that labour time - the mere quantity of labour - is posited by capital as the sole determinant element, to that degree direct labour and its quantity disappear as the determinant principle of production - of the creation of use values - and is reduced both quantitatively, to a smaller proportion, and qualitatively, as an, of course, indispensable but subordinate moment, compared to general scientific labour, technological application of natural sciences, on one side, and to the general productive force arising from social combination (Gliederung) in total production on the other side - a combination which appears as a natural fruit of social labour (although it is a historic product).<u>Capital thus works towards its own dissolution as the form dominating production</u>.(56)

This position, so heavily positivist, came some way toward the economic determinism which posited the theory that technological advancement led to the emergence of socialism. While Marx avoided this by stressing the role of labour, he did suggest that technological advancement was useful to socialism and not inextricably linked to capitalism. Moreover, he certainly suggested that such achievements

---

55. Marx, III, 1959, p. 817.
56. Marx, (1858), 1977, p. 700; emphasis added.

and advances in technology were central to any theories of transition from a capitalist mode of production to socialism.

Marx, however, did not suggest that the terrain of application of this technology (i.e. within the labour process) was an ontologically privileged site as Bogdanov and Stalin did. Like Lenin, Marx avoided such spurious assertions. However, such assertions can be derived from Marx. In Capital, what was assimilated in thought was a synthetic totality of social relations, a system of relations between social agents. In this system, the economic was conceived as the primary determinant of these social relations. The economic process generated necessary effects which were a part of the system; it affected how social agents perceived and acted. Thus, the economic secured its ideological conditions of existence. As Cutler, Hindess, Hirst and Hussain argue,

> It must do so because certain effects are necessary to it as a system and these effects take place through relations between men. Because capitalism is a system, certain definite acts are required of the men who live it, because its effects are necessary in its concept these acts must occur independently of the will of these men, and in consequence the conditioning of their will is necessary. Hence the theory of ideology is necessary to a concept of a system of social relations in which certain effects are necessary consequences of the system.(57)

These effects are generated through the category of experience. Social agents act as repositories for the effects of experience - experience determined primarily by the economic. The actions and consciousness of the social agents are determined by this experience. Thus, any social agent placed appropriately in the system will experience and act appropriately. In this sense, it can be said that the effects of experience are generated by the system of specific sites.(58) While Marx may well have argued that knowledge production must take place entirely in thought (precisely to avoid the effects of the experience of social agents generated by the system being appropriated in thought), it is easy to see how Bogdanov's position (his notion of 'living experience', his tectological conception of labour organisation, and his ontological privileging of the labour process as the site for the determination of consciousness and the construction of a 'knowing subject') could be derived from the rationalist discourse of

---

57.   Cutler, Hindess, Hirst and Hussain, 1977, I, p. 177.
58.   Ibid., pp. 117-8.

Marx's <u>Capital</u>; for the same tendency ontologically to privilege the economic existed there.(59)

Marx's positivist and technicist tendencies allow us to recognise something that Bahro has been at pains to point out: namely that Marx's conception of communism always presupposed a high level of industrialisation.(60)   On this point, all Bolsheviks, including Lenin, agreed.   In an underdeveloped social formation, such as the Soviet Union of 1917, a heavy stress upon industrialisation was not only understandable but also vitally necessary.   The problem is, however, that industrialisation and modernisation (or indeed collectivisation for that matter) are not by definition socialist or leading to socialism.   If all Bolsheviks are to be accused of confusing this point (and therefore constructing the Bolshevik problematic) then, as we have seen, so too is Marx.   But if we examine the various positions within Bolshevism, we can see there are major differences in the way this technicism was conceived.   These differences have massive implications for socialist strategies.

Lenin's position, like that of Marx, saw technology as neutral and therefore, by definition, contributing to socialism.   In his comments on the Taylor system, Lenin clearly demonstrated his technicist leanings.   Lenin said,

> The Taylor system - without its initiators knowing or wishing it - is preparing the time when the proletariat will take over all social production and appoint its own workers' committees for the purpose of properly distributing and rationalising all social labour.   Large-scale production, machinery, railways, telephone - all provide thousands of opportunities to cut by three-fourths the working time of the organised workers and make them four times better off than they are today.(61)

As Lecourt has shown, Lenin's treatment of capitalist techniques of labour organisation, as neutral and useful, certainly contributed to his weakness in combating the Bogdanovist tendency within the Bolshevik Party's ranks.   It would, however, be both unfair and untrue to lump Lenin, Bogdanov and Stalin together.   Lenin saw industrialisation as a prerequisite for socialism not as the process of its political construction.   He clearly saw the need for political and cultural work outside the labour process, that is as a separate site of activity.   With regard to the peasants, for example, Lenin saw the principal task as being one of cultural education.   The economic object of such cultural education was to organise the peasants into co-operatives.   Indeed, no

---

59.   <u>Ibid.</u>, p. 121.
60.   Bahro, 1978, p. 125.
61.   Lenin, (1914), <u>CW.</u>, XX, 1964, p. 154.

attempt to develop such co-operatives could be successful in the Soviet Union unless the Party was first able to raise the cultural standards of the peasants.(62) Thus, the economic instance was dependent upon the political level but, nevertheless, separate from it. There was no question here of calculating the level of political determination by simply reading it off the economic.

Stalin, however, whose theoretical position mirrored that of Bogdanov, clearly established an identity between the economic and the political instances. In relation to the peasants, Stalin argued,

> I should like to draw your attention to the collective farms, and especially to the state farms, as levers which facilitate the reconstruction of agriculture on a new technical basis, causing a revolution in the minds of the peasants and helping them to shake off conservatism, routine.(63)

As Bettelheim points out in relation to this quote, it is the modern 'scientific technique' which 'acts' upon the conservative peasants while they are merely 'acted upon'.(64)   They are 'acted upon' and 'proletarianised' both organisationally (in the actual labour process) and politically; (their 'consciousness' is 'raised' to that of a proletarian through their socially-organised experience in the labour process). Thus, it was this notion of socially-organised experience which was central to Stalin's epistemology rather than, as with Marx and Lenin, the notion of theoretical practice. For Stalin, theory could become experience because 'being' equalled 'consciousness'. 'Being' equalled 'consciousness' at the point of production; thus the working class, which had access to this site, became a collective knowing subject.

We can see now how far we have travelled from the position of Marx   and   Lenin.   The   difference   lies   not   in   the   stress   on industrialisation but rather on the way such a process was conceived. For Stalin, industrialisation was not simply a prerequisite for socialism; it was its political construction. Through its role in the labour process, the working class gained experience which was regarded as both revolutionary and scientific. The labour process was not only the point of economic production but also the point of knowledge production through the experiences of the collective knowing subject - the working class. What we argue here, then, is the importance of this theoretical conflation. The fact that Stalin privileged the economic instance is not, we believe, as important as the actual mechanism which <u>allowed</u> for an instance to be privileged. Hence arguments which counterpose theories of the productive forces to 'popular power'

---

62.   Lenin, (1923), <u>CW.</u>, XXXIII, 1966, p. 474.
63.   Stalin, (1928), <u>Works</u>, XI, 1954, p. 279.
64.   Bettelheim, 1976(b), p. 68.

essentially miss the point; they deal only with phenomenal forms. What is important is the epistemological mechanism which allowed a particular instance to be privileged; for it was this mechanism which became enshrined as Marxist-Leninist epistemology. This was a strange twist indeed; for, as we have tried to show, neither Marx nor Lenin held this position. We will now turn our attention to China and show that while the economism of Stalin might well have been overcome, the essentialist epistemology was, in fact, reinforced.

Mao Zedong: The Inversion of Stalin but the Continuance of Empiricism.

Mao's critique of Stalin stressed his economism and humanism and identified the basis of his deviation as the theory of the productive forces. This theory, Mao felt, reduced socialism to nothing more than state ownership of the means of production, together with the development of the productive forces. As such, once this state ownership had been achieved, class struggle became superfluous and revolution, in the political and ideological instances, meaningless. The Chinese were deeply critical of Stalin's position on these matters (see endnote 4),

> ...as Stalin departed from Marxist-Leninist dialectics in his understanding of the laws of class struggle in socialist society, he prematurely declared after agriculture was basically collectivised that there were 'no longer antagonistic classes' in the Soviet Union and that it was 'free of class conflicts', one-sidedly stressed the internal homogeneity of socialist society and overlooked its contradictions...(65)

Furthermore, the strategy pursued for developing the productive forces, that is emphasis on heavy industry (where, for Stalin and Bogdanov, the working class had access to the 'experience of labour') financed by taking the surplus from rural areas, had led to the virtual exclusion of the peasantry as a progressive class.(66) This Stalinist strategy, moreover, was theoretically informed, for peasants were regarded as inherently backward and not disciplined by the organisation of labour. Such criticisms led to the decentering of the theory of the productive forces; this theory being replaced by one which placed the relations of production at the centre. Thus, Bogdanov's notion of organisational and technical tectology was also displaced.

Central to Mao's position on the relations of production was the notion of exploitation and struggle in the determination of 'labour

---

65.   RMRB. and Hongqi, PR., 29, 17 July 1964, p. 11.
66.   Peck, 1977, pp. 12-15.

experience'. For Stalin and Bogdanov, it will be remembered, it was through 'socially-organised experience' in the labour process that one became 'proletarianised', that one developed the 'consciousness' of the proletariat. Thus 'labour experience' and 'class viewpoint' were 'read off' the economic instance. Mao unequivocally broke with this conception of the development of 'class consciousness',

> In many places in the textbook (i.e.   the Soviet textbook Political Economics), emphasis is laid on the part being played by machines in socialist transformation. However, if we do not raise the consciousness of the peasants and remould the ideology of man, how can it be possible to rely on machines alone? The question of the struggle between the two roads of socialism and capitalism and the question of employing socialist ideology to remould man and discipline him are a big problem in our country.(67)

Instead, he developed a somewhat different view of the determination of class attitude. He distinguished between class origin (defined by reference to one's relation to the means of production) and class stand.(68) Class stand was determined by one's attitude toward the revolution; indeed, by whether one was revolutionary or counter-revolutionary. The method of such categorisation was quite clear for Mao - it was to be done on the basis of willingness to integrate with the workers and peasants (with the exploited) and the extent to which this was actually done in practice.(69) Quite clearly, for Mao, there were experiental determinants in the formation of class attitude; namely, personal experience in struggle (class struggle, the struggle for production and scientific experimentation, with the first as the 'key link') and one's degree of exploitation (how 'poor and blank' one was). This concern with struggle and exploitation led Mao to a position where the 'experience of labour' was no longer confined, as a point of origin for the determination of strategy, to the working class (as for Stalin and Bogdanov), but rather was extended to 'the people' (workers, peasants, urban petty bourgeoisie and patriotic national bourgeoisie). It was the exploited 'people' who were locked in struggle against their enemies. The determination of experience, therefore, shifted from the workers' relationship with scientific technique, to the people's level of exploitation and degree of participation in struggle; it was no longer 'read off' the economic instance but rather off the political (see endnote 5).

Mao's shifting of the 'experience of labour' to 'the people', as well as his identification of contradictions among the people (overcome through 'peaceful struggle', that is, discussion, criticism, persuasion and

---

67.   Mao Zedong, (1961-62), in Mao, 1974, p. 262.
68.   Mao Zedong, n.d., in Mao 1974, p. 433.
69.   Mao Zedong, (1939), SW., II, 1965, p. 246.

education) and <u>between</u> the people and their enemies (which had to be overcome through class struggle), resulted in the avoidance of both the economism and the humanism of Stalin. What was obviously not overcome in Mao's epistemology, however, was the centrality of the Bogdanovist notion of 'living experience'. True, Bogdanov's concern for a scientific tectological conception of the labour process was removed, but the epistemological effects of the maintenance of the category of 'experience' remained. In this sense, there was a continuity between Stalin and Mao. There still existed an all-knowing subject which had, as its basis, what Bogdanov called socially-organised experience. It was only the site for the acquisition of that experience which had changed - namely, from the economic to the political. In this way, Mao's critique of Stalin never broke with the underlying epistemological position but remained firmly Bogdanovist, albeit in an inverted form.

This point is clearly exemplified by Mao's 'mass line' method of leadership which Mao himself characterised as the 'Marxist theory of knowledge',(70)

> This means: take the ideas of the masses (scattered and unsystematic ideas) and concentrate them (through study turn them into concentrated and systematic ideas), then go to the masses and propagate and explain these ideas until the masses embrace them as their own, hold fast to them and translate them into action, and test the correctness of these ideas in such action.(71)

This position was clearly Bogdanovist. The conception of study here was not theoretical elaboration, but rather the systematisation and organisation of the ideas of the masses. In this sense, Mao spoke of the necessity to 'synthesise the data of perception by arranging and reconstructing them',(72) and to 'systematise and synthesise ...experience and raise it to the level of theory'.(73) It is precisely at this point that we arrive at Bogdanov's argument that 'ordinary thought' and 'scientific thought' were essentially the same, merely distinguished by the organising of that thought.

Nevertheless, for Mao the movement of knowledge did not end here. The most important stage of the knowledge process, as far as he was concerned, was that of testing knowledge through practice. Practice was the only criterion of truth and only through the practice of revolutionary class struggle, production and scientific

---

70. Mao Zedong, (1943), <u>S W</u>., III, 1965, p. 119.
71. <u>Ibid.</u>
72. Mao Zedong, (1937), <u>S W</u>., I, 1965, p. 302.
73. Mao Zedong, (1942), <u>S W</u>., III, 1965, p. 42.

experimentation could knowledge be tested and developed.(74)   We have already seen that Mao's decentering of the theory of the productive forces resulted in an emphasis on the political, on class struggle and contradictions among the people.   Hence, truth for Mao - given that (political) practice was the sole criterion - was the organising form of experience.   This was precisely Bogdanov's position as Ballestrem explains,

> Bogdanov's theory of truth follows from his general empiricist premises.   The test of knowledge is to <u>organise experience</u> in the form of concepts, statements, theories. <u>There is no possibility of, but also no need for or interest in, looking outside the world of our experience for criteria to judge the adequacy of a statement or theory.</u>(75)

Quite clearly then, the elaboration of experience gained from political practice was regarded by Mao as 'theoretical practice'.   A theoretical practice which was relatively autonomous of the political was therefore, on this basis, unthinkable.   Mao made this clear on numerous occasions, and indeed characterised Marx in this way,

> Marx took part in the practice of the revolutionary movement and also created revolutionary theory...Marx undertook detailed investigations and studies in the course of practical struggles, formed generalisations and then verified his conclusions by testing them in practical struggles - this is what we call theoretical work.(76)

Hence, rather than eradicating the epistemological basis of Stalin's position, Mao merely 'substituted' the criteria for its determination. The experience of labour was no longer 'read off' the economic instance but rather was 'read off' political practice.

We can say, therefore, that Mao never broke with the empiricist epistemology of Stalin and Bogdanov which had experience as its centre.   In his essay 'On Practice', regarded as the central work of the Maoist theory of knowledge, Mao clearly identified experience in the real as the basis of knowledge,

> If you want knowledge, you must take part in the practice of changing reality...<u>All genuine knowledge originates in direct experience.</u>   But one cannot have direct experience of everything;   as a matter of fact, most of our knowledge comes from indirect experience...<u>Hence a man's knowledge consists only of two parts, that which comes from direct</u>

---

74.   Mao Zedong, (1937), <u>SW</u>., I, 1965, pp. 296-7; 304-5.
75.   Ballestrem, 1969, pp. 297-8;   emphasis added.
76.   Mao Zedong, (1942), <u>SW</u>., III, 1965, p. 40.

experience and that which comes from indirect experience. Moreover, what is indirect experience for me is direct experience for other people. Consequently...knowledge of any kind is inseparable from direct experience.(77)

One can see clearly that for Mao, the notion of 'experience' was central to any conception of knowledge. It was central because for Mao, knowledge production constituted little more than the systematisation of experience. Some have argued that Mao's description of the process of perception makes him a thoroughgoing empiricist, at least at the beginning of the process of cognition.(78) We hold that Mao was a thoroughgoing empiricist at all stages of the knowledge process.

It is tempting to defend Mao against charges of empiricism by arguing that he saw perception as only solving the problem of phenomena, and that he continually asserted that one had to go further than this and grasp the essence.(79) There is no doubt that Mao envisaged some process of interaction in the cognitive process between 'theory' or 'preconceptions' and perceptual data acquired through experience. Such preconceptions included Marxist-Leninist theory.(80) This theory was not to be used as 'lifeless dogma' or applied universally, rather it was to be combined with one's own perceptions, with 'concrete practice', so that some sense could be made out of one's experience.(81) However, there was absolutely no indication of theoretical practice in Mao's epistemology, despite this so-called 'interaction'. This body of preconceptions, this 'theory', was for Mao, nothing more than the 'summation of previous experience'.(82) Furthermore, only after people had studied theory, only once they had a grasp of this 'summation', would they be able to 'systematise and synthesise their experience and raise it to the level of theory', only then would they 'not mistake their partial experience for universal truth and not commit empiricist errors'.(83) And this was the central point for Mao. He argued that empiricism relied solely on direct experience, on phenomenal forms, for the production of its 'knowledge'. He, however, went beyond phenomenal forms by

---

77. Mao Zedong, (1937), S̲W̲., I, 1965, p. 300; emphasis added.
78. See e.g., Starr, 1979, p. 50.
79. Mao Zedong, (1937), S̲W̲., I, 1965, p. 299.
80. See e.g., Mao Zedong, (1942), S̲W̲., III, 1965, pp. 38-9; Mao Zedong, (1956), Schram (ed.) 1974, p. 86.
81. Ibid., and Starr, 1979, pp. 51-3.
82. See Mao Zedong, (1942), S̲W̲., III, 1965, p. 39; Mao Zedong, (1937), S̲W̲., I, 1965, p. 300.
83. Mao Zedong, (1942), S̲W̲., III, 1965, p. 42.

synthesising and reconstructing those perceptions which, he argued, were 'rich' and 'correspond to reality'.(84) Thus Mao stated,

> Fully to reflect a thing in its totality, to reflect its essence, to reflect its inherent laws, it is necessary through the exercise of thought to reconstruct the rich data of sense perception, discarding the dross and selecting the essential, eliminating the false and retaining the true, proceeding from the one to the other and from the outside to the inside, in order to form a system of concepts and theories - it is necessary to make a leap from perceptual to rational knowledge.(85)

Thus, the leap to rational knowledge for Mao, was no more than the interaction of direct experience and the 'summation and generalisation of previous experience' (both one's own experience, as well as that of others). It was no more than a leap based on an interaction between personal experience and experience of a higher order. The final result might no longer be 'narrow and partial' empiricism, but it was still empiricism. The failure to break with empiricism occurred precisely because there was no notion of autonomy between the theoretical and political instances.

This, then leads us to the conclusion that the category of subject had to remain in Mao's epistemology for, if classes or individuals had access to experiential knowledge (that is to the ontologically privileged site of experience as knowledge), then they must constitute a knowing subject. Mao might well have criticised the individualised subject of humanism, but the category of subject was not displaced, merely collectivised. This is clearly evidenced in his 1964 'Talk on Sakata's Article' where he discussed working-class cognition,

> A class is the subject of cognition. In the beginning, the working class was a class in and of itself, and it had no knowledge of capitalism. Later, it developed from a class in and of itself into a class that existed for itself, and, by that time, it began to understand capitalism. This was a case of the development of cognition based on class as the subject.(86)

Hence, for Mao, it was the experience of the working class which allowed it to 'know' itself as a class, as a subject. Here we see clearly the conflation of the object in thought, which is related to knowledge production, and the real object. In this process, the empiricist epistemology which enabled the tectological conception of labour under

84.   Mao Zedong, (1937), SW., I. 1965, p. 302.
85.   Ibid., p. 303.
86.   Mao Zedong, (1964), Mao, 1974, p. 399.

Stalin was not displaced, although the theoretical position argued by Marx and Lenin was.

The process discussed by Mao in the above quote is one of abstraction. The working class, through its experience in struggle, had become a knowing subject - it had gained the capacity to separate and abstract the essential from the inessential in the real, thereby establishing a part of the real as the site of knowledge production; it had become a class for itself. It had, in the same process, established itself as the subject of knowledge, as the agent which 'knew' the real. The working class would 'know' precisely because it had abstracted the essential from the inessential and, therefore, 'possessed' the real essence of the real object. At this point we again arrive at the conclusion that Mao, unlike Marx and Lenin, lacked any notion of theoretical practice. He therefore shared with Stalin and Bogdanov a basic commitment to the reductionist epistemology of empiricism. As with Bogdanov and Stalin, the 'real' object was 'knowable' for Mao, through the experience of the knowing subject. One must note with Mao, however, that while the gaze of the subject may well have remained ontologically privileged (and thus his position was similar to that of Bogdanov and Stalin), the basis of this privileging had altered dramatically. For Mao, the privileging was not due to one's interaction with advanced technology (as it was for Stalin and Bogdanov), but rather was based on one's level of suffering and oppression. The more one was oppressed, the more one had a revolutionary potentiality. In this sense the working class could more easily gain 'true revolutionary consciousness', not because it was disciplined and organised through the labour process but rather because it was an oppressed class. As a result, for Mao, classes such as the peasantry could, like the working class, have access to 'true revolutionary consciousness'. Moreover, for the most part, Mao's privileging of the working class was largely linguistic. In Mao's theoretical position there appeared to be no mechanism which would privilege the working class over other oppressed classes (e.g. the peasants). Thus, we find in Mao's analysis a much heavier use of terms such as 'the masses' and 'the people', for it was these groups which were oppressed enough to gain 'revolutionary "class" consciousness'. It was the masses, the people, who had 'true revolutionary consciousness' therefore, who would know the real. Mao hinted at this in his 1963 text 'Where Do Correct Ideas Come From?',

> In social struggle, the forces representing the advanced class sometimes suffer defeat not because their ideas are incorrect, but because, in the balance of forces engaged in struggle, they are not as powerful for the time being as the forces of reaction; they are therefore temporarily

defeated, but they are bound to triumph sooner or later.(87)

While practice might in most instances be the criterion of truth, the ultimate test of validity laid beyond the realm of practice. For Mao, the validity of knowledge was reduced to the question of who expounded the idea. As the discussion above makes clear, knowledge was considered to be true because it was held by members of the advanced class, that is by those who had suffered a high level of oppression and exploitation and who, therefore, had come to a realisation of their own oppression and ways to overcome it.(88)

We can see in this a determinism which allows knowledge production to be solely the preserve of the people. At the same time we can also see the reductionism inherent in Mao's epistemology. Mao designated one level of practice (the political) as the determinate site and tended to reduce all other instances to mere epiphenomena of that site. Failing that, the all-knowing subject could not know all levels of practice, it could only know the instances to which it had access; it could no longer be 'all-knowing'. Quite clearly then, Stalin's social spontaneism based on the economic had been removed, only to be replaced by Maoist spontaneism based on the political.

The Post-Mao Leadership: Another Inversion But Still Empiricism.

Similarly, post-Mao China is not free from those tendencies which engendered both Stalinism and Maoism. It is important to point out very clearly here that we are examining certain tendencies that have emerged since the death of Mao and the so-called 'overthrow of the Gang of Four'. In this sense, our examination of the intense period of theoretical and political debate about socialist transition is tentative and preliminary. The theoretical position of the post-Mao leadership has yet to be clearly defined. There are clear parameters to the debate, but within these confines differences do exist. There are also tendencies that cannot be conceived of as 'anti-socialist' per se - for example the specification of legal codes, the expansion of democracy, and increasing autonomy for enterprises.   With these qualifications and limitations in mind, this chapter will note that there are clear and disturbing tendencies within Chinese Marxism to invert Mao in precisely the same way that Mao inverted Stalin. This is evidenced by a tendency to collapse all levels of practice on to the economic and by the predominance of an empiricist epistemology with experience as its basis.

This section of the chapter will examine developments within Chinese Marxism since 1978, particularly since the Third Plenum of the

---

87.   Mao Zedong, (1963), Mao, 1971, p. 503.
88.   This conclusion is supported by Starr, 1979, pp. 62-3; 84-5; 87.

Eleventh Central Committee in December of that year. This is not to deny the extreme importance of the theoretical debates and associated political struggles that occurred in the 1976-78 period. During those rather complicated years, a number of theoretical positions on the question of socialist transition were put forward. The Third Plenum, however, marked a significant change in the policies pursued by the Chinese leadership. Indeed, the resolution 'On Questions of Party History' adopted at the Sixth Plenum stated,

> The Third Plenary Session of the 11th Central Committee in December 1978 marked a crucial turning point of far-reaching significance in the history of our Party since the birth of the People's Republic. It put an end to the situation in which the Party had been advancing haltingly in its work since October 1976.(89)

The Third Plenum discarded the slogan 'take class struggle as the key link' and shifted the focus of work to 'socialist modernisation'. It stressed the necessity of strengthening socialist democracy and the socialist legal system. Further, it upheld the principle of 'seeking truth from facts', proceeding from reality and linking theory with practice. It is to this epistemological question that we shall first turn our attention.

The campaign to promote 'practice' as 'the sole criterion of truth' and such slogans as 'seek truth from facts' testify to the empiricist epistemology of the present leadership. The epistemological debates since 1976 have relied heavily on Mao's texts 'On Practice', 'Rectify the Party's Style of Work' and 'Where Do Correct Ideas Come From?'. Central to the position Mao outlined in those works, as has been noted, was the notion of experience. The present leadership has appropriated this notion in toto and clearly identifies experience in the real as the basis of knowledge,

> In order to discover the laws of things, to forsee the extent of their progress, it is necessary to participate personally in practice, to become involved in realising the struggle, to become immersed in the inner nexus of things...Unless one starts with reality, participates in practice, and comes into direct contact with the study of

---

89.   CCP.CC., 27 June 1981, <u>BR</u>., 27, 6 July 1981, p. 26.

objective phenomena, it is not possible to discover the laws of things.(90)

Furthermore, just as for Mao, theory is seen as no more than the summing-up and generalisation of practical experience.(91) As has been shown, this position, this centrality of the notion of experience, is clearly Bogdanovist.

The empiricist nature of this epistemology has been unwittingly characterised, in terms reminiscent of Mao, by Lei Zhenwu,

> We all know that in the shaping of a theory, no matter from what kind of practice or under how correct a guiding ideology, a processing by way of man's brain is always required. The function of such processing through thinking means arriving at the formulation of concepts and theoretical systems through such steps as revising and regenerating on the basis of those rich, vivid sensual data derived from practice by absorbing the quintessential and eliminating the coarse, absorbing the true and eliminating the false, speculating from this factor to that factor, and penetrating from the superficial to the profound.(92)

The method of 'leaping' from perceptual knowledge to rational knowledge is exactly the same process that Mao outlined in 'On Practice'. Lei alludes to some process of interaction between perceptual data and the subject's 'standpoint', 'viewpoint' and 'approach'.(93) We can level precisely the same criticisms here as we did against Mao; this process of interaction between 'direct experience' and the 'summing-up and generalisation of (previous) practical experience' is not theoretical; it is clearly empiricist. This empiricist epistemology sees the real as the raw material, the starting point of knowledge production. It sees the subject abstracting the essence (the quintessential, the true) of the real object, eliminating all that is inessential (the coarse, the false), thus producing knowledge. Knowledge becomes nothing more than the essential part of the real object. Abstract theory, this 'summing-up and generalisation', becomes, at the very best, an approximation of reality. Clearly then, there is absolutely no conception, as there was in Marx and Lenin, of theoretical practice in the epistemology of the present Chinese leadership.

90. Li Xiulin, Ding Yelai and Zheng Hangsheng, Zhexue Yanjiu, 10, 1978, Chinese Studies in Philosophy, 3, 1980, p. 24.
91. Mao Zedong, (1937), SW., I, 1965, p. 300.
92. Lei Zhenwu, Zhexue Yanjiu, 9, 1979, JPRS., 74922, 14 January 1980, p. 27.
93. Ibid.

This point is also exemplified by the present leadership's position on the criterion of truth. Practice (experience) plays a dual role in the cognitive process - not only is it the source of all knowledge, but it also provides the sole test for the validity of knowledge. The practice referred to here is not individual practice but social practice (socially-organised experience) in material production, class struggle and scientific experimentation. Further, this test of validity seeks to ascertain whether or not the 'ideas of the subjective realm' achieve the anticipated results in practice - whether or not they are successful. How is such success to be measured? Offering practice as the test of knowledge takes no account of factors such as errors in work style or inability to implement the knowledge because of limited time or resources.(94) A far more serious criticism is that success can only be measured by perception, by the <u>first</u> stage of the knowledge process as it is conceived by the present Chinese leadership. The subject has to 'see' whether or not the anticipated results are achieved. This act of 'sighting' is itself empiricist, but now more clearly so; for in this instance knowledge collapses directly back into perception in the real. But the most telling criticism is that knowledge of the real is collapsed (both in its origin and testing) into social practice; into the real. There is obviously no notion of an autonomous level of theoretical practice in this 'knowledge process'; there is only 'practice in general' in the real. Knowledge is thus invested entirely in the real. We can see clearly how far the present Chinese leadership has moved from the epistemological position advocated by Marx. Just as with Stalin, empiricism continues to be enshrined as Marxist-Leninist epistemology.

Numerous references by Mao to the criterion of practice have been used by the present leadership to validate its position. Mao's 1963 text 'Where Do Correct Ideas Come From?' has been quoted approvingly in this regard.(95) This text's quite explicit reference to class struggle and its role in the criterion of practice has, however, been deleted from the present leadership's elucidation of Mao's epistemology. Does this indicate that the political, as the determinate site of practice (and therefore knowledge production), has been displaced? This chapter will go on to argue that tendencies in this direction appear to predominate. Furthermore, it will show that this tendency toward displacement of the political has been accompanied not by a notion of theoretical practice as outlined by Marx and Lenin but rather by a re-emergence of Stalin's theory of the productive forces with the economic as the determinate site of knowledge production. Stalin, inverted by Mao, appears to have been placed 'right-side up' by the present Chinese leadership.

---

94. E.g. This point, in relation to Mao, is suggested by Starr, 1979, p. 63.
95. Lei Zhenwu, <u>Zhexue Yanjiu</u>, 9, 1979, <u>JPRS</u>., 74922, 14 January 1980, pp. 29-30.

The communiqué of the Third Plenum announced that 'large-scale turbulent class struggles of a mass character have in the main come to an end'.(96) Furthermore, the communiqué decreed that the stress of the Party's work should shift to socialist modernisation. The basis of this argument was that the system of exploitation of man by man had been eliminated, and that exploiters no longer existed as classes.(97) This had been achieved through the transformation of the means of production from private ownership to public ownership. Ye Jianying argued,

> We have abolished the exploitation of man by man, transformed the system of private ownership by small producers, <u>set up comprehensive socialist public ownership</u> of the means of production and initially put into practice the principle of 'from each according to his ability, to each according to his work', <u>and thus it became possible</u> for the Chinese people...<u>to enter socialist society.</u>(98)

In this view, socialism becomes a question of ownership of the means of production. Once this ownership has been firmly established in the hands of 'the people', then the means of production become socialist. Thus, in determining whether or not the labour process is socialist, the question becomes solely one of judicio-legal ownership. Relations of production are not examined, nor are they considered pertinent to the question of socialist transition. The relations of production are 'placed on the socialist road' by the simple legal transference of ownership of the means of production. Once this simple transference of ownership to 'the people' has occurred, the increasing technical development of the productive forces 'acts upon' the relations of production to complete the socialist transformation of the labour process. Thus, it is the forces of production which, following the legal transference of the means of production, become the catalyst for the transformation of the form of the labour process. Technological advancement, then, becomes the dynamic for socialist transformation.

This reduction of socialism to a question of judicio-legal ownership of the means of production is not without its effects. There has been a clear tendency within Chinese Marxism to argue that, once the pattern of ownership has been transformed, 'objective economic laws', which operate in any mode of production, also change

---

96.   CCP.CC., 22 December 1978, <u>PR</u>., 52, 29 December 1978, p. 11.
97.   CCP.CC., 27 June 1981, <u>PR</u>., 27, 6 July 1981, pp. 13-4.
98.   Ye Jianying, 29 September 1979, <u>BR</u>., 40, 5 October 1979, p. 9; emphasis added.

fundamentally in nature; they become socialist in content.(99) (see endnote 6). Only by observing these 'objective economic laws', only by operating within them and not interfering with them, is it possible to guarantee the development of the productive forces and the success of socialism. Socialism is, in fact, threatened if politics interferes with the operation of these laws.

Thus, it is argued that socialism, defined as socialised mass production based on public ownership,(100) will emerge through the development of the productive forces. Ye Jianying continues,

> First, <u>for socialism to replace capitalism</u>, we must liberate the productive forces and achieve a constantly rising labour productivity to meet the people's material and cultural needs. This is the fundamental aim of socialist revolution. Once the proletariat has seized political power in a country, and especially <u>after the establishment of the socialist system</u>, it is imperative to place the focus of work squarely on economic construction, <u>actively expand the productive forces</u> and gradually improve the people's standard of living.(101)

This position is clearly guilty of both economism and positivism. It is only through technological advancement and the development of the productive forces that socialism emerges. A high level of technological development is not seen as a precondition for socialism (as it was for Marx and Lenin); rather it is seen as the mechanism which actually brings about socialism (as it was for Bogdanov and Stalin). Under this line, class struggle becomes redundant. In fact, it becomes an obstacle to the development of the productive forces and, thus, to the achievement of socialism. Quite clearly then, Mao's critique of Stalin's economism has been totally abandoned.

If class struggle is seen as an obstacle to socialist modernisation, then it becomes necessary to limit the role of class struggle in the process of socialist transition. Political stability and unity, therefore, are emphasised; anything which interferes with this stability and unity can not be tolerated. Class struggle is no longer regarded as the 'key link'; for such a position is seen to be unsuitable for a socialist society. Indeed, the present Chinese leadership's critique of Mao rests largely on what it deems it to be his 'theoretical and practical

---

99. See e.g., Hu Qiaomu, July 1978, <u>PR.</u>, 45, 10 November 1978, pp. 7-12; <u>PR.</u>, 46, 17 November 1978, pp. 15-23, and <u>PR.</u>, 47, 24 November 1978, pp. 13-21; Wu Jinglian, Zhou Shulian and Wang Haibo, <u>Jingji Yanjiu</u>, 9, 1978, pp. 15-25.
100. Hu Qiaomu, July 1978, <u>PR.</u>, 45, 10 November 1978, p. 9.
101. Ye Jianying, 29 September 1979, <u>BR.</u>, 40, 5 October 1979, p. 21; emphasis added.

mistakes' concerning class struggle in the socialist social formation.(102) After declaring that class struggle was no longer the 'principal contradiction' after the elimination of the exploiting classes, the Sixth Plenum's 'Resolution' went on completely to de-emphasise class struggle. It stated that, while class struggle would continue to exist 'within certain limits' for a long time to come and might even grow acute under certain conditions, most contradictions would not 'fall within the scope of class struggle'; and that 'methods other than class struggle must be used for their appropriate resolution'. If this were not the case, then social stability would be 'jeopardised'.(103) The class struggle that did remain was a struggle against remnant forces of the bourgeoisie. In waging class struggle against these remnants, it was necessary to 'centre around and serve the central task of modernisation'.(104)   The class struggle which remains, therefore, manifests itself in the economic instance,

> Class struggle in the past usually manifested itself directly in the struggle between those wanting to seize political power and those wanting to hold on to their political power, between those trying to take over and those fighting against it.   In the future, class struggle will mainly centre around socialist modernisation and be made to serve socialist modernisation, its main manifestation will be the struggle between those defending the four modernisations and those trying to undermine the realisation of these modernisations.(105)

Quite clearly then, the political has been collapsed into the economic.

Much of the debate on the nature and scope of class struggle in socialist society has taken place in the context of the re-evaluation of Mao's theory of 'continuous revolution'. While the term as such was upheld for a time, its meaning was interpreted widely. Hua Guofeng, for example, accepted the need for continued revolution in the superstructure so that it 'will correspond better with the socialist economic base', and for continued revolution in the realm of relations of production so that they 'will correspond better with the expanding productive forces'.(106) He also retained, although only in passing, the notion of newly emerging capitalist forces and bourgeois elements, and of their existence within the Party.   The danger of capitalist restoration remained.(107) However, Hua's elaboration of 'continuous revolution' owed much more to Mao's earlier notion of 'uninterrupted

---

102. CCP,CC., 27 June 1981, BR., 27, 6 July 1981, pp. 20 and 27.
103. Ibid., p. 37.
104. Hua Guofeng, 18 June 1979, NPC., 1979, p. 22.
105. BR., 47, 23 November 1979, p. 17.
106. Hua Guofeng, 12 August 1977, CCP., 1977, pp. 28-9.
107. Ibid., pp. 32-3.

revolution' in which the correct handling of contradictions among the people, rather than class struggle, was seen as the motive force of history. In Hua's version of 'continuous revolution', class struggle was not continually generated as a result of the material basis of the social formation, rather it was a result of remnant influences of the past and individual capitalist behaviour.(108)

Hua's views on the question of correspondence between the economic base and the superstructure were indirectly attacked by Wu Jiang: 'it is inconceivable that shortly after building its own economic base, our socialist superstructure should, wholly or in great part, be in disharmony with its base'.(109) The issue here was much more than disagreement over the degree of disharmony between the economic base and the superstructure. While Wu's comments were directed specifically against the 'Gang of Four', his position effectively negated Hua's perceived need for continued large-scale revolution in the superstructure. There may well be a need for 'readjustment' or 'change' in certain parts of the superstructure,(110) but the implication was that 'revolutionary activity' should primarily be restricted to the economic, specifically to the development of the productive forces; for these were the 'most active and revolutionary factors' which determined the nature of the social formation.(111) The Sixth Plenum's resolution endorsed this view and totally rejected the theory of 'continuous revolution'. This did not mean that the tasks of the revolution had been accomplished, nor did it signify that it was unnecessary to carry on revolutionary struggles. What it did mean was that the category of socialist revolution (i.e., the period from the overthrow of the system of exploitation to the realisation of communism) was redefined as an orderly process carried out within the system, not through class confrontation and conflict. In this view, it was not a question of eliminating systems of exploitation and exploiting classes, for such had ceased to exist with the transformation of the ownership of the means of production. Rather it was a question of greatly expanding the productive forces which would automatically lead to the improvement and development of socialist relations of production and the superstructure as well as to the elimination of class differences and social distinctions and inequalities, (which remained precisely because of the inadequate development of the productive forces).(112) Technological advancement and the development of the productive forces, thus, became the privileged mechanism through which socialism was actually achieved. The promotion of production was, in itself,

108. Hua Guofeng, PR., 19, 6 May 1977, pp. 15-27; for an analysis of 'uninterrupted revolution' and 'continuous revolution'; see Young and Woodward, 1978.
109. Wu Jiang, PR., 3, 20 January 1978, p. 7.
110. Ibid.
111. Ibid., p. 6.
112. CCP.CC., 27 June 1981, BR., 27, 6 July 1981, p. 39.

conceived of as a revolutionary process. The line of the Eighth Party Congress, which owed much to Stalin, was partially restored, namely that class struggle was not the principal contradiction of socialist society; rather the principal contradiction lay in the relationship between the 'backward productive forces' and the 'advanced socialist system'. The implications of that restoration will be explored in Chapter Two.

Quite clearly, 'continuing the revolution' has become nothing more than a question of developing the productive forces, of modernising and expanding technology. Politics has become nothing more than the promotion of production. Ye Jianying's speech on the thirtieth anniversary of the founding of the People's Republic made this clear,

> At present, the four modernisations constitute the pivot of our political life. The security of the state, social stability and a better material and cultural life for our people all hinge ultimately on the success of modernisation, on the growth of production. Our work in every field must revolve around and serve modernisation.(113)

The same point had been made much more explicitly in a Renmin Ribao editorial five months earlier,

> The four modernisations will not come about through idle talk, we must strictly avoid idle chatter and firmly give substance to politics in production, vocational and technical work. Those on the various fronts must see that every type of work we are now doing serves the realisation of the four modernisations and possesses the utmost political significance. From this point of view it can be said that extracting more oil is the politics of the petroleum industry, producing more coal is the politics of coal-miners, growing more grain is the politics of the peasants, defending the frontier is the politics of soldiers, studying diligently is the politics of students. 'The only criterion for the results of political education is the improvement achieved in economic conditions' (Lenin, 1921). We must persist in taking practice as the only criterion of truth, and actual results in work and the

---

113. Ye Jianying, 29 September 1979, BR., 40, 5 October 1979, p. 23; emphasis added.

situation of work as the measures of the political level of all units and individuals.(114)

As this quote makes abundantly clear, economic practice (for example, coal extraction, etc.) is always political practice. We would agree that economic activity is political to the extent that economic production (along with the ensemble of practices unified as 'socialist') aids the consolidation of a socialist economy. This quote, however, goes much further than that and appears to undermine, at least to some extent, the proposition that economic practice is always political practice. This is because if the politics of the economic instance is designed to increase economic production, then it appears that the political is, in fact, excluded from the economic instance altogether. This 'appearance' is informed by the fact that the criterion used in the determination of a so-called 'political activity' in the economic instance is stated to be purely economic (i.e. to expand and develop productivity). Politics then, by its own activity, appears to be excluded from the economic. Let us examine this argument as it unfolds before us; for appearances can be deceptive.

The major proposition is that politics appears to be excluded from economic practice by the assertion that politics is an economic practice. In other words, it is political activity which appears to exclude the political. But here we can see that the very act of exclusion of the political from the economic is itself a political activity; it is itself a politically-informed practice. Because the act of exclusion of the political is itself a political practice, we can say that the political remains within the economic in that it intervenes to allege its own exclusion. This political practice, however, is not directly visible; for its visibility is hidden by its own assertion of its own exclusion. It is, nevertheless, as we can now see, present and active in the economic. The employment of the political within the economic instance is, however, to highlight and specify the object of such a practice as economic and, in this sense, it operates as little other than a shadow of the economic. Its purpose is that of privileging politically economic practice and as such, it operates as a mere epiphenomenon of that site. The materiality of the political, then, can be said to be totally saturated by the economic which secures and maintains it. The criterion for political activity becomes economic. This means that 'political consciousness' must be inextricably linked to economic production for, as we have seen, politics is merely the epiphenomenon of the economic. Here is the basis for the re-emergence of Stalin's social spontaneism in that 'political consciousness' is seen as a reflection of economic conditions. 'Socially-organised experience' in the labour process is seen as the measure of one's political stand; for if 'political consciousness' is 'read off' the

---

114. RMRB., 11 April 1979, p. 1. The quote from Lenin, (1921), is in CW., XXXIII, 1966, p. 79; the translation varies slightly.

economic instance, then that instance must be the point of its determination. We thus return to the position of Stalin and Bogdanov, a position Mao broke with by centering on the notion of exploitation and struggle in the determination of 'labour experience'.

Much of the debate within Chinese Marxism on the relationship between politics and economics has dealt quite explicitly with Mao's position on this matter.(115)   The debate has centered around the question of the primacy of economics and whether or not politics can be decisive in certain conditions.   Lin Zili and You Lin, for example, have argued that while politics can have an important reflexive effect on economics, it can not determine economics. The primacy of politics under any conditions is totally condemned.(116)   In response to this position, Zhao Guoliang posits a dialectical relationship between economics and politics and argues that although economics is the ultimate determining factor, politics can in certain circumstances be decisive.   Politics can not be primary (this he sees as a fundamental error) even if in specific circumstances it plays a leading role, for he asserts the absolute primacy of economics in the last instance. Nevertheless, because of the dialectical relationship between them, politics and economics depend one on another, and in specific situations one or the other may be decisive.(117)   Zhao relies heavily on Mao for support for his more 'flexible' position.   He quotes approvingly from Mao's 'On Contradiction',

> Some people think that...in the contradiction between the productive forces and the relations of production, the productive forces are the principal aspect;   in the contradiction between theory and practice, practice is the principal aspect;   in the contradiction between the economic base and the superstructure, the economic base is the principal aspect;   and there is no change in their respective positions.   This is the mechanical materialist conception, not the dialectical materialist conception. True, the productive forces, practice and the economic base generally play the principal and decisive role; whoever denies this is not a materialist. But it must also be admitted that, in certain conditions, such aspects of the relations of production, theory and the superstructure in turn manifest themselves in the principal and decisive role.   When it is impossible for the productive forces to develop without a change in the relations of production, then the change in the relations of production plays the

---

115. For a fuller elaboration of the Chinese debate on this relationship, see Womack, 1981.
116. Lin Zili and You Lin, Jingji Yanjiu, 1, 1978, Chinese Economic Studies, 3, 1979, pp. 87-108.
117. Zhao Guoliang, Jingji Yanjiu, 6, 1979, pp. 33-8.

principal and decisive role...When the superstructure (politics, culture, etc.) obstructs the development of the economic base, political and cultural changes become principal and decisive.(118)

Duan Ruofei and Dai Cheng, in response to Zhao, claim that Mao really meant that politics had a reflexive effect on economics, not a determining effect, and that there is an essential difference between the two terms.(119) What Duan and Dai want, according to Womack, is an a priori exclusion of the primacy of politics in any situation.(120)

A number of points need to be made here. Whether Mao's position may be characterised as 'flexible' or not seems to us to be essentially irrelevant. Certainly that flexibility (primacy of the economic, but under certain conditions the political can be principal and decisive) seemed to become less and less evident as Mao's critique of Stalin's economism developed. The earlier discussion of Mao's critique of Stalin was not undertaken because we believe that Mao's thought was a consistent body of writing that exhibited no contradiction nor development. It was undertaken precisely because it has been seen as a totally new development within Marxist theory which has broken decisively with previous conceptions of socialist transition and thereby constitutes the means through which all the problems of socialism might be solved. Such is not the case! Nevertheless, whether Mao's position was flexible or whether 'continuous revolution' could be seen as a general model for socialist transition, the central point is that Mao always accorded privileged causality either to the economic or to the political. Such privileging, whether on the part of Mao or the post-Mao leadership, has been possible precisely because of their reductionist epistemology. What is important is the underlying epistemological mechanism which allows the ontological privileging of one site (either the political or the economic) to take place. This is not to say that no change in strategies of socialist transition occurs when one site rather than another is ontologically privileged. Rather it is to state that any dichotomy that may be established between the political and the economic, between base and superstructure, between forces and relations of production, is essentially false. All such dichotomies rest upon an underlying reductionist epistemology. Mao may have broken with the position of Stalin and Bogdanov by centering upon the political, but the underlying reductionist epistemology was maintained. It is the continued adherence to this epistemology by the present Chinese leadership which has allowed it to invert Mao and once again ontologically to privilege the economic. Obvious tendencies toward such privileging are clear in any of the theoretical debates on socialist transition that have taken place within Chinese Marxism since

118. Mao Zedong, (1937), SW., I, 1965, pp. 335-6.
119. Duan Ruofei and Dai Cheng, Jingji Yanjiu, 7, 1979, pp. 28-36.
120. Womack, 1981, p. 73.

1976. The debate on the relationship between politics and economics provides a clear example of this privileging and of the tendency to collapse the political into the economic.

Clearly, it is not only the political which has become an epiphenomenon of the economic; the same fate has also befallen the ideological. For the present Chinese leadership, ideological work has become nothing more than persuading the people of the need for socialist modernisation and the development of the productive forces, encouraging them to accept whatever changes are necessary to realise this goal and, further, encouraging them to work diligently for its realisation. Ideological and organisational work no doubt continue; but this work is only to ensure the success of the present 'political line' and of the policies and tasks for realising the four modernisations.(121) For Ye Jianying ideological work had to 'get down to realities'.(122) He argued that, 'we must proceed from the objective state of affairs and tackle actual problems which remain unsolved owing to failure in emancipating the mind'.(123) Emancipating the mind, for Ye, meant studying the objective economic laws governing socialist construction and acting in accordance with them. This was to be done so that one could study 'the new problems encountered in our advance and explore the best ways to develop the productive forces, enhance the people's enthusiasm for work and raise their living standards; we must readjust and reform our economic structure, management system and methods of work'.(124) One may see from this the tendency for the ideological, like the political, to become a mere epiphenomenon of the economic.

This section of the chapter has argued that there are disturbing tendencies within post-1976 Chinese Marxism to collapse levels of practice on to one site - the economic. The present line on the diminishing nature of class struggle, which is manifested only in the economic instance, and on the political nature of economic practice indicate the degree of conflation of these two instances. The same may be said for the ideological instance which, according to the present Chinese leadership, should directly serve economic production. Indeed, emancipating the mind can only be achieved, through solving economic problems and by observing 'objective economic laws'. In the words of Ye Jianying, work in every other field revolves directly around economic modernisation. Science and technology are bound ever more closely to production. They are characterised as part of the productive forces. Those engaged in scientific research are seen as part of the working people directly

---

121. Ye Jianying, 29 September 1979, BR., 40, 5 October 1979, p. 24.
122. Ibid., p. 27.
123. Ibid.
124. Ibid.

engaged in the labour process.(125) Similarly, the concern for the establishment of a socialist legal system emanates directly from the de-emphasis on class struggle and the need to promote stability and unity. As such, it is designed to advance the development of the productive forces and to ensure 'public order' in work and production.(126) Clearly, there are quite obvious tendencies in the present Chinese leadership's strategy of socialist transition which appear to tie it the abstract analytical method of Bogdanov and Stalin. To this extent then, we can see the tendency toward the tectological determinism central to Stalin's theory of the productive forces. We thus come close to Stalin's 1936 position that the transition to socialism was assured provided that the economy was fully developed.

For Stalin, industrialisation was regarded as having been basically completed by 1936 and, therefore, all 'people' had access to the experience of labour. Thus, all elements of society had access to the advanced techniques which produced not only higher productivity but also a higher socialist 'consciousness'. As the Soviet official history was later to outline, the period from 1924 to 1936 saw massive changes in all fields,

> During this period the relation of class forces within the country had completely changed; a new Socialist industry had been created, the kulaks had been smashed, the collective farm system had triumphed, and the Socialist ownership of the means of production had been established in every branch of national economy as the basis of Soviet society. The victory of Socialism made possible the further democratisation of the electoral system and the introduction of universal, equal and direct suffrage with secret ballot.(127)

This universal ballot was extended to 'the whole people', for it was now 'the whole people' which had access to the scientific organisation which was once the preserve of the working class. The official history continued,

> Thus the old class dividing lines between the working people of the U.S.S.R. were being obliterated, the old class exclusiveness was disappearing. The economic and political contradictions between the workers, the peasants and the intellectuals were declining and becoming

---

125. Deng Xiaoping, 18 March 1978, <u>PR</u>., 12, 24 March 1978, pp. 10-11.
126. Ye Jianying, 1979, NPC., 1979, pp. 224-30.
127. CPSU., 1939, p. 342.

obliterated.   The foundation for the moral and political
unity of society had been created.(128)

What had changed for Stalin between 1924 to 1936, was the subject of
history. It had increasingly moved from being simply the working class
toward the concept of 'the whole people'. 'The whole people' was
regarded by Stalin as increasingly gaining access to socially organised
experience.

In the present period in China, also, the conception of the subject
is increasingly being extended to include groups other than the working
class and the peasants. While there are major differences in the way
Stalin extended the definition of the 'people' in 1936 and the way the
extension is being carried out in China today, there are also striking
similarities. The development of the productive forces is seen by the
Chinese as the motive force of history. It is their development, then,
which is central not just to economic advancement but also to socialist
political development. The role of class struggle is decentered, since it
is no longer regarded as a constant and dynamic factor in socialist
advancement, but rather as a historical practice which is no longer
necessary. Class struggle is now seen as the motive force only in the
period of 'turbulent transformation' from the old society to the
new.(129) In a socialist society, after this 'turbulent transformation',
the emphasis must shift from class struggle to the development of the
productive forces. Class struggle must diminish because it is anathema
to the development of the productive forces. The development of the
productive forces is, in turn, central to socialist transition, not simply
because it is an economic prerequisite, but because it is believed that
it is the actual mechanism which leads to the successful establishment
of socialism.

From this point of view, the higher the development of the
productive forces, the more 'scientific' the 'living experience' of the
people becomes. As Lei Zhenwu points out,

> We know that man's ability to put things into practice does
> not always remain at the same level but develops forward
> continually along with the progression of history and
> advancements in science and technology.(130)

For the present Chinese leadership, it seems, knowledge develops along
with the increasingly technologically advanced labour process and,
given this, must emanate from it. The economic becomes ontologically
privileged. It once again constructs a knowing subject. Since practice

---

128. Ibid., p. 344.
129. Liu Danian, BR., 35, 1 September 1980, pp. 14-5.
130. Lei Zhenwu, Zhexue Yanjiu, 9, 1979, JPRS., 74922, 14 January
       1980, p. 28.

is the source of all genuine knowledge, since practice plays a promotive role in the development of cognition, since practice has been defined as that which develops the productive forces, and since all levels of practice have been collapsed into the economic, then those involved in the labour process (those with 'labour experience') become all-knowing subjects. We can see therefore, that the more developed the labour process, the more 'knowing' the subject becomes. Given the humanist tendencies of the present leadership (exemplified by its de-emphasis on class struggle, its attempts to end the restriction of 'bourgeois right', and its promotion of the concept of 'all people are equal before the law'), it is believed that the higher the level of the productive forces, the greater the access of the whole population to scientific experience. Thus, the theoretical basis of Stalin's 1936 Constitution re-emerges in post-Mao China where, to use Bogdanov's words, the whole people become collectivities. For the present Chinese leadership, the 'experience of labour' is no longer 'read off' political practice, as it was for Mao, but off the economic, as it was for Stalin and Bogdanov. The epistemological basis underlying their different positions, however, is exactly the same - the centrality of the notion of experience. Mao only changed the site for the determination of experience. But at least Mao in that way overcame Stalin's economism and humanism. The same cannot be said for the present Chinese leadership.

Conclusion.

This chapter has argued that the political and theoretical campaigns representing practice as the sole criterion of truth are simply devices for the elevation of the economic. But once this elevation has been understood and accepted, such political and theoretical devices will no longer be necessary. Indeed, their decline is assured by the fact that they may privilege other sites of practice. For the moment, the campaigns are, and can be little other than, underlabourers to the economic, for this site alone is ontologically privileged.

This chapter has argued that while Mao's position differs radically from that of the present leadership, the same theoretical and epistemological devices are used to privilege a particular practice (either the political or the economic). The maintenance of such epistemological mechanisms of conflation, we would argue, tie Mao, Stalin, and the present Chinese leadership to the same epistemological position. Clearly, we totally disagree with Corrigan, Ramsay and Sayer.

The work of Corrigan, Ramsay and Sayer, it will be remembered, centres upon the relations of production as the point for determining the nature of their 'social problematic'. They counterpose, on the one hand, Lenin, Stalin and the present Soviet (and Chinese) leadership and, on the other, Mao. They counterpose, moreover, the theory of the productive forces and popular power. The latter they regard as representing a major innovation and development within Marxist theory for which Mao was solely responsible. We argue that notions of popular power and popular will can, and have been, just as repressive and arbitrary as notions and practices more often represented as 'authoritarian'. As such, popular power (as a privileged site in the way it was characterised by Mao, for example,) is not necessarily any more 'socialist' than the so-called theory of the productive forces. It was the notion of popular power, after all, which underpinned and was used to justify many of the excesses of the Chinese Cultural Revolution. Moreover, popular power like the theory of the productive forces, was, and still is, used to validate the ontological privileging of 'the people' (and also the corollary - the repression of 'the non-people'). Popular power, like the theory of productive forces, is no guarantee of a democratic form of socialism.

Neither the theory of the productive forces nor the achieving of popular power should be seen as 'socialist' by definition. Both must be seen in the context of other factors in the social formation (such as the existence and operation of structures which ensure and secure the maintenance of democratic forms) and by reference to their role (privileged or otherwise) in theory. This is not to dismiss the notion of popular power, but simply to dismiss those arguments which posit it as the panacea for all the problems of socialism.

We must look beyond the dichotomy between the productive forces and the relations of production and examine the theoretical basis of such positions. Corrigan, Ramsay and Sayer fail to do this. Instead they argue that the concept of problematic is socially defined. From this, they are able to establish the Bolshevik problematic as one which highlights the role of the productive forces and which includes the theoretical position of all leading Bolsheviks. We have attempted to show, however, that one could extend this 'Bolshevism' right back to Marx. This positivist tendency is simply not the criterion one should use in specifying a Bolshevik problematic. Within Corrigan, Ramsay and Sayer's 'Bolshevik problematic', we can see major theoretical differences in the way this positivist tendency is conceived. Lenin, like Marx, stressed theoretical practice as a separate site of production. He conceived modernisation, again like Marx, as a prerequisite for socialism. He did not privilege the economic as a didactic device as Stalin and Bogdanov were to do. Both these latter figures used working class experience as the basis for their theories of cognition. Hence, their 'theory of the productive forces' had an ontological status which is not to be found in either Marx nor Lenin.

Mao, it has been argued, by decentering the theory of the productive forces, abandoned the economic as the site of ontological privilege, but he maintained the <u>mechanism for the production of knowledge based on this privileging of one instance</u>. He did little other than invert Stalin. Mao shifted the site for the production of a knowing subject (from the economic to the political) but did not abandon the mechanism for its production. This is not to deny that the Maoist 'shift' entailed quite substantial changes in the conceptualisation and theoretical elaboration of both politics and theory. Rather, it is simply to state that such changes were from within the same epistemological position and there are no indications that he broke from it. We can say that Mao worked within the same epistemology as Stalin because, theoretically, they both shared a position which privileged experience, which posited a knowing subject and which could allow, therefore, all practices to be read off a single site. Theoretically they shared the reductionist epistemology of empiricism. The terrain of knowledge production may have altered from Mao to Stalin but the mechanism which informed this production, and the devices of conflation which followed as a result, did not.

It is because Mao continued to espouse empiricist epistemology as truly Marxist-Leninist that his epistemology can now be used to validate practices he almost certainly would not have approved of. The present Chinese leadership has maintained Mao's epistemology; of this there is no doubt. All that the present leadership has changed is its terrain of application (from the political back to the economic) and, as a result, the location of its privilege (again from the political back to the economic). This is not to deny the massive changes which ensued as a result of such a change, nor is it simply a matter of denying their relevance.

It is the status of this relevance which must be questioned. Is it acceptable to dismiss the similarity of epistemological mechanisms and devices in the production of socialist strategies and focus instead upon the dichotomy between economic determinism and popular power? We believe not; for, as we have already argued, such dichotomies are dependent upon the epistemological position which organises them and through which they become intelligible. Without an understanding of this epistemology the dichotomy between popular power and economic determinism cannot even be posed. Nevertheless, with an understanding of this epistemology, as we have attempted to show the posing of such a dichotomy becomes questionable.

What is obviously not in doubt is the centrality of the epistemological to any discourse on socialist transition. It is epistemology which informs such discourses and it is the epistemological practices of socialist theorists which need to be examined far more rigorously and understood as being highly questionable. We argue against the epistemological practice of theoretical conflation which appears to predominate among these theorists. We argue against such practices in Marxist work, since such practices, as we have seen, can easily devolve into a form of economic determinism (i.e. economic development per se leads to socialism). On the other hand, through collapsing practices on to a different site (i.e. the political), a devolution into voluntarism can also easily occur. What must be challenged then, is not simply the economism or voluntarism of such practices, but rather the epistemological mechanisms which produce such practices. Here, then, it is necessary for us not only to assert the autonomy of practices (while at the same time not denying their inter-relatedness) but also to stress the need for specificity in the examination of particular practices. What we argue for is a rejection of the epistemological exercise, and a more precise, much more specific, set of calculations which are designed to examine these practices and their effects in quite specific conjunctures. It is with this very tentative proposition of the specificity of calculation in mind that we believe socialists can map out a body of practices which can then be called socialist. Such practices, we stress, however, are irreducible, as is the theoretical work which must be undertaken to articulate them. It is not our place here to map out in detail a proposed agenda for socialist transition. Such an exercise is however, not only necessary but also, given what we have said earlier, quite urgent. If socialism is to proceed in any given social formation it must be both theoretically informed and specifically located in the materiality of the various institutions of that social formation. To argue otherwise is not simply to weaken the socialist alternative, but to threaten its very existence.

Endnotes.

1. The central thesis of this chapter has been drawn from Dutton, 1983. An earlier version of this joint work was presented at the 4th National Conference of the Asian Studies Association of Australia, Monash University, Melbourne, 10-14 May, 1982. We should point out, however, that the central thesis, the arguments and indeed our basic position have been rigorously re-worked. New aspects have been added, others substantially revised and some deleted. This is particularly the case with those sections dealing with Marx, Lenin and the post-Mao leadership, and to a lesser extent with the sections dealing with Bogdanov, Stalin and Mao. In many ways, this chapter represents a substantial critique of our earlier position. We wish to thank Colin Mackerras, Bill Brugger, Jeff Minson, Peter Williams, Don McMillen, Nick Knight, Graham Young, Dennis Woodward, Anne Brown and Peter Costa for their critical and helpful comments and for their encouragement.

2. Corrigan, Ramsay and Sayer's position on the empirical basis of Marx's critique leads them to accuse Althusser and Balibar, in Reading Capital, of apriorism, (1978, p. 164). Following on from what we see as their serious misreading of Marx, we would argue further that their position is also based on a serious misreading of Althusser. To accuse Althusser of apriorism is to ignore that aspect of his work dealing with the distinction between the real object and the thought object. For Althusser, the real object exists outside, and independent of, thought. The thought object, on the other hand, is never a given. It is never concrete reality. It is already worked-up material (representations, concepts, 'facts') which are the products of previous practices, whether 'empirical', 'technical' or 'ideological'. This raw material may even be scientific, the product of past theoretical practice. Science (the process of theoretical practice) always works on the 'general', on the 'abstract', even if this has the form of a 'fact', and starting from here moves analytically towards the concrete in thought. It never works on some objective 'given' or on pure 'facts'. Indeed, theoretical practice elaborates its own scientific facts by working through theoretically the ideological facts expounded by earlier ideological practices. (See Althusser, 1979, pp. 167; 173; 183-4). Althusser argues that, in an already constituted science, theoretical practice 'works on a raw material (Generality I) constituted either of still ideological concepts, or of scientific "facts", or of already scientifically elaborated concepts which belong nevertheless to an earlier phase of the science (an ex-Generality III). So it is by transforming this Generality I into a Generality III (knowledge) that the science works and produces' (Althusser, 1979, p. 184). In this light, Corrigan, Ramsay and Sayer's attack on the 'apriorism of Althusser' seems untenable.

The raw material that theoretical practice labours on is not innate ideas nor concepts that the mind is constitutionally endowed with; it is the product of 'empirical', 'technical', 'ideological' and 'scientific' practices; it is already worked-up material. We would also posit that Althusser and Marx are in agreement on this issue. This is not to deny the massive problems of Althusser's position; it is simply to deny that <u>apriorism</u> is one of those problems.

3. Theories of social spontaneism emanate from economism in that they reduce all instances of the superstructure to mere epiphenomena of the economic. Hence 'class consciousness' becomes simply a reflection of economic conditions.

4. This section of the chapter deals primarily with Mao's position in the 1960s after he had developed his critique of Stalin and had begun to formulate the basic outlines of a theory of the generation of classes throughout the period of socialist transition, the increased danger of capitalist restoration and the urgent necessity for continued class struggle in socialist society.

5. We can see at this point that the effects of this dislocation correspond with the already articulated practice of previous Chinese Marxists who had emphasised the progressive role of the peasants. The determination of class on the basis of level of exploitation was, for example, a central tenet of Li Dazhao's theory of 'proletarian nation'. This theory, put forward in January 1920, basically argued that the Chinese nation as a whole was, because of its subservient and highly exploited relationship with the imperialist powers, a country of proletarians (Meisner, 1977, pp. 144-6). The reiteration of this position is also to be found in various forms of contemporary Chinese theories concerning foreign policy, such as Lin Biao's theory of people's war and Mao's 'thesis of the three worlds'. Lin's position, announced just prior to the Cultural Revolution, saw the wretched countryside of the world (the third world) surrounding the cities of the world (the imperialist powers) (Lin Biao, <u>PR.</u>, 36, 3 September 1965, pp. 9-30). Mao's thesis of the three worlds, set forth in 1974, saw the first world countries (the U.S.S.R. and the U.S.A.) as exploiters and oppressors, while the third world countries suffered the worst oppression. Because of their suffering, exploitation and oppression, the third world countries represented the main revolutionary force combating imperialism, colonialism and hegemonism. These oppressed third world countries were in a position to join with second world countries (those that oppress and exploit third world countries, but are themselves oppressed and exploited by the U.S.S.R. and U.S.A.) to form a broad united front in class struggle against the first world countries (<u>Renmin Ribao</u>, <u>PR.</u>, 45, 4 November 1977, pp. 10-41. See also Deng Xiaoping, <u>PR.</u>, 15, Supplement, 12 April 1974, pp. I-V). Thus, we can see that the politics of backwardness and underdevelopment, and the experience of oppression and exploitation, are seen effectively to

'proletarianise', or more correctly revolutionise, the third world. We can also see that the effect of the displacement of the theory of the productive forces was not only felt in Chinese domestic policy, but also in foreign policy.

6. Hu Qiaomu's discussion of 'objective economic laws' has also greatly influenced the debate on the relationship between plan and market. A number of formulations in this regard have emerged in the post-Mao era, for example 'integration of planning and market mechanisms'. Towards the end of 1981 a new position emerged, one that seemed to place more importance and far greater stress on planning, namely 'planned economy supplemented by regulation through the market'. This was the formula adopted by Zhao Ziyang in his report to the 4th Session of the 5th National People's Congress (Zhao Ziyang, 1 December 1981, BR., 51, 21 December 1981, p. 25), and also by Hu Yaobang in his report to the 12th National Congress of the C.C.P. (see CCP, 1982, p. 31). Soon after the Congress, an important Renmin Ribao article dealt at length with the issue, stressing the planned economy as the dominant factor. The article indicated that the 'guiding principle' of planned production was absolutely essential to the maintenance of China's 'socialist orientation',

> While it is beyond doubt that the state-owned economy must be predominantly planned, the collectively-owned co-operative economy, which is the principal economic form in the rural areas, must also be basically planned. If we do not regard planned production and circulation as the guiding principle, the unified state-run economy will disintegrate, the collectively-owned economy will deviate from serving the people's overall interests and from the socialist orientation, and the economy of the entire society will act recklessly under the domination of spontaneous market forces (RMRB., 21 September 1982, SWB/FE/7137/C/1).

Further, the article stressed 'relations inside the production process' as being most important because they determine 'the relations of exchange, of distribution and of consumption' (ibid., C/3). This led not to an emphasis on judicio-legal ownership in the determination of the form of the labour process, but rather to the question of 'control over production',

> If the state only takes part of the profits and allows enterprises to make their own decisions on production and operation, then the system of ownership by the whole people will not be embodied in the organisation and management of production. In that case it would be difficult to say that the state is still the owner of

the enterprises and that such enterprises are still state enterprises (ibid., C/4).

Thus, while it appears to us that tendencies toward the determination of the form of the labour process solely in terms of judicio-legal ownership as well as toward market regulation have predominated, it should be clear from this that such tendencies have been opposed and that some disagreement exists over basic principles central to the question of socialist transition. This leads us again to emphasise the tentative and preliminary nature of our examination of the post-Mao era.

Chapter 2

THE IDEOLOGY OF THE CHINESE COMMUNIST PARTY SINCE THE THIRD PLENUM

Michael Sullivan

The preceding chapter noted the importance of the Third Plenum of the Eleventh Central Committee in 1978 in laying to rest Mao's theory of continuing the revolution under the dictatorship of the proletariat and rehabilitating the line of the Eighth Party Congress of 1956. It noted also the Stalinist origins of that line. Back in 1936, when introducing the Draft Constitution of the U.S.S.R. at the Extraordinary Eighth Congress of Soviets, Stalin had argued that the,

> complete victory of the socialist system in all spheres of the national economy is now a fact. And what does that mean? It means that the exploitation of man by man has been abolished, eliminated, while the socialist ownership of the instruments and means of production has been established as the unshakeable foundation of our Soviet society.[1]

For Stalin, victory in the revolution had been achieved and a socialist system had come into existence with the successful transformation, in the main, of the system of private ownership of the means of production. In a similar vein, the 'Resolution on the Political Report of the Central Committee' (given by Liu Shaoqi) announced in September 1956 that,

> the contradiction between the proletariat and the bourgeoisie in our country has been basically resolved...The system of class exploitation has on the whole been brought to an end, and...the social system of socialism has, in the main, been established in China.[2]

The similarities between the above position and that of Stalin some twenty years previously goes far to explain why the Chinese Communist Party continued to respect Stalin as 'a great Marxist-Leninist', despite his 'several gross errors' [3], after he had been

1.   Stalin, (1936), Stalin, 1976, pp. 799-800.
2.   CCP., (1956), 1981, pp. 119-20.
3.   RMRB., 5 April 1956, Bowie and Fairbank (eds.), 1965, pp. 149-150.

denounced by Khrushchev at the Twentieth Congress of the Communist Party of the Soviet Union earlier in 1956. Indeed, notwithstanding its divergence from Soviet methods of planning and administration in the mid 1950s(4) and its stress laid at the Eighth Party Congress on the remaining 'revolutionary tasks' (the elimination of remaining counter-revolutionary elements and the liberation of Taiwan (5)), the C.C.P. remained locked into Stalinist orthodoxy. China had entered the stage of post-revolutionary development!

The above position was rehabilitated in late 1978 and it remains official orthodoxy. There was, however, another feature of the line of the Eighth Congress, rehabilitated after the Third Plenum, which is no longer official orthodoxy. This concerned the content given to the terms 'basic contradiction' (jiben maodun) and 'principal contradiction' (zhuyao maodun). In September 1938, in his 'Dialectical and Historical Materialism', Stalin had presented the victory of the socialist revolution as the resolution of the contradiction in capitalism between the relations of production and the productive forces. Socialism was seen as 'an instance in which the relations of production completely correspond to the character of the productive forces'(6). Thus, the task of Party leadership during socialism was to promote the progress of industry and agriculture in order 'to improve the material and cultural standards of the workers, peasants and intellectuals'.(7)   As the previous chapter noted, for Stalin the motive force of progress was economic development within the socialist 'system'.   The Chinese formulation of 1956 was identical: the basic contradiction (jiben maodun) of class societies between relations of production and productive forces and between base and superstructure had been resolved. In consideration of this, the Eighth Congress 'Resolution on the Political Report' proclaimed that the principal contradiction was,

> already that between the people's demand for the building of an advanced industrial country, between the people's need for rapid economic and cultural development and the inability of our present economy and culture to meet that need.   In view of the fact that a socialist system has already been established in our country, this contradiction, in essence, is between the advanced socialist system and the backward productive forces of society. The chief task now facing the Party and people is to concentrate all efforts on resolving this contradiction...(8)

---

4.   See Reglar, 1980.
5.   CCP., (1956), 1981, p. 120.
6.   Stalin, (1938), Stalin, 1976, pp. 860-1.
7.   Stalin, (1939), Stalin, 1976, p. 915.
8.   CCP., (1956), 1981, pp. 120-1; emphasis added.

Put like that, the 'basic contradiction' was telescoped into the 'principal contradiction'. A contradiction between the 'system' and the 'productive forces' was of the same order as one between the 'productive forces' and the 'relations of production' which supposedly had been resolved. The first part of the above quote, therefore, should be read as a statement of the principal contradiction and the second part as a restatement of the 'basic contradiction', at odds with orthodox thinking. This chapter will trace briefly the history of the above formulation after the Eighth Congress. It will note that changes were to occur in how both the 'basic contradiction' and the 'principal contradiction' were seen. These were to have profound implications for how the stages of socialist development were demarcated. Finally, through an analysis of the decisions of the Fifth and Sixth Plenums of the Eleventh Central Committee in February 1980 and June 1981 and of the Party Constitution adopted at the Twelfth Congress, it will show how the rehabilitated line of the Eighth Party Congress was modified. The first aspect of the above principal contradiction was retained but the second part - the contradictory statement of the 'basic contradiction' - was dropped in favour of a theory of 'undeveloped socialism'. This will establish the basis for the discussion of undeveloped socialism in Chapter Three.

From the Line of the Eighth Congress to the Theory of Continuing the Revolution.

Not long after the Eighth Congress, despite the strengthened recognition of Stalin's positive contributions, Mao began to define the victory of the revolution in different terms. In his famous and influential speech at the Eleventh Session of the Supreme State Conference in February 1957, entitled 'On the Correct Handling of Contradictions Among the People', Mao suggested that progress during socialism occurred through the ceaseless emergence and resolution of contradictions. This was the basis of what became known as his 'theory of uninterrupted revolution' (buduan geming lun).[9] According to Mao, the establishment of a socialist system in 1956 did not imply that the basic contradiction of class society had been resolved. The basic contradiction between the relations of production and the productive forces and between base and superstructure, remained. Having broken with the Stalinist formula concerning the basic contradiction, Mao was bound to come to a different conclusion concerning the principal contradiction and openly to criticise the Eighth Congress 'Resolution on the Political Report'. In his speech to the Third Plenum of the Eighth Central Committee in October 1957, Mao argued that the principal

---

9.   Mao Zedong, (1957), Mao, SW., V, 1977, pp. 384-421; see Young and Woodward, 1978.

contradiction in socialist society was still between the proletariat and the bourgeoisie, between the socialist road and the capitalist road.(10)

Mao's break with accepted orthodoxy was, however, not clear-cut. This is to be seen when one compares the official and unofficial versions of Mao's speech to the Third Plenum. The official version, published in 1977 in the fifth volume of the Selected Works of Mao Zedong, contains a blunt criticism of the 'Resolution on the Political Report',

(it) contains a passage which speaks of the principal contradiction as being between the advanced socialist system and the backward productive forces. This formulation is incorrect.(11)

This should be compared with an unnofficial version appearing in 1969 in the Red Guard compilation Mao Zedong Sixiang Wansui (Long Live Mao Zedong Thought). Here, Mao's assessment of the above contradiction was simply to the effect that, though Marx and Engels never put it like that, 'there is no harm in it'. The formulation of the principal contradiction was apparently a 'stylistic fault' rather than a major theoretical error.(12)   This chapter will return later to the context in which the official version was published. Suffice it to say at this point that though one may not know which version was correct, the ambiguity in Mao's thought was such that the unofficial version seems the more plausible. Mao's ambiguity after the Eighth Congress lies in his continued belief in the existence of socialism as a 'system' whilst feeling that the line of the Eighth Congress de-emphasised the importance of contradictions in socialist society. This is clear in the revised version of his 'Correct Handling...' speech which appeared a few months before the Third Plenum,

The sure triumph of our cause...does not mean that contradictions no longer exist in our society. To imagine that none exist is a naive idea at variance with reality.(13)

Mao, it seems, was reluctant to denounce the Eighth Congress because it had proclaimed the victory of socialism. He would not have wanted to undermine what was accepted as a significant historical turning point.   Nevertheless, his new stress on contradictions led him to conclusions diametrically opposed to the line of the Eighth Congress. This could be quite clearly seen in his arguments in favour of the Great Leap Forward. The 'form' of progress during socialism, Mao maintained at that time, was 'wave-like' since the ceaseless emergence and

10.   Mao Zedong, (1957), Mao, SW., V, 1977, p. 492.
11.   Ibid., pp. 492-3.
12.   Mao Zedong, (1957), Mao 1974, p. 75.
13.   Mao Zedong (1957), Mao, SW., V, 1977, p. 384; emphasis added.

resolution of contradictions determined the primacy of imbalance and disequilibrium in the economy. Moreover, since contradictions often took the form of class struggle, political, social and ideological factors were just as important in economic development as the balancing of inputs and outputs suggested by the sober formulation of the Eighth Congress.(14) Mao had not yet inverted the relationship between the economic and the political discussed in Chapter One. But he had moved away from the Stalinist position which had led most other leaders in the Communist Party to very different conclusions regarding contradictions, progress and economic development.

The ambiguity in Mao's thought between his Stalinist affirmation of the existence of a socialist 'system' and his un-Stalinist rejection of economic determinism with its linear view of progress remained throughout the Great Leap Forward. The collapse of the Great Leap and the growing Sino-Soviet dispute, however, led Mao to rethink his position. Mao began seriously to doubt whether a socialist 'system' really had come into existence in 1956 and whether the successful transformation of the system of private ownership of the means of production marked an end to revolutionary transformation. Mao's reassessment of the nature of the basic and principal contradictions after the Eighth Congress began to take on a new meaning. He began to talk about the need to 'continue the revolution'.

Chapter One has traced the evolution of Mao's thought in the early 1960s and has noted the importance of Mao's 'Reading Notes' on the Soviet textbook <u>Political Economics</u>. In his criticism of that text, Mao remarked that it,

> does not start from contradictions in its study of socialist economy. Actually it does not recognise the universality of contradictions, or the fact that social contradictions are the motivating force of social development.(15)

Mao's decisive step, reached by 1962, was his recognition that among the contradictions generated by socialist society were class contradictions. Thus, the basic contradiction between the relations of production and the productive forces took on a new meaning; the basic contradiction determined the necessity of continued revolutionary transformation. This was made quite clear in Mao's 'Talk at an Enlarged Central Work Conference' in January 1962 in which he argued that,

> in socialist society new bourgeois elements may still be produced. During the whole socialist stage there still exist

---

14. Mao Zedong, (1959), Mao, 1968-9.
15. Mao Zedong, (1961-2), Mao, 1974, p. 299, and Mao, 1977(a), p. 107.

classes and class struggle, and this class struggle is a protracted, complex, sometimes even violent affair.(16)

The tone was even stronger in Mao's speech to the Tenth Plenum of the Eighth Central Committee in September of that year,

We must acknowledge the existence of a struggle of class against class, and admit the possibility of the restoration of reactionary classes...A country like ours can still move towards its opposite...I think that right-wing opportunism in China should be renamed: it should be called Chinese revisionism.(17)

Underlying these claims was a definition of socialism different from either the Eighth Congress formulation or the subsequent theory of uninterrupted revolution. Socialism was not a system which came into being when private ownership of the means of production was transformed. That transformation was only the first necessary step in a protracted process of negating capitalist relations of production. Rather than being a system, socialism was the process in which those capitalist relations were negated. Capitalist relations, moreover, were constantly reproduced during the process of their negation; this gave rise to class struggle. The class struggle generated by socialist society itself was now seen as the principal contradiction. Its eventual resolution depended upon correct leadership now; otherwise 'revisionism' or retrogression would take place.

Mao's theoretical explorations were not coherently expressed in the early 1960s, though their broad contours had appeared in official Chinese polemics with the Soviet Union by the outbreak of the Cultural Revolution. As the previous chapter noted, many of these ideas became a part of what was known in the Cultural Revolution as Mao's theory of 'continuing the revolution (jixu geming lun) under the dictatorship of the proletariat'. This 'theory' was adopted as official C.C.P. ideology at the Ninth Congress in 1969 and reaffirmed as such at the Tenth Congress in 1973.(18) It also provided the starting point for the theories of transition explored during the mid-1970s by members of the so-called 'Gang of Four' and the 'Shanghai school of political economy'.(19)

---

16.   Mao Zedong, (1962), Schram (ed.), 1974, p. 168; PR., 27, 7 July 1977, p. 12.
17.   Mao Zedong, (1962), Schram (ed.), 1974, pp. 189-90 and 192.
18.   CCP., 1969, pp. 113-4; CCP., 1973, p. 62.
19.   Yao Wenyuan, Hongqi, 3, 1975, SPRCM., 814, pp. 16-26; Zhang Chunqiao, Hongqi, 4, 1975, SPRCM., 819, pp. 2-11; Wang (ed.), 1977; Christensen and Delman, 1981, pp. 2-15.

Official blessing for the theory of continuing the revolution resulted in sustained criticism of the formulations of the Eighth Congress throughout most of the 1970s. But an important point was often overlooked. The theory of continuing the revolution raised criticisms of a qualitatively different nature to those raised by the theory of uninterrupted revolution, even though the origins of both lay in Mao's stress on the ceaseless emergence of contradictions after relations of ownership had been transformed. The theory of uninterrupted revolution, it will be remembered, still affirmed the notion of socialism as a system. The latter theory, on the other hand, saw socialism as a potentially reversible process which required constant revolutionary action - action which went far beyond 'the correct handling of contradictions'. Adherents to Mao's views on uninterrupted revolution simply claimed that the line of the Eighth Party Congress was undialectical and therefore mistaken. Adherents to Mao's later views on continuous revolution, on the other hand, tended to see the line of the Eighth Congress as an ideological statement of those who sought retrogression. In this vein, it was argued that the contradiction between an advanced socialist system and backward productive forces was 'theoretically groundless'. Moreover,

> the fabrication of this 'principal contradiction' was to create a 'basis' for their fallacy of the 'dying out of class struggle' in order to negate Chairman Mao's Marxist-Leninist scientific thesis that the principal contradiction in China is the 'contradiction between the working class and the bourgeoisie', deny the existence of contradictions, classes and class struggle in socialist society, oppose continuing the revolution under the dictatorship of the proletariat, overthrow the proletarian dictatorship and restore capitalism.(20)

Though one is tempted to dismiss this style of criticism out of hand as just 'empty sloganeering' typical of the Cultural Revolution, one should acknowledge the tremendous symbolic significance, as a negative example, which the Eighth Party Congress line had attained once the theory of 'continuing the revolution' had been adopted as official policy. One suspects that adherents to the Cultural Revolution, mindful of their break both from Stalinist orthodoxy and Mao's own position of the later 1950s, were constantly worried about an ideological counter-attack in the name of the Eighth Congress line. They knew they were skating on thin ideological ice.

It was probably such fears which in the aftermath of the turbulence of the late 1960s, led to any deviation being tarred with the brush of the 'line of the Eighth Congress'. Thus, Zhou Enlai (celebrated

---

20.   PFLP., 1973, p. 20.

nowadays as a realistic adherent to the line of the Eighth Congress) told the Tenth Congress in 1973 that Lin Biao and Chen Boda (reviled nowadays as opponents of the Eighth Congress line) had sought to negate 'continuing the revolution' at the Ninth Congress (1969) in favour of promoting production. This was nothing more than,

> a refurbished version under new conditions of the same revisionist trash that Liu Shaoqi and Chen Boda had smuggled into the resolution of the Eighth Congress, which alleged that the major contradiction in our country was not the contradiction between the proletariat and the bourgeoisie but that 'between the advanced socialist system and the backward productive forces of society'.(21)

One may probably take with a pinch of salt the notion that collusion took place at the Eighth Congress to distort Mao's analysis of contradictions; indeed Mao rejected a similar type of criticism during the Cultural Revolution.(22)   It is important, however, to note the symbolic importance of the Eighth Congress line throughout the 1970s.

It is important also to bear in mind that both adherents to Mao's theories of uninterrupted revolution and continuous revolution were opposed to the Eighth Congress line. It is possible, therefore, that some leaders might have remained highly critical of that line whilst not necessarily supporting the 'Gang of Four' or the 'Shanghai school'. Perhaps the above quote from Zhou Enlai might be seen in that light. Consider also, for a moment, the programmatic outline for the modernisation of industry, agriculture, science and technology and national defence (the four modernisations) put forward by the State Council under the de facto leadership of Deng Xiaoping in 1975. The 'General Programme of Work for the Whole Party and the Whole People' was criticised by the 'Gang' in 1976 as one of Deng's 'three poisonous weeds' and praised in 1977, after the 'Gang's' demise, as a 'fragrant flower'.(23)   This document was, of course, highly critical of policies associated with the 'Gang of Four' but was very careful to distance itself from the formulations of the Eighth Congress,

> Adhering to Marxist theory, we criticise the theory of the productive forces peddled by political swindlers such as Liu Shaoqi. The core of their fallacy lies in their saying that after the completion of the socialist revolution in the ownership of the means of production, the principal contradiction in the country is no longer between the proletariat and the bourgeoisie, or between socialism and

21.   Zhou Enlai, Xinhua, 31 August 1973, SWB/FE/4387/C/1-2.
22.   Mao Zedong, (1966), Schram (ed.), 1974, p. 269.
23.   Xuexi yu Pipan, 4, 1976, SPRCM., 873, pp. 1-12; Hongqi, 8, 1976, SPRCM., 886, pp. 43-50; PR., 33, 12 August 1977, pp. 28-32.

capitalism, but that between the progressive relations of production and the backward productive forces... Criticising this theory of productive forces is completely correct and imperative. We have to criticise it today, and continue to do so in the future.(24)

One commentator, Kenneth Lieberthal, explains this attack in terms of Deng Xiaoping's concern to adorn the document with suitable Cultural Revolutionary language in order to enhance its political respectability.(25) This may be so; but there are good grounds for taking the criticism at face value. There were significant differences between the formulations of the Eighth Congress and the theory behind the plans of 1975 to implement the four modernisations. The differences found concrete expression during the first two years after Mao's death, (1976-78).

When one considers ideological developments in China in the period immediately following Mao's death, one must remember that the theories of uninterrupted revolution and continuous revolution offered different criticisms of the line of the Eighth Party Congress. In December 1976, the new Party Chairman, Hua Guofeng, seemed to reject not only the arguments of the 'Gang of Four' but also the line of the Eighth Party Congress. The latter is implied in his criticisms of Stalinist orthodoxy. Stalin,

> did not look at socialist society from a materialistic dialectical viewpoint of the unity of opposites, but saw it as an integrated whole where there is only identity but no contradictions.(26)

During the late 1950s, according to Hua, Mao 'fundamentally negated the metaphysical view that contradictions do not exist in socialist society and that there is no longer any need to make revolution'.(27) Hua stressed the importance of Mao's arguments that the basic contradiction of socialist society was between the relations of production and the productive forces and between base and super-structure and that the contradiction between the proletariat and the bourgeoisie and between the socialist road and the capitalist road was the principal contradiction in socialist society.(28) Liu Shaoqi and Chen Boda, on the other hand,

> said that the bourgeoisie had been eliminated and the question of which would win out, socialism or capitalism,

---

24. Chi Hsin, 1977, p. 222.
25. Lieberthal, 1978, p. 37.
26. Hua Guofeng, 1977, p. 11.
27. Ibid., p. 15.
28. Ibid., p. 14.

had already been settled. They spread the theory of the
dying out of class struggle precisely for the purpose of
writing off the socialist revolution.(29)

Similar arguments were put at the Eleventh Congress in August 1977,
which attempted to consolidate the Hua Guofeng leadership, and at the
First Session of the Fifth National People's Congress in February
1978.(30)   Hua's explicit aim was to implement the 'four modernisations' within the framework of 'continuing the revolution'. This was,
in fact, not the theory which Mao would have recognised after 1962.
The 'theory' was, of course, purged of Mao's ideas of that time under
the rubric of eliminating the influence of the 'Gang of Four'. What
passed for 'continuous revolution' was what had once been called
'uninterrupted revolution' and took for its inspiration Mao's ideas of the
late 1950s. But one must stress: though this theory was very different
from the theory of 'continuous revolution' described earlier, it was still
critical of the line of the Eighth Congress. The developments of 1976-
78 underline the point that hostility to the line of the Eighth Congress
might come not only from advocates and beneficiaries of the Cultural
Revolution but also from many who were not renowned as its adherents
- including sworn enemies of the 'Gang of Four'.

We see here a continuity in the years 1977-78 with the proposals
in the 1975 'General Programme'. We can thus understand the
unambiguous wording of the version of Mao's speech of October 1957
which appeared in the official text of Mao's Selected Works published
in 1977 and which was referred to at the beginning of this chapter. The
mood of the time might also explain why the official version was given
the title 'Be Activists in Promoting the Revolution'.

For two years, the post-Mao leadership placed great emphasis on
developing an ideological position different from that of both the 'Gang
of Four' and the line of the Eighth Congress. The quasi-leap forward of
1978 should be seen in the context of an 'uninterrupted revolution'
version of promoting the 'four modernisations'. We now know that the
legitimacy of Hua Guofeng's chairmanship rested on this formulation
and that, even whilst the 'Gang' was being arrested, some members of
the C.C.P. leadership proposed changes more far reaching than those
pursued by Hua.(31) By 1978, these people were in the ascendency and
could claim legitimacy as the quasi-leap ran into trouble. By 1978,
more and more leaders felt increasingly that despite the wide-ranging
campaign against the 'Gang of Four', many of the changes had only
been cosmetic. The return to 'uninterrupted revolution', in reality if
not always in name, had restored the idea of a socialist 'system'. The

29.   Ibid., p. 12.
30.   CCP., 1977, p. 123; Hua Guofeng, NPC., 1978, pp. 1-118.
31.   Issues and Studies, 2, 1979, p. 88.

next step was to redefine the principal contradiction. The groundwork was being laid for a reassessment of the line of the Eighth Congress.

In June 1978, Deng Xiaoping argued that the 'starting point and fundamental point' of Mao Zedong Thought was not the theory of continuing the revolution but 'seeking truth from facts'. Practice was the 'sole criterion of truth'.(32)   But what was practice?   Practice boiled down to achieving anticipated results - a pragmatist rather than a Marxist notion. Thus, because a socialist system had been established in 1956, it was now possible to plan social development.   Practice existed in real economic production and not in making revolution. As Deng put it, whether the Party's line is conducive to the development of the productive forces...is the only arbiter of the correctness of this line'.(33) Hua would certainly not have disagreed that it was important to develop the productive forces and, as has been noted, had come to see the importance of doing this within a socialist 'system'; but the idea of developing the productive forces as the only arbiter of correctness was too much to swallow.   In the official media, the criticisms of Stalin's failure to understand contradictions as the motive force of progress went on.(34)

The veteran Party historian and social scientist Hu Qiaomu supported Deng's views in a very important speech to the State Council in July 1978.   Here Hu brought back the old Stalinist argument that the task of leadership was to ensure that economic work proceeded in accordance with 'objective economic laws'. Since the establishment of a socialist system had resolved the major political problems, the remaining problems were scientific; how best to run the economy.(35) It was adherence to objective economic laws which would establish a framework for correct economic policy, not the theory of continuing the revolution.   In effect, Hu's speech constituted a direct criticism of the plans for the quasi-leap announced by Hua in February 1978. One may understand why its publication was delayed.

Soon, however, Hu's speech and other advocacy of Deng's new position appeared in the official press.   Such open expressions of dissent on the public stage were to mobilise much additional dissent below the surface and confrontation occurred. The crunch came at a Work Conference in November 1978 and, of course, at the famous Third Plenum. Large scale turbulent class struggle was now declared, once again (as in 1957), at an end.(36) The Party's focus shifted explicitly from revolution to modernisation and in everything but name, the Plenum revived the formulation of the Eighth Party Congress.

32.   Deng Xiaoping, PR., 25, 23 June 1978, p. 15.
33.   PR., 28, 14 July 1978, p. 8.
34.   PR., 50, 15 December 1978, p. 8.
35.   Hu Qiaomu, PR., 45, 10 November 1978, p. 8.
36.   PR., 52, 29 December 1978, p. 11.

The Reassessment of the Line of the Eighth Congress: The Cat Changes Colour.

In the 1970s, Deng Xiaoping had been criticised for the remark that it did not matter whether a cat was white or black so long as it caught mice. After the Third Plenum 'catching mice' - achieving economic results - was the order of the day. As adjustments were made to economic strategy at the Second Session of the Fifth N.P.C. in June 1979 and new plans were unveiled at the Third Session in August-September 1980(37), however, considerable attention was still paid to the colour of the cat. In March 1979, Deng Xiaoping in an important speech, was careful to point out that during the 'new stage' of socialism heralded by the Third Plenum, economic modernisation should continue to be guided by four time-honoured principles: adherence to the socialist road, the dictatorship of the proletariat, the leadership of the Communist Party and Marxism-Leninism Mao Zedong Thought.(38) Deng clearly sought to head off criticism from two different directions. On the one hand, he had to deal with the disatisfaction with C.C.P. leadership and the socialist system expressed in the Democracy Wall Movement. After encouraging the movement during the meetings which led up to the Third Plenum in 1978, Deng now made it clear that criticism would be tolerated so long as it did not violate the above four principles. To give force to this point, orders were given on 29 March 1979 for the arrest of Wei Jingsheng, the author of a famous 'big character poster' of 5 December 1978 entitled 'Democracy is the Fifth Modernisation'.(39) On the other hand, Deng had to contend with those members of the Party who regarded the resolutions of the Third Plenum as an excessive move to the right.(40)

In treading a middle road, Deng had recourse to time-honoured formulae. Yet the content of those formulae underwent considerable change. We have already seen how Mao Zedong Thought was bent in a pragmatist direction under the guise of 'seeking truth from facts'. We have seen also how adherence to C.C.P. leadership was redefined in terms of economic modernisation instead of continuing the revolution. As for the dictatorship of the proletariat, this was now seen as identical with the old formula of 'people's democratic dictatorship', a formula more conducive to the establishment of a socialist legal system where rights were assigned to 'the people' rather than being class-specific and more conducive to representative forms of democracy in which all non-proscribed sections of the people were to

---

37.   Hua Guofeng, BR., 27, 6 July 1979, pp. 5-31; Yao Yilin, BR., 38, 22 September 1980, pp. 30-43.
38.   Deng Xiaoping, (1979), Deng, 1983, pp. 150-1.
39.   Gardner, 1982, pp. 141-53.
40.   RMRB., 7 September 1979, JPRS., 74250, 25 September 1979, p. 45.

have access.(41)

It was the remaining principle - 'adherence to the socialist road' which provided the overall theoretical context for all other changes in C.C.P. ideology. The symbolic importance of the Eighth Congress line as a negative example made it difficult to rehabilitate. The Third Plenum had vindicated the Eighth Congress decisions in a general sense, but considerations of the switch of emphasis at the Third Plenum did not soften the impact of an article in the April 1979 edition of <u>Lishi Yanjiu</u> (Historical Research). The article noted that the analysis made at the Eighth Congress was scientific and conformed to the objective reality of the Chinese situation. The principal contradiction between proletariat and bourgeoisie had indeed been basically resolved in terms of political power and ownership.(42) The Third Plenum was seen as a continuation and promotion of the spirit of the Eighth Congress; moreover, the 'false charges' brought against it had already been 'exposed for what they were'. It was anticipated that 'the glory of the Eighth Congress' would shine with increasing brilliance.(43) It was in the same spirit that an article in <u>Guangming Ribao</u> noted in August 1979 that Stalin's 1936 'Report on the Draft Constitution of the U.S.S.R.' had drawn the correct conclusion. Stalin's error had not been to play down the importance of class struggle, as Hua Guofeng had stressed as late as 1977, but rather his belief that class struggle had become more acute.(44) Indeed, the spirit of reassessment was given glowing official endorsement by Ye Jianying in his speech in September 1979 on the eve of the thirtieth anniversary of the People's Republic.(45)

It seemed then that the Stalinist formulae of 1956 had been totally revived. Saich, one of the few Western scholars to remark upon the importance of this restoration, noted that,

> the 'good name' of the Eighth Party Congress (1956) had been restored. The Congress is a symbolic occasion for the present leadership because it...finds its echo with the present leadership. Consequently, the basic contents of the documents adopted by the congress are still considered to be of relevance.(46)

But it was not quite that simple! Agreement that the basic contradiction had been resolved and that the principal contradiction

---

41. Sichuan Ribao, 28 May 1981, JPRS., 78505, 14 July 1981, pp. 55-8; Faxue Yanjiu, 23, February 1980, JPRS., 76141, 30 July 1980, pp. 36-9.
42. Lishi Yanjiu, 4, 1979, SWB/FE/6147/B11/5.
43. Ibid., B11/8.
44. GMRB., 22 August 1979, SWB/FE/6207/B11/4-5.
45. Ye Jianying, BR., 40, 5 October 1979, p. 13.
46. Saich, 1982, p. 25.

was no longer a matter of class did not necessarily imply acceptance that the principal contradiction was 'between the advanced socialist system and the backward productive forces'. In its initial reassessment, <u>Lishi Yanjiu</u> observed that the socialist system established in 1956 'could not but be considered advanced', but the Eighth Congress 'might not have been sufficiently precise and exact' in defining the principal contradiction.(47) Throughout 1979, other academic journals attempted to lend precision to that formulation to the point where the 'advanced' nature of the socialist system was denied. What, after all, did the word 'advanced' mean? This point was taken up in an article by Su Shaozhi in the June 1979 edition of the Shanghai journal <u>Xueshu Yuekan</u> (Academic Monthly) entitled 'On the Principal Contradiction Facing our Society Today'. Su began by noting that although the repudiation of the Eighth Congress formulation of the principal contradiction during the Cultural Revolution 'was not based on facts', it was not necessary to revive it now.(48) This was because socialist relations of production might only be said to be advanced when they met the demands of the 'expanded productive forces' and facilitated their development. It had often been argued that the commune system of ownership in the Chinese countryside was more 'advanced' than ownership by the production team. In practice, given the level of development of the productive forces when the communes were established, only the production team could meet the demands of the productive forces and facilitate their development. In the late 1950s and 1960s, clearly the production team was more advanced than the commune. Indeed, Su argued strikingly, since the productive forces 'can never be overtaken by the relations of production in any sense'(49), what was defined as 'advanced' in the late 1950s might not be advanced at all. The same sort of argument applied to the socialist system itself. For Marxists, Su argued, the criterion of advanced socialism was that laid down by Marx in his 'Critique of the Gotha Programme' - the first stage of communism. The current stage of socialism was 'not yet well developed' and the 'imperfect aspects of the social system' had yet to be transformed and adapted to the needs of production.(50)

Arguments such as those of Su Shaozhi suggested that either the use of the term 'advanced' to describe the relations of production was misplaced or else some relations of production should be described as 'too advanced'. This is a point to which we will return. Suffice it to note here that it was arguments like these which were to lead to the formulations concerning 'undeveloped socialism' - where the relations of production were modified to suit what were acknowledged to be the low level of the productive forces. Clearly, an affirmation of the

---

47.   <u>Lishi Yanjiu</u>, 4, 1979, SWB/FE/6147/B11/6.
48.   <u>Xueshu Yuekan</u>, 7, 1979, <u>JPRS.</u>, 74813, 21 December 1979, pp. 13 and 15.
49.   <u>Ibid.</u>, p. 14.
50.   <u>Ibid.</u>, p. 15.

Eighth Congress had to dispense with the notion that there was a principal contradiction between the advanced socialist system and the backward productive forces.   No mention was made of this contradiction when a Renmin Ribao commentary endorsed both Su Shaozhi and the Eighth Congress in August 1979.(51)

The Line of the Eighth Congress and the Correct Handling of Contradictions.

This chapter argued earlier that Mao's initial reaction against the line of the Eighth Party Congress in 1957, whilst affirming socialism as a system, was to reject the notion that the basic contradiction had been resolved and, of course, to reject the notion that the principal contradiction was 'between the advanced socialist system and the backward productive forces'.   By 1979, the official position of the C.C.P. was to affirm socialism as a system, to argue that the basic contradiction had indeed been resolved and, of course, to reject the formulation of the principal contradiction in terms of the advanced socialist system and the backward productive forces.   The position was very different from Mao's 1957 views in substance, though there were some formal resemblances.   Though Deng disagreed with Mao's 1957 views as to the solution, he could still maintain that the contradiction between relations of production and productive forces was 'basic'. Deng had come to repudiate the Eighth Congress formulation of the principal contradiction in favour of a version of undeveloped socialism, expressed in the Eighth Congress language of a gap between aspirations and capabilities.   Mao had come to reject it in favour of class struggle. The point is that both rejected it.

We may see here how Mao's 1957 speech 'On the Correct Handling of Contradictions' might be pressed into service by the current C.C.P. leadership.   We may understand too the profound irony of juxtaposing elements of the undialectical Eighth Congress formulation with what was originally intended as a dialectical advance on that formulation. As Deng Xiaoping put it,

> It is better to expound the basic contradiction according to Comrade Mao Zedong's explanation in his article 'On the Correct Handling of Contradictions Among the People'... He spoke a lot about this question, and it is not necessary for me to repeat it...Anyway, experience over the past twenty years and more has shown that Comrade Mao Zedong's explanations of this contradiction are more proper than others.(52)

---

51.   RMRB., 28 August 1979, SWB/FE/6210/B11/3.
52.   Deng Xiaoping, (1979), Deng, 1983, p. 168; emphasis added.

Deng's views were fed very quickly into official C.C.P. pronouncements indicating how 'On the Correct Handling...' was to be read. The 'Report on the Work of the Government', adopted by the Second Session of the Fifth N.P.C. in June 1979, stressed the importance of Mao's analysis of contradictions, arguing of course that the principal contradiction was not class struggle as Mao believed but the tasks of economic modernisation as called for by the Eighth Congress.(53)

But once the principal contradiction had been reduced to economic modernisation, the content given to the word 'contradiction' changed. The analysis ceased to be dialectical and became mechanical. The correct handling of contradictions was no more than fine-tuning the social mechanism. As the Introduction to this book pointed out, handling a contradiction among the people was treated as responding to a disfunction. From the dialectical proposition that change in a totality was the result of the interplay of internal countervailing forces, one was presented with something resembling Western functional analysis.(54) Though Mao was not wholly innocent of the charges of functionalism in 1957, he would have been shocked to see his approach reduced simply to exercises of problem-solving in a static system. The establishment of institutions to ensure socialist democracy and law, therefore, were merely mechanisms to handle any system disfunction. Defined out of existence was Mao's dialectical view of progress and his entire struggle dynamic.

But no Marxist-Leninist may define class struggle out of existence, as Stalin found to his cost in the late 1930s. Class struggle had to be given a place in the new ideology; but what place? This was to be one of the most contentious issues in formulating the new ideo-logical line, since for many years under Mao class struggle had been seen as the principal contradiction or the 'key link'. As has been noted, the revived position of the Eighth Congress that a socialist system had been established, by definition reduced class struggle to a secondary position. The Eighth Congress, it was argued, recognised the funda-mental unity of the people, though its 'correct call' to shift the focus of Party work was not heeded until the Third Plenum in 1978.(55) Given that fundamental unity, the class struggle which existed after 1956 was now seen to differ greatly from that which existed before the socialist system came into being. This is shown in Table 2.1.

---

53.   Hua Guofeng, BR., 27, 6 July 1979, pp. 9-11;   see RMRB., 28 August 1979, SWB/FE/6230/B11/13.
54.   Deng Xiaoping, (1979), Deng, 1983, p. 168.
55.   Tianjin Ribao, 7 August 1979; JPRS., 74552, 9 November 1979, p. 3.

Table 2.1: Class Struggle Before and After the Transformation of the System of Ownership.

THE SYSTEM OF OWNERSHIP

	Before Trans- formation	After Trans- formation
Class struggle		
Scale	Against exploiting classes as a whole	Against a small number of counter-revolutionaries, new exploiting elements, remnants of the 'Gang of Four', and a 'very small' number of unreformed remnant elements of the exploiting classes.
Form	On a large and turbulent mass scale	Solved in accordance with state laws.
Type	Violent	As the number has decreased, and the scope narrowed, it is relaxed rather than sharp.

Source: Xinhua, RMRB., 22 July 1979, JPRS., 74012, 15 August 1979. p. 34.

One may see from Table 2.1 that class struggle was accorded a secondary position because it could not destroy the socialist system. It now occured amongst individuals who, for whatever reason, threatened or undermined socialism. By definition their efforts had to fail. Here a curious content was given to the word 'dictatorship of the proletariat'. That 'dictatorship' was manifested not in mass mobilisation nor in collective political struggle but through the institutions of socialist law which applied equally to everybody.(56) Since dictatorship of the proletariat was taken to be the same as 'people's democratic dictatorship' and since the ranks of the people had been expanded to include almost everybody, the theoretical content of the term boiled down to the dictatorship of almost everybody over everybody else. This had not much to do with the proletariat, but neither did the formulation current during the Great Proletarian Cultural Revolution. In official accounts, it was said that 'the most important task of the dictatorship of the proletariat is no longer to suppress class enemies but to protect and develop the forces of social production'. Marx would have been astonished! The dictatorship of the proletariat had become synonomous with the rule of law. This position harked back to that taken by Dong Biwu at the Eighth Congress, to whom honour was now paid.(57) Continuity had once again been established.

This chapter has already noted that the official assessment of class struggle was the most strongly resisted of all the new ideological formulations. Resistance often harked back to pre-1978 assessments. Some cadres, it was argued,

> worry that if class struggle is not taken as the key link, we will be unable to guarantee the socialist direction of economic construction...Some comrades feel that if we do not 'take class struggle as the key link, there will be no political work to do.(58)

In academic journals it was stressed, for example, 'that at present and for a long time to come in the future, we must remain vigilant against revisionism'. 'The proletariat must still persist in class struggle to prevent the degeneration of the socialist country'.(59) All this was a far cry from the official position that there existed no class struggle of the type implied, no possible danger of 'revisionism' and no possible danger of degeneration while the social system was intact.

By 1982, the official regional press was warning of the dangers of 'peaceful evolution' back to capitalism and of the C.C.P. 'changing political colour'. Though the Cultural Revolution had been a mistake,

---

56. Wenhuibao, 1 September 1979, JPRS., 74468, 29 October 1979, p. 6.
57. Dong Biwu, CCP., 1956, pp. 79-97; RMRB., 10 December 1979, JPRS., 74974, 22 January 1980, p. 6.
58. Beijing Ribao, 14 September 1979, JPRS., 74748, 11 December 1979, p. 14-5.
59. Xueshu Yuekan, 3, 1979, JPRS., 74334, 9 October 1979, p. 12 and 14.

the Party,

> must not go to the other extreme, negate the correct
> things in Mao Zedong's standpoint and deny that the danger
> of 'peaceful evolution' still exists in China(60)

To refute the above criticisms, the Party affirmed once again in 1982
the secondary nature of class struggle. Though the basic contradiction
was still between the relations of production and the productive forces,
it did not manifest itself as class struggle. As the Party mounted a
major onslaught against 'spiritual pollution' in 1983, one suspects that
the official formulation was, and will continue to be, under severe
strain.

Going Backward in order to Go Forward.

The previous discussion of the dictatorship of the proletariat and
the rejection of the Eighth Congress line on the 'principal
contradiction' may seem no more than an exercise in splitting semantic
hairs. This is far from the case. There were many important practical
consequences of the new formulation. Once it was accepted that
relations of production might be too far in advance of the productive
forces, then it became possible to go back to earlier forms of social
organisation without acknowledging that one was fostering capitalism.
The ideological formulations might well be in large measure a rationalisation of policies already decided. But ideology and policy surely have
a reciprocal rather than just a one-way relationship.

Arguments we have already encountered in the article by Su
Shaozhi were developed after 1979 into theories of stages of development between undeveloped and advanced socialism. Theorists felt it
will be remembered, that a system of planning and management had
been adopted which was too advanced for the level of the productive
forces. Thus, when criticism was made of 'old forces of habit' which
hindered the four modernisations, reference was surely being made not
just to the residues of the old society but also to habits stemming from
an inappropriately 'advanced' system adopted in the 1950s.(61) It was
felt at that time that rapid economic progress might be achieved not
by patiently improving the productive forces but by constantly
improving the system. According to the veteran political economist Xu
Dixin,

> We had originally determined that the process of
> transformation should take some fifteen years. However,

---

60.   Dazhong Ribao, 1 April 1982, JPRS., 81260, 13 July 1982, p. 23.
61.   Xinhua, RMRB., 22 July 1979, JPRS., 74012, 15 August 1979,
      pp. 34-5.

because of a subjective desire to speed things up...the transformation was achieved within four years. We were particularly overhasty in pressing on with agricultural co-operation and the transformation of the handicrafts and small businesses. The changes were too fast.(62)

Because of this emphasis on speed, the 'basically correct' economic policy changed to one which impeded the development of the productive forces. But, one might ask, since the policies adopted since the Third Plenum were designed to correct mistakes going back to the period in the 1950s when the Party 'closed the door too tight', how was economic policy in the early 1980s any different from that of the early 1950s during the period of 'New Democracy'?   Xu side-stepped the question.   He differentiated the two periods not in terms of the concrete policies implemented but in terms of the existence of a dominant socialist system.(63)   But if that system were inappropriate, it could only have been so as a result of policy. In any case, once one separates policy from the operation of the system, it is but a short step to arguing that any policy which develops production improves the system.   Could one then argue that capitalist relations of production would improve the socialist system if one concludes that they facilitated output?

Xu Dixin's arguments harked back to a little-talked-about speech made by Chen Yun to the Eighth Congress. The speech was quite unlike any other in the Congress documents.   At that time, Chen acknowledged the successful transition to socialism which he saw purely in terms of a change in formal ownership. He warned, however, against undue haste in transforming other aspects of the relations of production. Instead, he called for a relaxation of the restrictions which had been imposed on market relations during the 'New Democratic' period.   These restrictions had facilitated the transition to socialism but now the system of ownership had changed, they were no longer necessary.   In fact, their continuance could hinder the further development of production and undermine socialism. State-capitalist enterprises, restricted during the transition process, should now have those restrictions lifted since they had become 'socialist'.(64) By the late 1970s Chen seemed to be saying: 'I told you so'. He, of course, is now seen as one of the principal architects of recent changes.

Current policies therefore, are seen as an 'ample retreat' from 'an abnormal form of development to a more rational structure'.(65) The abnormal violation of what is now seen as the 'objective economic

---

62.   Xu Dixin, Xu et.al., 1982, p. 14.
63.   Xin Shiqi, 8, August 1981, JPRS., 79344, 2 November 1981, pp. 27-8.
64.   Chen Yun, CCP., 1956, pp. 157-76.
65.   Beijing Ribao, 15 June 1981, JPRS., 78709, 10 August 1981, p. 35.

law' that the forces of production should correspond completely to the level of the productive forces (66) is being rectified, and the relations of production are being restructured to achieve that correspondence. This is the rationale for dismantling the commune structure in agriculture and promoting the rural responsibility system.(67) Similar arguments are used to support enlarged enterprise autonomy, increasing integration with foreign trading and financial institutions, joint operations with transnational corporations and the growing individual economy. It is argued that although the individual economy and the 'special economic zones' are not socialist, they contribute to increasing output and thus contribute to consolidating the socialist system.(68)

The retreat to policies associated with the early stages of socialist transition is justified by adherence to the 'objective economic law' that relations of production should always be in accord with the development of the productive forces. But once such is seen as an 'objective economic law', then how may it be seen as a 'basic contradiction' which has been resolved? Clearly, if policies are being pursued to return to the smooth operation of the 'objective economic law', then it has not been resolved. But then, neither could it be said to have been resolved at the time of the Eighth Party Congress. This was quite clear in the arguments put forward by Su Shaozhi. In 1956, it will be remembered, it was implied that the backward productive forces would catch up with the advanced relations of production because of the socialist system. After 1978, it has been argued that the requirements of the socialist system were such that the relations of production should be scaled down to correspond to the level of the productive forces.(69) Obviously, what is meant by the socialist system is of a much lower order than that of the 1950s.

One of the clearest expositions of the stages of development was made in 1981 by Feng Wenbin, Vice President of the Central Party School. Feng distinguished between the principles which defined a socialist system and the form public ownership took. So long as public ownership of the means of production was dominant, so long as exploitation had been brought to an end with labour power no longer a commodity and so long as distribution was according to work done, one might talk about the existence of a socialist system.(70) The form public ownership took, however, depended on the level of the productive forces. The form of public ownership adopted in agriculture

---

66. Jilin Daxue Xuebao, 2, 1979, JPRS., 74595, 19 November 1979, p. 19.
67. O'Leary and Watson, 1980; O'Leary and Watson, 1982.
68. Xin Shiqi, 1, 1981, JPRS., 78733, 12 August 1981, p. 6.
69. Wenhuibao, 13 January 1980, JPRS., 75320, 17 March 1980, pp. 25-6. See also discussion in Schram, 1981, pp. 428-31.
70. BR., 23, 8 June 1981, p. 21.

had been inappropriate. Future socialisation of agriculture depended upon raising the level of the productive forces, by de-collectivisation in some degree now.(71) So long as the overall principles defining the socialist system were maintained, this could not be seen as a return to capitalism.(72) Expanding on such arguments, other articles spoke of 'the stratified state of the productive forces', requiring 'pluralistic forms of ownership'.(73)   All these features of 'incomplete and impure'(74) socialism were still governed by the 'overall principles'. The overall system was not capitalist.

It was obvious however, that not everyone was convinced by such arguments. As one may see from Table 2.2, the line between the policies listed on the left and the deviations listed on the right was not easy to draw.

Table 2.2: Policies and Deviations.

Policy	Deviation
Responsiblity system in agriculture.	Denunciation of need for collectivisation of the 1950s.
Decentralisation of economic management to the enterprise.	Refusal to observe central plans by practicing 'selfish departmentalism'.
Enlivening rural markets.	Speculation, profiteering and black market.
Emancipating the mind.	Anarchism and ultra-individualism.

Source: Changjiang Ribao, 28 May 1981, JPRS., 78678, 5 August 1981, p. 11; Ningxia Ribao 6 May 1981, JPRS., 78709, 10 August 1981, p. 33.

---

71.   BR., 26, 29 June 1981, p. 18.
72.   Jinghan Luntan, 1, 1979, JPRS., 75919, 20 June 1980, p. 35.
73.   Wenhuibao, 20 August 1981, JPRS., 79210, 15 October 1981, p. 16.
74.   Ibid., p. 17.

Indeed, some cadres considered that the restoration of capitalism was already a reality and some actually welcomed it,

> ...some twenty years ago, some people went so far as to say that with a backward economy and culture, our country is not qualified to promote socialism, and now is the time for us to move back to take some refresher courses in capitalism.(75)

One may understand why those cadres came to that position. Adherence to the formal principles defining the socialist system, whilst allowing great variety of forms of ownership, offered no guide as to just how far the reforms ought to go. Once it was accepted that 'private enterprises with large-scale equipment and operations will have lost capitalist characteristics' once they 'operate within our legal system and under the state plan',(76) then anything goes. Both Lenin and Mao spoke at various times of having to go backwards in order to go forwards later. But one has to have some guide as to how far backwards one may go. Just how may one read off the appropriate configuration of the system from the state of the productive forces? We are back to the problem discussed in Chapter One.

The Codification of the New Ideological Position: From the Fifth Plenum to the Twelfth Congress.

At the Fifth Plenum in February 1980 and the Sixth Plenum in June 1981, attempts were made to weld together the various strands of ideology discussed earlier. The Fifth Plenum was noted for its posthumous rehabilitation of Liu Shaoqi. Celebrating that rehabilitation, Renmin Ribao praised Liu's 'Political Report' to the Eighth Congress and the resulting 'Resolution'; they contained 'important standpoints (which) are correct and Marxist', whether 'viewed at that time or now'.(77) Renmin Ribao was careful, however, only to quote that part of the resolution which talked about 'the contradiction between the people's demand for the building of an advanced industrial country and the realities of a backward agricultural country' and the contradictions between aspiration and capabilities.(78) The 'advanced' socialist system had been laid to rest. Official commentaries on the Fifth Plenum went on to assert the identity between the Eighth Congress 'Resolution' and Mao's speech 'On the

---

75.   Chengdu Ribao, 16 June 1981, JPRS., 78678, 5 August 1981, p. 17.
76.   Minzhu yu Fazhi, 4, 1981, JPRS., 78450, 6 July 1981, p. 29.
77.   BR., 16, 21 April 1980, p. 20.
78.   Ibid., pp. 19-20.

Correct Handling...'(79)   A similar position was taken by the Sixth Plenum which adopted a new official interpretation of the history of the C.C.P. since 1949, entitled 'Resolution on Certain Questions in the History of the Party Since the Founding of the People's Republic of China'.(80)   The functionalist reading of Mao's 'correct handling of contradictions' was celebrated (81) and the way was open for Mao to be indicted for 'going against Mao Zedong Thought' in the 1960s and 1970s - a position which Hua Guofeng had inherited in the two years following Mao's death.(82)

The Fifth and Sixth Plenums cleared the ground for the drafting of a new Party Constitution to be adopted by the Twelfth Congress which met in September 1982.(83)   It was apparently a slow and painful process which generated much debate and disagreement.(84)   It was originally announced that the Twelfth Congress would convene early(85), but probably because of disagreement it did not convene until the due date.

This chapter has already discussed the erroneous interpretation of some Western analysts that it was not until the Twelfth Congress that the line of the Eighth Party Congress was seen as 'flawed'.   One such scholar, Lowell Dittmer, argues further that reluctance to criticise the Eighth Congress was in part due to the fact that it was that Congress which elevated Deng Xiaoping to the central leadership.(86)   He ignores the evidence that Deng himself was a prime mover behind the re-interpretation of the line of the Eighth Congress in 1979 and of the marriage of its 'Resolution' with the functionalist reading of Mao. Deng, it seems, was all along ready to re-assess the Eighth Congress and significantly, in his opening speech to the Congress on 1 September, Deng compared the importance of the Twelfth Congress, not so much with the Eighth, but with the Seventh in 1945.   The Seventh Congress had been 'the most important in the period of democratic revolution', summarising correctly the democratic revolution's twenty-odd years of tortuous development. It had proposed 'a correct programme and correct tactics' for victory.(87)   Similarly, it was hoped, the Twelfth Congress would be seen as the most important during the socialist stage.   It too summarised twenty-odd years of tortuous development and established 'a correct programme' to ensure

---

79.   Ibid., p. 20.
80.   BR., 27, 6 July 1981, p. 17.
81.   Ibid., p. 18.
82.   Ibid., p. 26.
83.   Dittmer, 1983, pp. 110-11.
84.   Gardner, 1982, pp. 173-7.
85.   BR., 10, 10 March 1980, p. 3.
86.   Dittmer, 1983, p. 109.
87.   CCP., 1982, p. 2.

the victory of socialism.(88)   The Eighth Congress, on the other hand, had been held when the 'Party was not adequately prepared ideologically for all-round socialist construction'.   Though the overall orientation of the Eighth Congress was felt to be correct, if one compared the situation in 1982,

> with the time of the Eighth Congress, our Party has gained a much deeper understanding of the laws governing China's socialist construction, acquired much more experience and become   much   more   conscious   and   determined   in implementing our correct principles.(89)

Deng's elevation of the Seventh Congress was in accord with the principle of going backward in order to go forward. But, of course, no-one was advocating a return to the policies of the time of Liberation. The Eighth Congress still had to be affirmed as celebrating the transformation of the system of private ownership. As <u>Renmin Ribao</u> put it on the eve of the Twelfth Congress,

> The Eighth C.C.P. National Congress was a great meeting of profound historical significance, called at a crucial moment when there was a great turning point in the history of our country...It pointed out a clear direction for the development of the socialist cause in the new period and the building of the Party.   The correct general and specific policies defined at the Eighth National Congress made a brilliant contribution towards finding a path of socialist construction compatible with the conditions of our country.(90)

The 'General Programme' of the Party Constitution, adopted on 6 September 1982, codified most of the elements brought together at the Fifth and Sixth Plenums(91), but one element in the discussions of previous years was remarkable for its absence. This was the discussion of stages of development from undeveloped to advanced socialism. Perhaps, any explicit discussion of undeveloped socialism might promote an invidious comparison with the Soviet Union, in which its own Communist Party had formulated its own version of advanced socialism. This comparison will be explored in Chapter Three. Suffice it to note here that though there are marked similarities in the economic determinism of both the ideologies of the C.C.P. and the Soviet Communist Party, memories of past disputes prevent the full exploration of those similarities.   For example, in practice both the C.C.P. and the Soviet Party affirm a 'Party and state of the whole

---

88.   <u>Ibid.</u>, pp. 2-3.
89.   <u>Ibid.</u>, p. 3.
90.   <u>RMRB.</u>, 30 August 1982, SWB/FE/7121/C/11.
91.   CCP., 1982, p. 94.

people' but after years of polemic, the C.C.P. is not going to acknowledge it explicitly.

A second possible reason why the 'General Programme, failed to mention the stages of socialist development was simply that controversy still raged. There was much discussion in 1981 and 1982 about those who could not tell the difference between socialism and capitalism. This became particularly important as the Party tightened up its control in the industrial sphere and launched the major movement to create a new 'socialist civilisation'. Considerable disquiet has often been noted in Army circles. The Army newspaper Jiefangjunbao asked on the eve of the Twelfth Congress,

> How can we overcome the inroads by bourgeois and other non-proletarian ideas and still retain the glorious title of...worthy communists?   If this is considered 'ultra-leftist', then upholding the Party's leadership and the four basic principles is also ultra-leftist.(92)

In 1983, moreover, further signs of a backlash against some of the economic reforms became evident. There is much evidence that the stages of socialist development are still very controversial.

The Restoration of Capitalism.

The hazy line of distinction between socialism and capitalism was not just an abstruse question of ideology. It was to have an important effect on the way lower-level cadres went about their business. In agriculture, for example, cadres were never sure just what the limits of official policy were and just how capitalist the relations of production were supposed to become. Cadres were often accused of abandoning their leadership role in following peasants in the excessive dismantling of the collective economy. Such people were held to be guilty of 'tailism'.(93)   But what was 'tailist' in 1978 was 'correct' in 1980. Consequently, those who had been 'correct' in 1978 could be denounced as 'commandist' as the household responsibility system expanded.(94) What, for example, were cadres of the Sichuan Education Bureau to do when they observed that one of the results of the success of the household responsibility system was that primary school students

---

92.   Jiefangjunbao, 28 August 1982;   reprinted in Jiefang Ribao, 27 August 1982, SWB/FE/7145/B11/4.
93.   Changsha, Hunan Provincial Service, 8 May 1981, SWB/FE/6723/ B11/19-20.
94.   Kunming, Yunnan Provincial Service, 18 May 1981, SWB/FE/6737/ B11/4.

preferred to return to farming rather than finish school?(95) The lack of clear policy directives should ideally be compensated for by cadres using their common sense in accordance with the ideological line. But when that line was unclear, what were cadres to do?

Similar sorts of problems arise when one considers 'economic crime'. One might adopt a positivist position and say that all economic crime is what the law says it is. But the law (especially a new body of law) cannot specify everything and the distinction between 'enlivening the individual economy' and 'economic crime' becomes hard to determine. This was clearly the case in Guangdong province in which, Nanfang Ribao noted, economic crime was 'rather extensive', criminal elements were 'very savage', corruption among cadres was 'severe', and where 'the capitalist ideology that "everything depends on money"' had become rampant.(96)   The severity of the problem was such that Nanfang Ribao compared the struggle against economic crime with the 'Three Anti' and 'Five Anti' campaigns of the early 1950s.(97) Ironically, the struggle against economic crime was described as one aspect of class struggle in a situation where official ideology held that turbulent class struggle was a thing of the past. Here one is reminded of a similar situation in the Soviet Union in the late 1930s after Stalin had made a similar point.

The underlying reasons for the above difficulties were explored in a number of articles pointing to the dangers of 'bourgeois liberalisation' and 'spiritual pollution' produced by the inroads of international and domestic ideology.(98) The prime culprit was overseas influence which was particularly dangerous in Guangdong because of the 'special economic zones' (99); but clearly there was also an assignation of blame to the reform policies going on at home. One major source of trouble was 'small scale production' which was bound to continue for a long time.   This provided the 'soil' for 'rightist deviation'.(100)   One is reminded here of the old complaint of the 'Gang of Four', though this time the spread of small scale production was the direct result of government encouragement.

As attempts were made to strengthen the planning system, it became increasingly clear that the concessions to capitalism since the Third Plenum had been excessive. For example,

> If we do not regard planned production and circulation as the guiding principle, the unified state-run economy will

---

95.   Xinhua, 9 June 1982, SWB/FE/7052/BII/3.
96.   Nanfang Ribao, 13 March 1982, JPRS., 80773, 11 May 1982, p. 22.
97.   Ibid.
98.   Xinhua, 1 July 1982, SWB/FE/7072/BII/2.
99.   Nanfang Ribao, 13 March 1982, JPRS., 80773, 11 May 1982, p. 23.
100. Shehui Kexue, 1, 1982, JPRS 80794, 12 May 1982, p. 73.

disintegrate, the collectively-owned economy will deviate from serving the people's overall economic interests and from the socialist orientation, and the economy of the entire society will act recklessly under the domination of spontaneous market forces.(101)

Even more suggestive was the statement,

If the state only takes part of the profits and allows enterprises to make their own decisions in production and operation, then the system of ownership by the whole people will not be embodied in the organisation and management of production. In this case, it would be difficult to say that the state is still the owner of the enterprises and that such enterprises are still state enterprises.(102)

How else may one read the above quote except as implying that the formal official distinction between capitalism and socialism was inadequate, and that some forms considered 'socialist' were really capitalist. In 1981 and 1982, discussions of this question were quite openly conducted,

In brief, we are firmly upholding the socialist system of ownership but, as required at this stage of socialist development, allow individual economy and other operational patterns as supplements. Can the socialist system admit capitalist ownership? Do our present joint enterprises constitute state capitalism? These questions are worth our further study.(103)

No less a person than the veteran economist Xue Muqiao demanded serious consideration of the limits to capitalist forms,

Individual ownership has been recognised by law, and enterprises jointly operated with Chinese and foreign capital and even a small number of foreign enterprises have also been recognised. Now that we may take in foreign capital and welcome investment by overseas Chinese, are people who have large deposits with the bank permitted to invest in state enterprises? At present some enterprises encourage their staff and workers to join them as partners; many co-operatives have been newly established by commune members raising funds themselves

---

101. Xinhua, 20 September 1982, RMRB., 21 September 1982, SWB/FE/7137/C/1.
102. Ibid., C/4.
103. Minzhu yu Fazhi, 4, 1981, JPRS., 78450, 6 July 1981, p. 29.

and they issue bonuses to labourers according to work done
and to investors according to the amount of capital
contributed. Some well-off rural people's communes have
also set up enterprises outside the original scope of their
businesses, or have invested in state enterprises. In some
localities, some enterprises have been established with the
capital of individuals and each hires ten or more staff
members and workers. To what extent can these semi-
socialist or non-socialist sectors of the economy develop?
This question is very important and complicated and needs
serious discussion.(104)

Some of the warnings about the restoration of capitalism harked back
to some variation of the old ideology of 'continuing the revolution
under the dictatorship of the proletariat' and extended pre-1978
criticism of the Eighth Congress to take post-1978 formulations into
account.(105) Most warnings however were more moderate. It was
argued, for example, that the cornerstone of C.C.P. ideology - the
principle of correspondence between relations of production and
productive forces - was arbitrary; it could hardly be called an
'objective economic law',

There is no denying the fact that production relations must
suit the development level of productive forces, but it
must not be mechanically interpreted...Since it is only a
relative concept to say that the level of productive forces
is high or low or...advanced or backward, nobody can
possibly determine a clear and unambiguous...demarcation
line for bringing about a change to old production
relations.(106)

It was also argued that one should not rigidly separate the relations of
production from the productive forces,

Strictly analysed, productive forces and production
relations are two abstractions derived from our analysis of
social production. In...production there is no separation.
The two together always constitute a dialectical
unity.(107)

Underlying the above criticisms was the fear that the implicit belief
that anything which contributed to production also contributed to
socialism would in fact lead to capitalism. By any Marxist standard,

---

104. GMRB., 19 May 1982, JPRS., 81041, 14 June 1982, p. 24.
105. Xin Shiqi, 6, 1981, JPRS., 78847, 27 August 1981, p. 30.
106. Shanxi Ribao, 14 August 1981, JPRS., 79320, 20 October 1981,
     p. 27.
107. Xueshu Yuekan, 7, 1979, JPRS., 74450, 25 October 1979, pp. 6-7.

hiring and firing workers and returns on investment were exploitative in a capitalist sense.(108) One could not explain them as 'supplements' to the socialist economy unless one specified very clearly the degree of permissible supplementation, the conditions under which they would be tolerated and for how long. It was no use saying they would be tolerated so long as they developed the productive forces; capitalism may do that very well. It was also no use saying that the socialist system was superior because the relations of production could be shaped to fit in with the level of the productive forces, whereas under capitalism the contradiction between them became more acute, unless one specified beforehand how one knew when the one correspond to the other. The mistake, as was noted in Chapter One, and has been remarked on again in this chapter, stems from the reductionist belief that one can simply read off the relations of production from the productive forces.

Even if we assume that the present mix of socialist and capitalist relations is appropriate for the present stage of development, once one creates an edifice of law to safeguard property rights without any legal mechanism to carry out the upgrading of production relations, then one must either violate the law in the future or give up the idea of socialist transition. What, for example, is one to make of Chapter I, Article 13 of the State Constitution, promulgated on 4 December 1982, which holds that 'the state protects the right of citizens to inherit private property'?(109) Commenting on this, the jurist Wang Shuwen outlined four types of inheritable property,

(1)   citizens' lawful income, private houses, bank deposits and various kinds of articles that they use in their individual and family life
(2)   the personal income of commune members from their private plots, private tracts of mountain land, private livestock breeding and family sideline occupations
(3)   the means of production of individual labourers
(4)   the legal property of Overseas Chinese.(110)

What, one might inquire, is the class position of an individual who lives off dividends from invested capital inherited from parents who accumulated their capital from shares invested in a state-owned

---

108. RMRB., 17 September 1979, SWB/FE/6225/BⅡ/1-2;   Fuzhou, Fujian Provincial Service, 27 August 1981, SWB/FE/6817/BⅡ/9; Guangzhou, Guangdong Provincial Service, 3 September 1981, SWB/FE/6823/BⅡ/8;   Xinhua, 25 August 1981, SWB/FE/6814/BⅡ/1-3.
109. Xinhua, 27 April 1982, SWB/FE/7014/CI/5.
110. Xinhua, 9 May 1982, SWB/FE/7027/BⅡ/5-6;   wording changed for stylistic reasons.

enterprise, a tract of land farmed by hired labour and a private bicycle repair shop employing four workers?   Even the possibility of this question arising, because of the important structural changes in China since 1978, might confirm the belief of those who argue that China has abandoned socialism and will increase the fears of those who see problems with the C.C.P.'s distinction between capitalism and socialism.

Conclusion.

In contrast to the sparse secondary literature on ideological reform in China since the Third Plenum, this chapter has argued that the positive assessment of the line of the Eighth Party Congress was qualified right from the time of its rehabilitation. The reformulation involved its marriage with a functionalist reading of Mao Zedong's speech 'On the Correct Handling of Contradictions...'. The line of the Eighth Congress had such an important symbolic importance that the post-1978 C.C.P. leadership were bound to come to terms with it.

The process of ideological reform centred on such issues as the basic and principal contradictions, class struggle and the stages of development from undeveloped to advanced socialism.   After much discussion at the Fifth and Sixth Plenums of the Eleventh Central Committee, a new formulation was agreed upon at the Twelfth Congress in 1982. What apparently could not be agreed on, however, was a precise formulation of what constituted undeveloped socialism and how one proceeded from that to its advanced form.

This chapter has argued that, having thrown out the theory of 'continuing the revolution' either in its original 1960s form or in the revised 'uninterrupted revolution' form of 1976-78, the C.C.P. has established a very formalistic distinction between socialism and capitalism which is clearly inadequate. One may understand why the hazy distinction has been opposed and why many in China believe that capitalism is being restored. In the last two years, a backlash has occurred and it is possible that questions of class structure might become important once again.

Chapter 3

UNDEVELOPED SOCIALISM AND INTENSIVE DEVELOPMENT*

Bill Brugger

Advanced and Undeveloped Socialism.

I have described elsewhere two ways in which socialism has been conceived in the Soviet and Chinese traditions: as a process or as a model.(1) The previous chapter noted that Mao Zedong, in the last decade and a half of his life, and those people associated with the 'Gang of Four' were concerned with the former, albeit somewhat incoherently. For that reason the line of the Eighth Party Congress, which saw the principal contradiction in society as being between the 'advanced socialist system and the backward productive forces' was rejected (eventually) in favour of what I described as 'the generative view of class'.(2) In my earlier work, I noted that socialism as a process consisted in the progressive negation of capitalist relations of production. My critics quite correctly pointed out that the formulation, associated with the 'Gang of Four', was inadequate. The process of negation could lead in a number of directions - to communism, to a form of feudalism or even to barbarism. Much of recent Chinese discussion of the theories of the 1960s and early 1970s dwells on the feudal consequences of the 'Gang of Four's' prescriptions for the negation of capitalism. Consideration of Kampuchea under Pol Pot clearly demonstrates the possibility of barbarism. For socialism to make sense as a process one needs a clear statement of a telos, and this Mao and the 'Gang of Four' failed to provide.

Official Marxist-Leninists have usually been wary of spelling out a telos for both theoretical and practical reasons. Considerations of orthodoxy lead theorists away from the taint of 'utopian socialism', and memories of Khrushchev's 'communism in one country', to be achieved by 1981(3), make practical politicians unwilling to stick their necks out. This is particularly the case in China today, where the reaction against what is considered to be utopianism leads to much the same

---

*A version of this chapter was presented at the conference 'New Directions in the Social Sciences and Humanities in China', Adelaide University, 20-22 May 1984. Thanks are due to the participants.
1.   Brugger, 1981(b).
2.   Brugger, 1978, pp. 20-7.
3.   CPSU., 1961.

kind of atheoretical fetishisation of 'the real world' that we find among increasingly conservative Western social scientists. The prevailing mood amongst Chinese political economists is a deterministic scientism. When socialist transition is discussed, the primacy of the 'forces of production' is asserted and the development of those forces to certain levels provide necessary (and in the cruder arguments sufficient) conditions for the achievement of arbitrarily defined moments of 'socialism'. Chapter Two made it clear that this is in the tradition of Stalin's 'basic achievement' of socialism in 1936(4) and the 'advanced socialism' of the Brezhnev era.(5)

Though the methodology is similar, there are clear differences between Soviet and Chinese positions on the level at which the moments of socialist transition are pitched. There are differences too in the causal weight given to the forces of production. Many Chinese political economists now believe that Stalin's 1936 formulation pitched socialism at too low a level. They feel also that his 1952 work, Economic Problems of Socialism in the U.S.S.R., laid too great a stress on the relations of production. Whilst endorsing Stalin's criticism of Yaroshenko for collapsing the relations of production into the forces of production, they feel that Stalin then went too far in the opposite direction.(6) Their views oppose Mao Zedong's position both before and after his formulation of the generative view of class.(7)

Although Chinese political economists are no longer obliged to engage in a ritual denunciation of the Soviet Union, there is a relative silence on the Soviet version of 'advanced socialism' which has been claimed as the creation of Leonid Brezhnev. Nevertheless, the more determinist Soviet claim of the 1970s that a new stage in the development of socialism depends upon the integration of production with the 'scientific and technological revolution' is similar to Chinese thinking. It is the level at which this new stage is reached that is in doubt. This is clearly shown in the position taken by Su Shaozhi, noted in the previous chapter, and in an article by Wang Guoping which both see developed socialism as no less than the 'first stage of communism' as described by Marx in his 'Critique of the Gotha Programme.'(8) Here there is one form of ownership; society is one huge factory and planning is so perfect that distribution according to work no longer takes the form of wage payment. In Marx's words the worker,

---

4. Stalin (1936), Stalin, 1976, pp. 799-800.
5. See Evans, 1977.
6. Xiong Yingwu and Wang Shaoshun, 1980, pp. 8-12.
7. These are scattered through Mao, 1974. See in particular Mao's criticism of Stalin in 1957 to the effect that Stalin could not see the socialism could be negated, (pp. 49-50).
8. Wang Guoping, Shehui Kexue, 6, 1983, JPRS., 84330, 15 September 1983, pp. 7-14.

receives a certificate from society that he has furnished such and such an amount of labour (after deducting his labour for the common funds), and with this certificate he draws from the social stock of means of consumption as much as costs the same amount of labour. The same amount of labour which he has given to society in one form he receives back in another.(9)

Wages are eliminated because the worker receives a dividend based on work. But this is not communism since the law of value still operates. The law of value, it is stressed, is a law of all commodity production and not, as the 'Gang of Four' was supposed to maintain, only of capitalism. Because that law operates to ensure equal distribution of unequal amounts of labour (i.e. is still a source of inequality), a further step is required before communism may be reached.

I have argued elsewhere that the status of 'the law of value' as an 'objective economic law' is a matter of considerable doubt.(10) Unless one has a solution to the transformation problem, one is never quite clear how it is supposed to operate. My purpose here, however, is not to consider its theoretical validity but to examine the ideological consequences of views as to how it is claimed to operate at different stages of socialism. In the official Marxist-Leninist tradition one should distinguish three views. The first is that the law of value does not operate at any stage of socialist society and one should immediately set up a planning system which operates solely according to use values and needs. This view is rarely encountered nowadays and is usually invoked by its critics to discredit a 'left' which never maintained it in the first place. The second view is that the law of value should progressively be negated as one moves towards communism. This position still has many Chinese adherents, though such people are worried about the possibility that their position could be bent in the direction employed by the 'Gang of Four' to 'restrict bourgeois right'. The third position is that the law of value operates more perfectly as one moves towards the final stage of commodity production. Thus, it may be inferred, advanced socialism is a situation where the law operates perfectly and may be utilised by the omniscient planner, and undeveloped socialism is a situation where it operates imperfectly.

This third view gives rise to a number of important problems. Is an expanded role for the market a temporary expedient of undeveloped socialism, permitted in order to facilitate the more perfect operation of the law of value? Or is market regulation a permanent feature of all forms of socialism directed by the need for planners to have perfect information? I suspect that the latter view is more strongly held. The

---

9.   Marx, (1875), Marx and Engels, <u>SW.</u>, III, 1970, p. 18.
10.   Brugger, 1984(b).

question then arises: how could communism ever be possible? Will there be a transcendental leap when the 'perfect' operation of the law of value is miraculously transcended and the kingdom of God is established on earth? If negations really are negated, they are surely not negated so easily.

Since the transformation problem remains, what the above view boils down to in practice could be one of two positions. The first position is simply making prices correspond more to costs in which the price of labour is taken as given. But surely no believer in 'objective economic laws' would be content with wages which are completely arbitrary. The second position is to allow for the partial development of a labour market. But although commodity relations are not necessarily capitalist, the commodity nature of labour power is central to any definition of capitalism. It is pure sophistry to claim that the buyers and sellers of labour power have no class significance just because legal forms are different. Is advanced socialism then a form of capitalism?

Advanced socialism, defined in the sense of Marx's 'first stage of communism', clearly exists nowhere and is a far more lofty notion than the Soviet version of 'advanced socialism'. One is not at all sure therefore, what Wang Guoping means when he claims that some socialist societies, which have developed on the basis of mature capitalism (as Marx envisaged), already do practice remuneration according to labour.(11) He surely cannot be thinking of countries like Czechoslovakia which had the highest degree of capitalist development when the Communist Party came to power. Nor may we be at all sure just what technical conditions (forces of production) might be necessary to bring this advanced socialism into being. This is presumably why many Chinese political economists advocate the study of futurology (weilaixue). All this is great fun, but one has to have a peculiar faith in technology to believe that a socialist equivalent of the credit card could solve the technical problems of accounting according to work.(12)

The purpose of many discussions in China of the nature of advanced socialism is clearly the opposite of Soviet discussions. It is not to celebrate what exists but to point to the fact that China is an underdeveloped country, and that there are limitations on what is economically feasible. Few would disagree with that observation. There is a world of difference, however, between the idea of constructing socialism in an underdeveloped country (which refers to a process) and the creation of an 'ideal type' called undeveloped socialism. The key element of this ideal type is the same as in the

---

11. Wang Guoping, Shehui Kexue, 6, 1983, JPRS., 84330, 15 September 1983, pp. 7-14.
12. Xiong Yingwu and Wang Shaoshun, 1980, p. 81.

Stalin model of 1936 - the co-existence of different forms of ownership - by 'the whole people' (i.e. the state), the collective and the individual. One wonders why this piece of Stalinist orthodoxy is still necessary. Once it is conceded that commodity relations exist within the state sector and that the means of production are themselves commodities (denied by Stalin) and this is so even under conditions of advanced socialism, then why does the distinction between state ownership and collective ownership matter?

The answer is unconvincing. It is maintained that wages in state enterprises are set with a view to the totality of all state enterprises, whilst wages in collective enterprises are dependent upon the enterprises being responsible for their own profits and losses. Consequently, workers at identical levels who belong to enterprises under different systems of ownership may have different incomes.(13) Such a statement ignores the huge variety of forms collective enterprises take. In some of the 'large collectives' basic wages are worked out according to administratively-formulated norms not too different from those which apply in the state sector. In many of the 'small collectives', however, income levels differ widely. The crucial line of demarcation is not between the state-owned and collectively-owned units but the point at which the state can effectively exercise control. But to define the difference between undeveloped socialism and advanced socialism in terms of the effectiveness of state control is theoretically rather barren and not particularly Marxist.

In any case, I have argued elsewhere that the line of demarcation between state-owned and collectively-owned enterprises is breaking down.(14) The increase in enterprise autonomy in recent years has meant that, in state enterprises, the proportion of workers' income deriving from profits has increased markedly. Thus, payment according to work in particular enterprises with different profits will lead to wide disparities in remuneration according to work across the nation. The adoption of corporation income tax to replace in part the remittance by state enterprises of profits to the state (yishuidaili) has done much to put state enterprises on a footing similar to collective enterprises.

The Law of Planned and Proportionate Development: Agriculture and Industry.

It has been argued above that considerations of the law of value and of the structure of ownership are not of much use in establishing the dividing line between undeveloped and advanced socialism. A more sophisticated argument concerns the second of the 'objective

13. Wang Guoping, Shehui Kexue, 6, 1983, in JPRS., 84330, 15 September 1983, pp. 7-14.
14. Brugger, in Young (forthcoming).

economic laws' celebrated by Stalin. This is the law of planned and proportionate development which Stalin thought was one of the most important 'laws of socialism' and one peculiar to it. But, as some Chinese political economists have pointed out, there is nothing particularly socialist about it at all.(15) What economy can get by for long with serious disproportions? If proportionate development is really to enjoy the status of a law, there should be some indication as to what determines appropriate proportions at various stages of development and under what conditions; otherwise the 'law' is no more than a principle of the order 'porridge should not be too sweet nor too salty'.

Amongst political economists, both Marxist and non-Marxist, discussions of proportions take the form of a bewildering variety of growth models as different theorists disagree on what are dependent and independent variables. In the Marxist-Leninist tradition, debate on this issue commenced in the 1920s. Complaints of the 'genetic' school in the Soviet Union that its 'teleological' opponents were guilty of 'utopianism' and of the latter that the genetic school was unduly passive or conservative were repeated in the Chinese debates of the 1970s. The early Soviet political economists, Bazarov and Groman, maintained that the Soviet economy was determined by its weakest link - agriculture. The industrial growth rate was dependent upon the 'unapproachable fortress in which, despite all the counter-currents in our planned economy, hides the mouzhik like a snail in his shell, easily and simply escaping beyond all attempts of planning to reach him'.(16) An extrapolation of the 'natural equivalents' between the marketed surplus of pre-war agricultural and industrial products led Groman to advocate the magic 37:63 ratio to apply to the Soviet Union of the mid-1920s. Stalin's response to this 'conservatism' was to assail the mouzhik and forcibly to attempt to alter the relations of production in agriculture. Growth models à la Fel'dman, which stressed the future potential for consumption of current investment in heavy industry, became de rigeur.(17) The result was the achievement of remarkable growth rates in Soviet industry amid agricultural stagnation.

The demise of the genetic school in the Soviet Union left Soviet theorists of planning with no external criterion by which one could monitor the operation of the law of planned and proportionate development. In the 1930s and thereafter, a complex set of material balances were worked out and discussions of planning dealt with how well the various balances fitted together rather than external determination. The danger of this form of objectivism is obvious. Its practitioners acquire greater and greater degrees of power through their knowledge

---

15. Xiong Yingwu and Wang Shaoshun, 1980, pp. 104-8.
16. See Dobb, 1948, p.328. On the arguments of Bazarov and Groman, see Jasny, 1972, pp. 89-138.
17. See Domar, 1957, pp. 223-61.

of technological relationships to the point where <u>technique</u> itself is seen not only as the determinant of how the system operates but also its own <u>telos</u>.(18)   Moreover, when the system fails to operate smoothly, it is seen merely to be the result of imperfect knowledge.

A diagnosis of the problems in Soviet planning in terms of imperfect knowledge led to two responses in the mid 1960s. The first of these sought to enlarge market forces as a way of supplementing planners' information. The second sought to employ new mathematical formulae and to use computers to specify more accurately the myriad balances which constituted the planning system.   Both of these approaches were felt to be ideologically suspect. The first evoked fears of capitalist behaviour in the pursuit of the profit motive and suggested that planners might lose their ability to chart the course of a new balance. The second approach involved the use of formulae which covertly implied that factors other than labour might be designated as productive inputs. This challenged the received orthodoxy.(19) More important to the argument here, once the objective of political economy shifted to the Western notion of the allocation of scarce resources among competing ends according to a utilitarian calculus, then however sophisticated the balances might be and however 'optimal' the resource allocation, the ends of planning seemed forever reduced to the internal logic of the existing system. The only future was greater and more efficient growth. One may call that 'advanced socialism', if one wishes, but one wonders what content is given to the word 'socialism'.

The above discussion of planning is important when one considers the charge that the law of planned and proportionate development was disrupted in China during the Great Leap Forward. I have argued elsewhere that a good many objective laws of science were violated in the Great Leap; but what is usually meant by violation of the law of planned and proportionate development referred to the collapse of the hitherto relatively coherent set of subjective balances which constituted the plan. In other words, incoherent subjectivity replaced relatively coherent subjectivity. If one is going to make any sense out of the claim that Great Leap strategies ignored objective reality in an economic as opposed to a natural scientific sense, then one has to reintroduce some kind of external determinant which makes sense of the original balances in the first place. And here we are back to a Chinese equivalent of the original genetic school of the Soviet Union. Amongst contemporary Chinese political economists, instead of an extrapolation from a pre-war situation and pre-war 'natural equivalents', we have an extrapolation from the early 1950s and '1950s natural equivalents'.   The ratios of the early 1950s are taken as

---

18.   This kind of argument may be found in Ellul, 1967.
19.   See Campbell, 1968. For a detailed discussion of the use of mathematical economics, see Ellman, 1973.

appropriate and deviations from them taken as distortions, the key element being the relatively unchanging nature of the Chinese peasant. Thus, the attempts to change the relations of production in the mid and late 1950s were superficial. The 'agricultural fortress' was stormed but in the end proved to be as resistant to change as Bazarov and Groman felt the agricultural sector to be in the Soviet Union. Thus, Chinese theorists now actively support measures to restore the more 'healthy' relations in agriculture of the 1950s. As the previous chapter has discussed at great length, this is said to be in accordance with the 'law' that, 'the relations of production should correspond to the productive forces'.(20)

Just like Chen Yun, Bazarov and Groman would have said: 'I told you so'. That indeed is also the conclusion of many later Soviet theorists. One is reminded of an official Soviet denunciation of Mao Zedong written in the early 1970s,

> To try to establish new relations of production without relying on a development of the productive forces is to establish these relations of production only in formal terms, without the substratum on which alone they can be consolidated and developed.(21)

But what happens when you admit you have committed the above error? Do you de-collectivise, as the Chinese appear to be experimenting with, and rehabilitate the conservative economists of the 1950s? Or do you struggle on in the manner of the Soviet Union, until a time comes when you can blame all your present ills on the dead leader who got you into trouble in the first place without rehabilitating the conservative economists who opposed his way of thinking? Of course, the Soviet leadership can not rehabilitate the ideas of the genetic school. That would be to ignore what is said to be 'Lenin's idea that developing industry is the basis of the transformation of the national economy along socialist lines'. It was with this in mind that official Soviet comments criticised Mao's stress on 'agriculture as the base with industry the leading factor'.(22) So, if in the Soviet economy agriculture is not the determinant which specifies the objectivity of the law of planned and proportionate development, what is? Unless that question can be answered, there is no point talking about planned and proportionate development as a law.

In China nowadays one sees a modern version of the old genetic school of the Soviet Union. This is coupled with market socialist proposals which echo and go beyond those of the Soviet Union in the mid 1960s. Such proposals are accompanied also by a desire to tread

---

20. See Watson, 1983.
21. Krivitsov and Sidikhmenov, 1972, p. 212.
22. Ibid., p. 237.

the path of mathematical sophistication followed by the Soviet Union some two decades ago.   There is, as yet, not much of an ideological backlash but Soviet history suggests the form it might take.   The genetic approach will be criticised as 'conservative'.   Fears that the state might lose control over a decentralised economy have already led to a modification of the decentralisation plans for industry and could lead to more.   Finally, the non-Marxist assumptions in some of the mathematical models being studied could produce severe criticism.   We may only hope that the criticism will not just arise out of a yearning for comfortable orthodoxy and that a new teleological approach to balance might be achieved.   If this means abandoning elements of the traditional Marxist-Leninist approach to value theory, so be it; though the utilitarian road is not the only one to take.

Extensive and Intensive Development.

The law of planned and proportionate development is central to the distinction between undeveloped and advanced socialism. Here, it may be argued, as with the law of value, advanced socialism suggests an economy in which balance is more 'perfect' than undeveloped socialism.   But that does not help us decide when one has moved from one stage to another.   To make sense out of the distinction, we must consider another dichotomy proposed by socialist political economists - between extensive expanded reproduction and intensive expanded reproduction, (or to simplify things between extensive and intensive development).(23)

Extensive development is a response to economic backwardness. An ample supply of resources and an abundant supply of labour results in a concentration on the maximisation of output rather than the efficiency of inputs.   At an early stage of economic development efficiency does not matter very much. The administrative structure, appropriate to a socialist society experiencing such extensive develop- ment, is that developed by Stalin.   A centralised system is created which maintains high rates of accumulation (usually, though some disagree, more at the expense of the peasants than the workers).   The rural surplus is syphoned off by a pricing system which discriminates against rural produce, and the resulting 'scissors crisis' is dealt with by administrative coercion.   At this stage of development, the law of planned and proportionate development can tolerate a greater stress on heavy industry than on light industry and a greater concentration on industry in general than on agriculture. A high ratio of national income is devoted to accumulation and a high proportion of accumulation is

23.   A classic discussion is Sik, 1967. For a Chinese discussion, see Xu Fulan, Shehui Kexue, 6, 1983, JPRS., 84404, 26 September 1983, pp. 19-24.

devoted to investment in production. Of that investment in production, a high proportion is devoted to capital construction.

A point comes, however, where either the supply of labour dries up or material supply (and energy) problems become acute. There is, therefore, a need to switch to a more intensive strategy of development which concentrates on the efficiency of factors of production. At this point, supposedly the law of planned and proportionate development demands a different mix. The accumulation rate should be lowered with greater attention given to consumption; non productive investment should be given greater stress and more attention paid to the renovation of equipment than to investment in capital construction. As consumption is boosted there is greater incentive for workers and peasants to improve labour productivity. Greater investment in light industry with faster rates of turnover increases the efficiency of output, and the renovation of equipment yields returns faster than simply expanding capital construction.

In the 1970s, many theorists in the Soviet Union felt that the transition to their own form of advanced socialism involved the shift to intensive development. Using the reductionist methodology described in Chapter One, they offered a linear view of development where the transition point could simply be read off the current state of the productive forces. By the late 1960s and early 1970s, a new balance was said to be emerging between agriculture and industry, between investment in productive capacity and the growth of consumption funds, and between investment in capital construction and in equipment renovation.(24) The development of the 'scientific and technical revolution' was an inexorable linear process.

Some East Europeans, however, noted that the linear pattern of development was inadequate as a description of what was happening. The shift from extensive to intensive development and to advanced socialism ought to be seen in terms of a number of cycles. The work of Kalecki is of note here, and McFarlane has recommended his approach to the analysis of China.(25) Three sorts of cycle are proposed. The first of these - the economic cycle - derives from the fact that the centrally planned system developed under Stalin, is geared to very rapid growth in manufacturing which outstrips the ability of the primary sector to produce raw materials and energy. Periodically, therefore, central planners are forced to respond to a crisis of proportions by restricting growth and attempting to produce a new balance. Thus, in China two major cycles are discerned: 1953-61 and 1962-78. The crucial determinant here is not just agriculture (as the old genetic school maintained) but the whole primary sector which produces raw materials and energy. Such cycles may be expected to

---

24.   See Evans, 1977, and Bergson, 1973.
25.   McFarlane, 1983; my interpretation is somewhat different.

recur unless the centrally planned system is drastically reformed and the path opened for intensive development, without which any form of 'advanced socialism' is impossible.

A second type of cycle is determined by inputs of technology. In China the importation of Soviet technology in the early 1950s inaugurated a cycle which came to an end when new inputs from that source dried up. Then in the late 1950s, a new cycle commenced; the original Soviet technology was copied but there was also a massive development of intermediate technology. The inefficiency of this intermediate technology led to demands to step up technological imports from the West and Japan; and this process, after fitful starts, inaugurated a new cycle in the mid-1970s. This time, the inability to make full use of that new technology and to provide necessary infrastructural support led to a drastic curtailment of the cycle in 1979-80.

The third type of cycle is a socialist version of Kalecki's 'political trade cycle'. In Kalecki's original formulation a crucial determinant was elections. This is not the case in China, though it is clear that under certain conditions a leadership oriented to rapid growth will appeal to a mass audience; either to existing enthusiasts or, failing that, to those who seek to mobilise the masses to develop a synthetic 'u' (motivation) factor. The crucial point, where such a leadership will inaugurate a cycle, is when what is felt to be an unsatisfactory rate of growth persists at a time of rising expectations. Such was the case in 1958, 1969-70 and 1978. One must stress that the attempt to inaugurate a radical push is not made in years of economic or political crisis (e.g. 1961 and 1976), but in periods of rising expectations as the situation improves. I have discussed elsewhere my methodological doubts concerning what the social psychologists call 'aspirational relative deprivation'. I am even more skeptical about the 'principal contradiction' in socialist society being expressed in such terms.(26) Nevertheless, with McFarlane, I believe that a fuller explanation of the problems of moving from extensive to intensive development may be obtained by integrating this third type of cycle with the other two.

In the current Chinese literature, scant attention is given to the cyclic view. One might see why considerations of the political cycle might be disquieting. One might have to conclude that the 'Gang of Four' was responding to different moments of the cycle rather than being consistently 'bad eggs'. The linear view is frequently considered, though most Chinese accounts discuss the concepts of extensive and intensive development without any reference to historical stages at all.(27) It is as if intensive development is characteristic of socialism in any form and of capitalism too. Thus, when Chinese theorists talk

---

26.   Brugger and Hannan, 1983, pp. 45-8.
27.   E.g.   Xu Fulan, Shehui Kexue, 6, 1983, JPRS., 84404, 26 September 1983, pp. 19-24.

about high accumulation rates, they usually mean anything over 30 per cent regardless of time; when they speak of high productive investment rates in state-owned industry, they usually mean anything over 20 per cent regardless of time. Nevertheless, some concessions are made to the linear view in discussing the proportion of investment devoted to capital construction in state owned units. It is usually acknowledged that this had to be high in the early 1950s but that the rate of decline was too slow.

Table 3.1: Accumulation and Investment by Five Year Plan

Five Year Plan	Year	Accumulation Rate	Productive Investment Rate in State Owned Units	Balance	Proportion of Investment in Capital Construction*
1	1953-57	24.2	14.8	9.4	96.2
2	1958-62	30.8	23.3	7.5	92.3
	1963-65	22.7	14.0	8.7	84.5
3	1966-70	26.3	15.5	10.8	80.7
4	1971-75	33.0	20.6	12.4	77.5
5	1976-81	33.4	21.2	12.2	73.5

* proportion to total investment in state-owned units.

Source: State Statistical Bureau: Abstract, JPRS., 84111, 12 August 1983, p. 115, and Liu Huiyong, Jingji Yanjiu 6, 1983, JPRS., 84013, 1 August 1983, p. 24.

Conventional Chinese analyses of the figures in Table 3.1 praise the First Five Year Plan period but note that considerable difficulty was experienced thereafter in the transition from extensive to intensive development. In part this was because of 'leftist' errors, particularly during the Great Leap Forward, the Cultural Revolution and the quasi-leap of 1978. These errors are seen either (in the linear sense) as subjective deviations from the true path, or ahistorically as a product of ignorant 'utopians'. No attempt is made to look at any systemic causes of 'leftist' behaviour such as the exponent of cycles would demand.

The official account goes like this. In the first period of 'leftist' fervour (1958-60) there was much talk of telescoping stages of development and of 'liberating' productive forces which were just waiting to be unleashed by the appropriate changes in the relations of production. Mass mobilisation would solve the materials barrier and one could push that sector and heavy industry for all one was worth. A very high 'u' factor (morale) would allow for very high accumulation and investment rates. Thus, the accumulation rate for 1958 was said to be 33.9 per cent, rising to 43.8 per cent in 1959. The investment rate in state-owned enterprises was 25 per cent in 1958, rising to 28.9 per cent in 1959 and 33 per cent in 1960.(28) As a consequence, a large amount of capital was tied up in construction work and factories could not operate at full capacity.

In the Cultural Revolution a different picture emerged. It 1966, at the outbreak of the Cultural Revolution, the accumulation rate was 30.6 per cent and for years it remained high despite a declining growth rate caused in part by the turmoil of the Cultural Revolution. The fear of war at that time led to a huge amount of productive investment in the interior (the so-called 'third line'), where infrastructure was insufficient and therefore, efficiency was low. Yet, for all that, the investment rate in state-owned productive enterprises overall actually declined to 10.8 per cent in 1968 and was only 15.5 per cent for the Third Five Year Plan.(29) We may only conclude from this that there was proportionally greater investment in non-productive sectors and a greater stress on building up reserves. The concern with defence and preparedness for war was summed up in the slogan 'store grain everywhere, dig tunnels deep and guard against revisionism'. This was a different kind of extensive development from that of the late 1950s, and it was not until the 'flying leap' of 1970 that the 'left' excesses of the Great Leap began to appear once again. Though the flying leap was short-lived, the imbalances associated with a 'left' version of extensive development persisted to some extent throughout the Fourth Five Year Plan and were exacerbated once again by the quasi-leap of 1978. It was only after that experience that a fundamental change in strategy occured. Drastic attempts were made to reduce the scissors gap by raising agricultural prices and fostering a rural market, and there was a dramatic shift in investment away from heavy industry. By 1981, it was seen that the shift was too rapid and a more cautious policy of readjustment was pursued. Nevertheless, current policy is still to hold down the rate of growth in order to achieve a new balance.

---

28. Liu Huiyong, Jingji Yanjiu, 6, 1983, JPRS., 84013, 1 August 1983, pp. 19-25.
29. Ibid.

Many economists have interpreted and evaluated the above official description.(30) My aim here, as a student of politics, is simply to draw out the ideological implications. Unless the words 'left' and 'right' are related to particular configurations of the productive forces or to particular moments of the various cycles, it is difficult to give them any objective meaning. 'Left', in the Great Leap, meant a high growth rate, a high accumulation rate, a high rate of investment in state-owned enterprises and a high proportion of capital construction investment in total investment. 'Left', in the Third Five Year Plan, meant a lower growth rate, a high accumulation rate, a lower invest-ment rate in state-owned enterprises and investment in the wrong kind of capital construction (the 'third line' enterprises). In 1982, the accumulation rate was still 29 per cent with an investment rate in state-owned enterprises of 19.8 per cent. This should be compared with a prescribed ideal accumulation rate of just under 30 per cent and an investment rate of 17-18 per cent.(31) At first sight, this is about as 'left' as in the height of the Cultural Revolution; but is not so considered because now there is greater priority given to agriculture and not so much wasteful investment in 'third line' enterprises.

As for the proportion of total investment in state-owned units devoted to capital construction, this has declined steadily over the years. It was 74.9 per cent in 1978, 1979 and 1980, declining to 66.4 per cent in 1981 and 65.7 per cent in 1982. If, however, one takes seriously an official comment that the three 'left' years of 1958, 1970 and 1978 were singled out as such partly because investment in capital construction surpassed the previous year by over ¥10 billion, then 1982 must also be a 'left' year, because then, investment in capital construction surpassed the previous year and the budgeted amount by ¥11 billion, reaching ¥55.5 billion.(32) Even more seriously, investment in capital construction for the first four months of 1983 was 18.3 per cent higher than for the same period the previous year. Extensive development seems to be flourishing.

To be sure, China's economic planners are doing all they can to combat excessive capital construction, but they have a problem. Up to the late 1970s, high rates of investment in capital construction were largely the result of planning decisions based on 'mistaken' theories of extensive development, whereas those after 1978 were in large measure a result of enlarged enterprise autonomy, designed to move to a form of intensive development. The growth of extra-budgeted funds has been dramatic. In 1957, the ratio of extra-budgeted funds to state financial revenue stood at about 10 per cent. By 1965, this had risen to 17.7 per cent. In 1982, it stood at 60 per cent and then did not include

---

30. See e.g. Ishikawa, 1983.
31. Jiang Wei, GMRB., 26 June 1983, p. 4.
32. State Statistical Bureau, Abstract, JPRS., 84111, 12 August 1983, p. 115.

loans concluded outside official credit plans and receipts and payments handled by units themselves.(33) The fact that a lot of these extra-budgeted funds find their way into new capital investment has led the state to formulate measures in 1983 to tighten its grip on credit. A Comprehensive Plan for Credit and Finance has been proposed to prevent the blind expansion of capital construction and to facilitate planning for equipment renovation.(34) It is apparently extremely difficult to get out of the stage of extensive development.

The preceding paragraph suggests that there is now a willingness to look at systemic causes of 'left' behaviour in the present (when the leadership is not defined as 'left'), but a continuing tendency to ignore systemic causes of 'left' behaviour in analysing the various leaps of the past. This approach is reminiscent of the post-Stalin period in the Soviet Union where the systemic troubles of the past could more often than not be reduced to quirks of Stalin's personality.

A lot of work needs to be done if we are to make sense of Kalecki's cyclic approach. I suspect that the major economic cycles portrayed by McFarlane are too broad. Applications of Kalecki's approach to Eastern European countries show cycles of shorter duration,(35) though one must note that in most of those countries there are relatively large manufacturing sectors and much poorer supplies of raw materials. I have, moreover, already indicated my methodological unease about the political cycles. But the techno-logical cycles do offer much food for thought. Each of the three cycles identified stressed different types of technology, and the technologies inaugurated in each of the three cycles have produced different problems. Technology, introduced during the first cycle, is now characterised by obsolescence. In 1982, it was noted that of the ¥440 billion in fixed assets held by enterprises, one third was acquired in the 1950s and 1960s. The backbone of heavy industry was still the 400 or so enterprises set up during the First Five Year Plan. The equipment was obsolete and the consumption of energy high. In the Anshan Iron and Steel Corporation, the key enterprise of the First Five Year Plan, for example, two thirds of the equipment was still of 1930-1950 vintage; as a consequence, steel plates were uneven in thickness and internal and external strengths varied. In the Changchun No.1, Motor Vehicles Plant (China's first and most prestigeous), more than 60 per cent of the equipment had been in service for more than twenty years and has undergone at least two and up to ten major repairs. Combination machine tools, which in developed industrial countries only have a life of eight to ten years, after fifteen to twenty years service in China were considerably worn down. Similarly in the three

---

33. Duan Yun, Zhongguo Jinrong, 5, 1983, JPRS., 83989, 27 July 1983, pp. 76-82.
34. Caizheng, 6, 1983, JPRS., 84388, 22 September 1983, pp. 64-7.
35. See e.g. Goldmann, 1968.

major ballbearing plants (Harbin, Wangfangdian and Luoyang), over 45 per cent of machine tools had been in service for twenty years; in the Harbin plant 60 per cent were officially designated sub-standard. Chemical works built in the late 1950s were grossly inefficient. The Jilin Chemical Fertiliser Plant for example, had increased its productive capacity over those years from 75,000 to 300,000 tonnes of synthetic ammonia, but its energy consumption per tonne produced (17-18 million kilocalories) was twice that of plants of similar size imported in the 1970s (9-10 million kilocalories). Of the 1.56 million civilian motor vehicles in the country, 60 per cent consisted of two types of truck based on 1940s designs with fuel consumption 20-30 per cent higher than foreign imported vehicles. According to China's leading industrial economist, Ma Hong, only 20 per cent of technical industrial equipment in the country was up to the standards of the 1960s and 1970s, 20-25 per cent was technically backward but could be improved, 20-25 per cent was really obsolete but had to be saved for the time being and the remaining 35 per cent should be scrapped.(36)

The appalling state of the older industrial plants, it is said, is due to the influence of the 'left' who behaved like slash and burn cultivators. Their strategy was to 'fish the pond until it became dry' and then to move on to another one. As a result of their influence, it is claimed, 90 per cent of the foreign exchange earmarked for importing technology between 1950 and 1979 went on whole sets of equipment (and much on complete plants) instead on advancing the technological level of existing equipment.(37) This ahistorical telescoping of 'left' behaviour across three cycles is misleading. In the first cycle (the 1950s), there was little disagreement about importing complete sets of equipment speedily to build up an industrial base at a time of economic blockade and Cold War. The central planning structure adopted at that time has always been seen as a historical necessity; but what needs to be acknowledged is that built into it was a logic of extensive development which was bound to cause problems of obsolescence later. The failure to transform existing equipment was not just a question of 'left' thinking; it was also the consequence of the way decisions on capital construction investment were made. It was also, paradoxically, the result of attempts to reform the sclerotic centrally planned system. If one decentralises authority to provinces (as was done in 1957), then local governments engage in competition to produce the most impressive modern new development and, in so doing, enlarge expenditure on capital construction. As I have noted above, if one decentralises power to the enterprise itself, the growth of extra-budgeted funds weakens the grip the central planners have over capital construction expenditure.

---

36. Ma Hong, Zhongguo Jingji Nianjian, 1982, JPRS., 84059, 8 August 1983, pp. 88-101.
37. Ibid., p. 94.

Indeed, many large factories have recently been criticised for spending funds earmarked for technical transformation on capital construction projects; and they have been able to get away with this precisely because of their enlarged autonomy. It is clear, moreover, that the state does not trust enterprises sufficiently to engage in the transformation of existing equipment.(38)   This is evident in the insistence on state control over depreciation funds. Of the ¥440 billion of fixed assets in state-owned enterprises, some ¥20 billion is drawn out annually as depreciation funds.   The advocates of increasing enterprise autonomy have urged that these funds should be handled by enterprises themselves; though considerations of controlling capital construction has resulted in the present pattern of distribution (50 per cent to enterprises, 20 per cent to local industrial departments and 30 per cent to the state treasury) being maintained. It is pointed out that, if enterprises were to handle all the depreciation funds, their relative independence would be converted into absolute independence.(39) Behind this important theoretical point, I suspect, is simply government worries that depreciation funds will be misused.   Quite clearly, if technical transformation is to be given much greater attention, then depreciation rates must be increased; but the decline in state revenue, which is a direct result of allowing enterprises to retain a greater share of profits, makes this very difficult to bring about.

Much of Chinese industry, therefore, has all along been locked into the pattern of extensive development inaugurated during the first technological cycle, however 'left' or 'right' its leaders might have been.   Now what about the technology introduced during the second cycle?   When they were introduced, the 'five small industries' of that time were praised because they were closer to raw materials and helped solve the problems of bad communications and transport. To be sure, a lot of them were grossly inefficient according to normal economists' arithmetic; but if one really wants to assess their worth, one has to consider the long-term effects of educating people in industrial techniques and the fact that sometimes small industries managed to mobilise funds which could never have become productive capital in any other way.   Calculating the productivity of such industries is fraught with immense problems.   But that is not my brief.   My argument here is that, although many of these have been closed down, large numbers will remain for a long time, indefinitely locked into a pattern of extensive development.   Even if it were possible for the large enterprises to switch to an intensive pattern, there is no way one can see this spilling over to the small and inefficient enterprises in the xian in the foreseeable future.

---

38.   Jingji Ribao., 25 July 1983, JPRS., 84188, 25 August 1983, pp. 62-8.
39.   Caizheng, 6, 1983, JPRS., 84388, 22 September 1983, pp. 68-72.

As for the enterprises in the 'third line' areas, established during the Third and Fourth Five Year Plans, there is certainly a glaring manifestation of the problems of extensive development. According to Ma Hong, the level of mechanical equipment per worker in large and medium sized enterprises in those areas was 27 per cent higher than in the old industrialised areas (the 'first line' of Bejing, Shanghai, Tianjin, Liaoning and Jiangsu), but the output value per worker was 52 per cent lower and the fixed asset utilisation coefficient (the output value per ¥100 of fixed assets) was 54 per cent lower.(40) Short of massive new capital investment in infrastructure, there is no way of remedying this - and the state is hell bent at the moment on minimising such expenditure.

Is it fair to criticise the establishment of these 'third line' enterprises as 'left'? A lot here depends on whether the perceived Soviet threat of the 1960s and early 1970s was simply 'subjective' fantasy or an objective reality. Had there been a major conflict at that time, then these enterprises would surely have been seen as cost-effective. Like so much of the alleged 'subjectivism', we only really define it as such long after the event.

Finally we come to the 'left' error of importing complete sets of equipment and complete plants from the West. This really got under way in the 1970s and laid the basis for the third cycle. If one really wants to call this 'left', one has to consider that one of the 'crimes' of the 'Gang of Four' was to 'threaten to damage foreign trade' by the insistance that foreign plants embodied capitalist relations of production, and that they should not be imported. Put that way, it looks like a 'left' error. But if one poses the problem differently and notes that the 'Gang of Four' was concerned (as are many political economists in the third world) that it would be difficult to integrate complete plants into a technologically-dualist economy ('walking on two legs'), then the arch 'leftists' appear as on the 'right' side. One can only repeat: 'left' and 'right' here have no meaning unless one specifies which technology one is talking about and at what time it was imported.

One must observe that in a country such as China where the levels of productivity vary so much between locality and industry, it is extremely difficult to determine at what point the whole economy may be said to move from the stage of extensive to intensive development. Tables 3.2 and 3.3 show widely differing patterns of productivity growth.

---

40. Ma Hong, Zhongguo Jingji Nianjian, 1982, JPRS., 84059, 8 August 1983, p. 92.

Table 3.2: Growth in Productivity

Year	Output in yuan per worker p.a.	Index (1952 = 100)
1949	3,016	72.1
1952	4,184	100.0
1957	6,362	152.1
1965	8,979	214.6
1978	11,130	266.0
1979	11,838	282.9
1980	12,080	288.7
1981	11,863	283.5
1982	12,133	290.0

Table 3.3: Productivity by Industry (1952 = 100)

Industry	1957	1965	1978	1981	1982
Overall	152.1	214.6	266.0	283.5	290.0
Metallurgy	208.2	303.1	233.6	250.8	257.1
Electric Power	156.3	248.9	386.0	336.2	322.8
Coal	150.8	98.9	110.8	100.7	103.6
Petroleum	174.9	317.7	624.3	520.2	494.7
Chemicals	231.7	501.2	552.4	654.6	694.5
Machinery	199.5	287.4	404.0	380.2	425.8
Building Materials	171.1	313.5	328.1	341.3	365.9
Forestry	98.6	95.9	79.7	80.6	78.7
Food	141.7	162.5	158.2	176.2	175.5
Textiles	114.5	168.9	208.7	238.9	213.6
Paper	174.5	209.1	155.4	142.3	144.3

Source: State Statistical Bureau, Abstract, 1983, JPRS., 84111, 12 August 1983, pp. 100-101.

One would, indeed, expect high levels of productivity in the chemical industry, where many new factories have been imported, and one would expect the antequated coal industry to reveal the opposite picture. The question is what one does about it. One may complain about the 'iron rice bowl' and the anti-economic effects of employment for life and one may adopt measures to employ most new workers on a contract basis. I fear, however, that the short-term effects on employment would mean that intensive development will be purchased by the achievement of a society which is less socialist, at least in the terms of Stalin's fundamental 'law' of socialism - of providing for the needs for an ever-expanding number of people. But here we are back to the point raised in the first part of this chapter and the point raised by Sullivan in the preceding chapter. Does the move towards advanced socialism require a temporary abandonment of the socialist telos? If so for how long?

Conclusion.

The extension of the contract system and granting enlarged hiring and firing rights to enterprises brings us back to the earlier argument about the development of a labour market in which forms of capitalism appear long before any 'advanced socialism'. For many orthodox Western economists the conclusion is clear; intensive development is only possible under capitalism where enterprises go bankrupt if they neglect the efficiency of factors or production. Thus, the transition from extensive to intensive development in China will occur if and when China returns to the only truly efficient economic system. Because of this belief, these 'real world' theorists dismiss the debates about advanced and undeveloped socialism as ideological nonsense. A few armchair Mensheviks shrug their shoulders, deciding that the transition from extensive to intensive development may only take place before any attempt is made to socialise the economy. Their Bolshevik critics will point out that however disproportionate and inefficient the Soviet economy may be, it has achieved a degree of intensive development which, whilst not appropriate to the standard for advanced socialism proposed by Su Shaozhi and Wang Guoping, certainly qualifies the Soviet Union as an industrially developed country: on this basis they defend the version of 'advanced socialism' of the Brezhnev years.

The latter have a point! The Soviet Union's achievements should not be under-rated. A lot, moreover, was achieved in the Soviet Union under decades of extensive development. Nevertheless, although few would deny that the Soviet Union is 'advanced' in a sense, many would disqualify it as socialist. The current Chinese leadership can no longer do this because it shares the same definition, which takes as its starting point the productive forces and one relation of production (ownership). There are, of course, other relations of production in the Marxian formula, not the least of which is the relationship between people at work. And what about the relationship of producers to the products of work, which is outside the customary distinction between forces and relations of production? I am talking here about alienation which was discussed for a brief moment in China around the time of Marx's centenary and then stamped out. Yet surely there are many in China who question the validity of a Clark Kerr-type, 'logic of industrialism',(41) which will operate like 'an objective economic law' until miraculously the kingdom of God is ushered in. There needs to be more thinking, therefore, on the idea of socialism as process. This does not have to be a 'socialism of poverty'; but any thinking about a <u>telos</u> does involve a degree of utopian thinking which Engels would not have approved of; as for Marx, we may only guess. But does it matter what Marx would have thought?

---

41.   Kerr et.al., 1962.

Chapter 4

ECONOMIC REFORM: LEGITIMACY, EFFICIENCY AND RATIONALITY

Kate Hannan

Chapter Two argued that Chinese theories of 'continuing the revolution', current in the 1960s and early 1970s, laid great stress on avoiding trends which might lead to a restoration of capitalism. Though the content given to the term 'continuing the revolution' changed after 1976, the possibility of a capitalist restoration was still a major concern. That danger could be expected to remain so long as the productive forces were relatively undeveloped. There was some discussion at that time of whether labour power continued to be a commodity in any sense and in what way the commodity nature of labour power might be reproduced in a society experiencing socialist transition. After 1978, however, attempts were made to define socialism not as a process but in terms of economically-determined models. Considerable fears about a capitalist restoration were still voiced by critics of the official position who felt that the line of demarcation between capitalism and socialism had become blurred. For all that, the official position appeared as a theoretical rationalisation of promoting the development of the productive forces.

The preceding two chapters traced the Stalinist origins of the model-building approach in considering the stages of socialist development. It was Stalin's 1936 position(1) which was emulated (even though it was considered that Stalin had pitched his model of 'socialism' at too low a level). Stalin's more flexible position of 1952(2) was criticised by some scholars precisely because Stalin was insufficiently determinist; he apparently gave excessive weight to the relations of production. Mao, of course, went to even greater extremes in telescoping the stages of development in the late 1950s; and his 'timing theory', sketched out in his 'Reading Notes' on the Soviet textbook Political Economics,(3) was an attempt to reconcile a concern with stages with the idea of socialism as a flexible process. After 1978, such thinking was simplified (indeed, oversimplified) by the adoption of the simple two stage model described in the preceding chapter.

---

1.   Stalin, (1936), Stalin, 1976, pp. 799-800.
2.   Stalin, (1952), 1972.
3.   Mao, 1974, pp. 247-313; Mao, 1977(a).

By 1979, it was increasingly acknowledged in official circles that China was in a stage of undeveloped socialism, characterised by the co-existence of state ownership and collective ownership. In this stage, commodity production and circulation would continue and there would remain marked differences in living conditions between workers and peasants. Clearly, the adoption of an economically-determined notion of undeveloped socialism was more useful in rationalising the quest for economic growth than the previous notion of socialism as a process of transforming both forces and relations of production. The C.C.P. sought to enhance its legitimacy by delivering the goods.

By the late 1970s, the problem of legitimacy was very real. The Cultural Revolution allegations that the 'vanguard' was leading the revolution backwards had dealt a serious blow to the Party's authoritative claim to be practising domination in the name of the 'dictatorship of the proletariat'. It was during those turbulent years, when everyone claimed loyalty to Mao, that Mao Zedong's actual views were prised apart from the official ideology called 'Mao Zedong Thought'. During the political movements of the early 1970s, many people became confused as to what Mao Zedong Thought really was and whether the Party was articulating it. Then, as the functional orientation articulated by Party leaders switched after the demise of the 'Gang of Four', it was announced officially that Mao Zedong Thought was very different from that envisaged by most Party members. Weberian theorists would explain this situation in terms of the use of the legitimating function of Mao Zedong Thought by those seeking political dominance. Such theorists would then almost certainly take note of the damage done to the legitimacy of the Chinese Communist Party by Party factionalism, by the prior public critique of the policy and functioning of the Party caused by Mao's 1960s theoretical position and by the subsequent critique of 'vested interest groups' and 'Party people in authority taking the capitalist road'.(4)   Mao's theoretical position of the 1960s, and that later articulated by the 'Shanghai school'(5) saw socialism as a transition period - a period of revolutionary change. Such a view was not conducive to the preference for political stability inherent within the functionalist interpretation of social processes. Mao's and later the 'Shanghai School's' theoretical position had a notion of progress predicated on a vision of 'what ought to be'. A Weberian has no such notion of 'progress'. The Weberian theorist is confined to attempting an understanding of 'what is'.

With the demise and show-trial of the 'Gang of Four' it might have been expected that C.C.P. legitimacy would have been sufficiently repaired. But, as previous chapters have noted, the Party felt the need for a 'strategic decision' which could hasten the repair.

---

4.   Young, 1978.
5.   See Christensen, 1983.

Against this background the role of the C.C.P. was re-defined. No longer was the role of the Party seen in terms of attaining a classless society. Now, the role of the Party was to be the promotion of 'socialist modernisation' by means of a primary focus on the development of the productive forces. Development of the productive forces was identified as being in the objective interest of the proletariat. 'The economic requirements of the broad masses' were to be promoted. Most attention was now directed at immediate economic problems rather than broad questions of socialist transition. The attention of China's planners focused on what the preceding chapter described as the quest for 'optimal resource allocation'. In functional Weberian language, the C.C.P. had ceased to articulate a substantive (value-orientating) goal. It had re-defined its functional orientation in terms of formal or purposive (means appropriate to given ends) rationality.(6)

Such an interpretation must be regretted by those who reject the functional theorist's addiction to 'what is' and who prefer a Marxist - a priori - informed objective notion of 'what ought to be'. But a less obvious criticism of the Weberian position must be made. From within the functionalist paradigm, it has been argued that pure purposive rationality, in the sense used by Weber, offers an insufficient grounding for legitimation. Here it is posited that there needs to be a general consensus grounded in a rational orientation to values.(7) This argument can be extended to suggest that purposive .rationality can only be seen as a degenerate form of substantive rationality. In pure form purposive rationality appears value-neutral. As such, it is a distorted form of rationality. If this criticism of the Weberian division between substantive and purposive rationality holds, then one should not understand the post 1978 C.C.P. position as a bald switch from substantive rationality to purposive rationality (even allowing for the Weberian use of the 'ideal-type'). It was a change in the C.C.P.'s functional orientation from one which was in accord with the attainment of the substantive rational goal of a classless society to one in which the functional orientation was in accord with the attainment of the substantive rational goal of 'socialist modernisation'. Both goals, in turn, can be seen as resting on the authority accorded to the C.C.P. by those it dominates by virtue of its knowledge and ability to identify the objective interest of the masses. But, in the case of the latter goal of 'socialist modernisation', an undignified reduction has taken place whereby this goal is presented as value-neutral. Then a further reduction has taken place to the point where means justify ends and ends justify means. In this situation, as the preceding chapter noted, it is the case that the ends of planning seem forever reduced to the internal logic of the existing system.

---

6.   Weber, 1968, pp. 809-38.
7.   Habermas, 1976.

Clearly the concern in this chapter with legitimacy, domination and rationality is Weberian. Thus, what Dutton and Healy call the 'privileging of the economic instance' reflects a switch to remunerative policies desired to achieve legitimate domination. This is opposed to the normative appeals of earlier years, which in Althusserian language might be seen as the privileging of the ideological instance. It is opposed also to the coercive appeals involved in the primacy given to class struggle, which Althusserians prefer to call the privileging of the political instance.

In Weberian language, the use of remunerative policies to achieve legitimation is best achieved by legal-rational (purely purposive) forms of domination. Charismatic domination of the past is criticised for its arbitrariness and for its tendency to be routinised in traditional rather than legal-rational terms. Such Weberian concepts are useful in understanding recent Chinese literature which talks about the 'feudal' aspects of authority before 1976. Furthermore, as Brugger notes,[8] no Weberian would be surprised that undeveloped socialism would inevitably be presented as an 'ideal-type' once socialism was conceived of as a system and contradictions were explained in functional terms.

The conceptual apparatus used in this chapter will be Weberian, though the conclusions will not necessarily be so. Let us start, in true Weberian tradition, by attempting an understanding of the mechanics of China's economic reform policies, rather than passing judgement on what such a programme for reform ought to be.

The Strategy for Economic Reform.

When the economic reforms were set in motion after 1978 it was intended that the Chinese economy should be based on 'objective economic laws'. The most prominent of these was the law of value which was seen as being an essential feature of both capitalist and socialist economies. The law could be said to operate when the supply of a commodity met the demand for that commodity; under such conditions the price of the commodity would correspond to its value (the amount of socially necessary labour time embodied in its production and distribution). Under capitalism, the 'law of value' regulated prices spontaneously, thus reflecting scarcity. Under socialist conditions, the spontaneous element was qualified. Spontaneity often produced temporary disquilibrium as capitalists engaged in speculation. Now the role of the capitalist was replaced by the planning mechanism and exploitative behaviour was deemed to have been eliminated. Thus, a flexible planning structure which responded to scarcity could ensure steady equilibrium. Under socialist conditions, a plan which responded to the law of value could ensure the

---

8.   Brugger, 1981(b).

rational distribution of labour amongst different departments of the economy and would promote labour productivity.

Both capitalism and socialism are presented here as ideal types. The capitalist ideal type is drawn from Marx's reading of Adam Smith. A Weberian might comment that it ignores the fact that prices are historically determined as much as they are determined by supply and demand. This must also be true of a transitional socialist economy. The socialist ideal type is constructed by imagining what a commodity system would look like once exploitation is removed and in which it is assumed that the price of labour itself corresponds to its value. The problem with this ideal type is that exploitation is removed by definition (the workers who own the enterprise cannot exploit themselves). It ignores Weber's point that all concepts are historically specific and under a bureaucratic system which claims to be socialist, exploitation might take on different forms. It was probably a consideration of such a conclusion that the Party ideologues were quick to clamp down on any talk about 'alienation' under socialism. After all, didn't Weber talk about alienation from the means of administration.

A second 'objective economic law' was supposed to be the 'law of the identity of interests between the state, the enterprise and the individual'. Only when it was adhered to might one expect optimum labour productivity. In the past, it was felt that that law had been violated both when vertical rule ('administration by lines') and dual rule ('administration by lumps') held sway. Both were administrative rather than 'economic' means of running an economy and both laid excessive stress on the interests of the state rather than on those of the enterprise or the individual. Looked at from the perspective of the enterprise, both of the above forms of administration were forms of rule by command. The vertical method of allocating resources led directly to inefficient stockpiling and the slow completion of capital construction projects. Now, a more efficient system was to be created, promoting horizontal co-operation between enterprises which were to exchange goods and services under a legally enforceable contract system. Administrative reorganisation of industry was to create conditions for this kind of horizontal co-operation and was also to promote specialisation of functions. The old 'large and all inclusive' or 'small and all inclusive' forms of enterprise were to be reshaped. The interests of the enterprises would be enhanced by allowing a greater proportion of profit to be retained and allowing greater freedom to sell on the open market; and the interests of the workers would be served by greater bonus payments and an element of representative democracy. The result, it was hoped, would be greatly improved labour productivity.(9)   Students of Eastern Europe will be familiar with such proposals. The Stalinist stress on payment according to work and anti-egalitarianism in general had been joined to 1960s-type arguments about the regulating role of the market.(10)

In order to make industry function more economically, it was proposed to strengthen the role of China's centrally-controlled banking system. Rather than relying on past methods of direct state allocation of enterprise funds, it was proposed that industry move gradually to a system where the banks granted funds in accord with the enterprise's ability to meet scheduled repayments from enterprise profits. Enterprises would be expected to enter into contracts with state organs and these would be enforceable by law; enterprises, however, would be granted much greater freedom in planning activities outside the scope of mandatory contracts. It was felt especially that funding capital construction projects through the banks would be a more effective way of curtailing and controlling expenditure. By implementing project-loans for capital construction, banks could ensure that capital construction expenditure would be limited by an enterprise's estimated capacity to generate a quick return on capital construction projects to meet repayments. A concern to repay loans, moreover, might be expected to give an incentive for enterprises to boost profits.

To facilitate the expanded role for the banking system, China's specialised banks were re-constituted. It was stressed, however, that these banks were to be regulated and controlled by the People's Bank which was directly answerable to the State Council and charged with regulating the circulation of money. In monetarist vein, it was argued that by controlling the money supply inflation could be curbed. The People's Bank, moreover, was expected to monitor the equilibrium between state income and expenditure.(11)

The above picture was modified somewhat by the decision to put the Bank of China, charged with overseas economic relations, directly under the State Council rather than under the People's Bank. The notion of export-led growth, floated for a time during the 'quasi-leap' of 1978, was replaced by a more sober policy of overseas borrowing and direct foreign investment in export industries (particularly in the 'special economic zones'). The Bank of China was to play a major role in such activities. It was felt that although foreign investment would not produce the miracles expected in 1978, it could help to generate foreign exchange earnings and facilitate the importation of technology

9.   Hu Qiaomu, PR., 45, 10 November 1978, pp. 7-12; PR., 46, 17 November 1978, pp. 15-23; PR., 47, 24 November 1978, pp. 13-21; Xue Muqiao, 1981.
10.   See Feiwel (ed.), 1968.
11.   Wu Qiyu, Jingji Guanli 2, 1980, JPRS., 75735, 20 April 1980, pp. 55-8.

with a relatively fast rate of return on capital. The development of joint enterprises, moreover, could help raise the level of skills in the workforce and would be attractive because of China's relatively low labour costs by international standards.(12)

Most of the above proposals have respectable Marxist-Leninist credentials even though they constituted a radical departure from policies identified with Mao Zedong. Lenin set great store on the regulating role of the banks and prior to the War Communism period, was not adverse to foreign investment. Banking control over a more decentralised economic system had also been among the reform proposals in several East European countries. The special economic zones, however, were a new departure in a socialist country, however 'undeveloped', and did raise fundamental questions about China's Marxist orientation. These have already been discussed in Chapter Two.

From a Weberian perspective, one must ask: what is the likelihood of success of policies designed by bureaucrats to combat the excessive rigidity of the bureaucracy? In the mid-1950s, Khrushchev transferred many of the functions of the central planning and control apparatus to other bodies, only to find that those other bodies, staffed by the same sorts of people, behaved in just the same way. Is there some kind of bureaucratic logic which subverts structural change? Now the banking system is to be given functions hitherto exercised by ministerial departments, will it behave in the manner intended? There is no easy answer to such a question. In the capitalist world, treasuries have usually been responsive to monetarist policies. Despite its being coupled with a stress on small government, the idea that the state apparatus is able to steer the economy simply by controlling the money supply is attractive to the bureaucratically naive. Banks in capitalist countries, on the other hand, often depend for their success on the money supply not being controlled. If socialist banks are to be given this control function, then will they not just behave like extensions of government financial departments? Furthermore, the idea of the central bank monitoring the equilibrium between government income and expenditure suggests an activist role which can only be fulfilled by a body which acts like a government ministry? To put it bluntly, if banks act like capitalist banks, they will not fulfil the control function allocated to them; on the other hand, if they act like government departments, they will not be banks.

---

12. For a general account of the proposed reforms in banking, see Watson, 1980.

Efficiency and Rationality.

The preceding discussion has given the impression that bureaucracies are always inefficient and that inefficiency is always unambiguously a bad thing. The first part of the sentence may be true but the second part need not be. In the Introduction to this book, it was pointed out that sometimes efficiency might be at odds with the (formal) rationality of a system. The preceding chapter, moreover, pointed out that under certain conditions, the inefficient system characteristic of extensive development might be more rational than one based on intensive development. Let us return then to the question raised in the Introduction. Could it be the case that Chinese planners, in their single-minded pursuit of efficiency, might be contributing to bureaucratic irrationality? Or is it the case that the pursuit of bureaucratic rationality is contributing to new inefficiencies?

Consider, for a moment, the arguments about the law of value. If profit is truly to be an indicator of efficiency then prices, it is argued, must reflect value. This involves removing subsidies on those goods and services which are considered to be basic necessities. If one removes the subsidies, then the goal of efficiency is purchased at the cost of severe dislocations in people's standard of living - the opposite of what Stalin felt to be the 'basic law of socialism'. A rational bureaucrat, therefore, will not purchase efficiency at that price. Such considerations led planners to draw a distinction between a market governed by the law of value - 'a broad market' - and 'a market regulated by the plan'. Only the latter was seen as offering no threat to rational socialist modernisation. The consequences are profound. On the one hand, the government has decided that, for the time being, it is not able to afford the degree of enterprise autonomy necessary to bring about intensive development. On the other hand, such programmes as exist for the intensification of the production process depend on increased productivity triggered off by labour incentives without adopting a pricing structure which reflects scarcity. This intensification is very limited and will remain so as long as central pricing policy undermines enterprise autonomy.

Currently the price of goods and services which are designated as having the greatest effect on the national economy and people's livelihood remain fixed. The price of those goods are formulated according to the stable cost-plus structure of the past. In part, these costs were historically determined though since moves were made to close the 'scissors' between agricultural and industrial prices after 1978, the element of subsidy has increased. Such prices conform to the planners' rationality but are clearly inefficient. A second category are prices which are allowed to fluctuate within limits above and below a state-set median. A third category are prices which are supposedly determined by supply and demand, though in reality are simply historically determined prices adjusted at enterprise level to allow for the particular enterprise's costs plus a profit of two or three per cent. This third category is usually the price at which an enterprise sells directly to consumers after the state quota has been met using prices in category one or two.   It is only the fourth category that is directly determined by supply and demand.   Both categories three and four, which   make for efficiency, are described as 'supplements' rather than basic.(13)   Rationality is valued more highly than efficiency. Clearly, since the vast majority of prices are in the higher categories, the real effect of enterprise autonomy is limited.   Enterprises are urged to intensify the qualitative aspects of accounting but often are not given the means so to do. Rationality demands that the grant of those means be selective.

The above categorisation of prices determines the way industrial enterprises themselves are categorised.   The first group are those enterprises, occupying key positions in the national economy, which continue to be directly subject to state plans.   The goods produced by such enterprises are deemed vital to the economy and to the living standards of industrial workers and are governed by fixed prices. Though the variety of goods produced by these enterprises is small, the output value constitutes the greater part of the national total.   The second group of enterprises are subject to conditions similar to the first except that flexible provision is made for them to organise production over and above the state quota.   The third group, usually small enterprises, is free to sell the bulk of its products on the open market with only a small portion coming under the state plan.   The final group is unfettered by the state plan and operates with the fourth category of price.   These last two categories only produce a small percentage of national ouput.(14)

If the 'law of value' is to operate and enterprise autonomy is really to be meaningful, then the above system of pricing must be reformed.   But how may this be done without undermining the 'stability and unity' according to which formal rationality is measured?   East European experiences are most instructive.   Prior to the economic reforms in several East European countries, there was a considerable degree of mobility between rural and urban areas.   Policies of extensive development promoted the drift to the cities of an under-employed rural work-force.   This push factor, however, was less important than the pull factor.   Since the prices of agricultural products were low, rural incomes likewise remained low in comparison to urban incomes.   City life was very attractive to those who wished for a better standard of living - a standard of living dependent on the relatively open 'price scissors'.   Considerations of adhering to the law of value, however, led to a rise in the price of agricultural staples and

---

13.   Su Xing, 1982(a).
14.   Zhao Ziyang, 30 November and 1 December 1981, <u>BR.</u>, 51, 21 December 1981, pp. 6-36.

to a decline in real wages in the urban sector. At the same time, the switch to more intensive patterns of development curtailed the opportunities for expanding urban employment. The price rises were not sufficient to provide a disincentive for farmers to go to the cities and coercive controls were strengthened. But they were sufficient to cause much disquiet among industrial workers. Both farmers and workers were angry! In Poland, urban unrest in the 1970s began with the protest of industrial workers about higher food prices. By the 1980s, simple grievances about prices had developed into the demand by workers for an institutional means through which they could influence the planning process. Solidarity became a threat to Party legitimacy! From the point view of a ruling Communist Party, the Hungarian experiences were more encouraging. Nevertheless, there too, the hopes of economic reformers have been diluted as the government allowed 'social policy considerations' to militate against enterprise efficiency. Workers showed a considerable resistance to anything which would undermine price stability. They always saw a rise in prices as a threat to their standard of living. The Party, for its part, saw worker unrest as more important than economic efficiency. Both industrial workers and the Party acted rationally and both contributed to inefficiency.(15)

In the Weberian tradition, Zygmunt Bauman has pointed out that in socialist societies, problems arise because industrial workers are oriented towards formal (means-ends) rationality whilst the Party is oriented towards substantive (or value) rationality.(16) The argument here is different. As has been noted, in many socialist societies the telos appears to have been set aside. The cleavage between Party and workers appears reduced to formal rationality. An efficient economic system oriented towards growth, in the short run, requires curtailing the privileged standard of living of industrial workers by raising agricultural prices. It is rational for workers to protest and it is rational for the government to suppress their protests. The means justify the ends and the ends justify the means. An efficient political system, on the other hand, demands order and stability and above all legitimacy. It is, therefore, rational for the government to place 'social policy considerations' before economic efficiency.

The above suggests why cautious policies were adopted in China and why the reform of the pricing structure has been delayed. Back in 1978, the government raised significantly the procurement prices of agricultural products in accordance with the 'law of value'. To offset any unrest in the urban areas, the government then increased subsidies on basic necessities. These escalated from 7.6 per cent of national income in 1978 to 32 per cent in 1981. The peasants were relatively happy and the industrial workers were not dissatisfied, but any political

---

15.   See Szelenyi, 1979; Pravda, 1979; Haraszti, 1977.
16.   Bauman, 1974.

economist must observe that the programme of subsidisation was in violation of the law of value. Far from a situation where the law of value acted to promote efficiency, price control was continually strengthened. But because of the stratified nature of the pricing system, this control was limited to a range of basic necessities. The law of value could only be said to operate at the margins of the economy and could only promote efficiency in the least important sectors.

The Chinese government is currently very concerned about escalating price subsidies and attempts are being made to limit them. Government action is felt to be needed not just out of some theoretical commitment to the operation of the 'law of value' but because subsidies are creating real fiscal problems.(17) These problems are exacerbated by the decline in state revenues resulting from limited enterprise autonomy. It is felt, however, that the gains to the Party in terms of legitimacy, from the new remunerative appeals might be lost once the effects of the inflationary spiral, sparked off by the agricultural price-hikes, really bite into the standard of living of urban residents. The ideological rationalisations are most confusing. It is claimed, for example, that 'socialist inflation' is better than capitalist inflation because the state can control the price of necessities. Such arguments, as has been noted, contradict those about the law of value. Socialist inflation is also supposedly less serious, because the state can control the money supply. To be sure, the socialist state has a greater capacity to do this than a capitalist state, but such action may only make the banks more like arms of government, contradicting the belief that freeing up the banks is a crucial step in moving from administrative to economic methods of management. Here may be the roots of a legitimation crisis.

One response to a crisis of legitimation, noted by some Western political scientists, is to deliver contradictory messages to different audiences. Thus, the public may be told that 'price subsidies embody the superiority of the socialist planned economy' in preventing 'sharp contradictions' in people's livelihood. Some enterprise managers might be told that limited price subsidies are a way of rewarding enterprises

---

17. Price subsidisation for retail sales of agricultural products is recognised as having contributed to the 1979 budget deficit of ¥17.06 billion and the 1980 budget deficit of ¥12.75 billion. See Wang Bingqian, 1 December 1981, BR., 2, 11 January 1982, pp. 14-23. See also Xu Yi and Chen Baosen, 1981; Huang Da, 1981; Li Kehua, Wenhuibao (Hong Kong), 5, 6, 7 July 1983, JPRS., 84310, 13 September 1983, pp. 28-36; Sichuan Ribao, 26 May 1983, JPRS., 84188, 25 August 1983, pp. 14-16.

with good management but which operate at a planned loss.(18) Financial departments, however, know that price subsidies are the major cause of China's budget deficits and are expected to take solace in measures taken to limit them and the fact that China has not suffered the social disorder of some other socialist countries. Ordinary people in Xinjiang, however, who see that the price of grain transported hundreds of kilometres from other parts of China is cheaper than local grain, might question this aspect of the 'superior' socialist system. Managers in highly efficient petrochemical plants, moreover, might feel that the coal industry, inefficient by anyone's standard, is featherbedded by the system of subsidies designed, amongst other things, to help efficient enterprises which run at a loss. Finally, officials in financial departments, seeing subsidies continually increasing, might come to a conclusion diametrically opposed to official thinking. Rather than preventing disorder, a good deal of social disorder could actually be caused by the perception that different quantities of the same commodity are governed by different degrees of subsidy.

Systemic Problems of the Command Economy and Excessive Capital Construction.

This chapter has argued that, if one adopts the functional economic view of China's planners, then the intention of 1978 to move from an extensive (quantitative) form of development to an intensive (qualitative) form of development, has not been realised. This is because the prevailing notion of administrative rationality has prevented prices reflecting scarcity. The initial moves towards decentralising the economy have been countered by a recentralising trend. This is quite clear when one considers that the key branches of the economy are now required to respond to mandatory state plans, rather than the indicative plans proposed in the early days of the reform. The categorisation of prices and types of enterprise, discussed earlier, are those of a command rather than of any other type of economy. Though incentives in the form of monetary payments are used to support commands, 'success' at enterprise level is still largely measured by quantitative target fulfillment. With prices determined as they are, profit still can not be an indicator of the most economical use of inputs to achieve the best output.

Given the continued tendency to measure success in quantitative terms, one will expect investment priority to return to the heavy industrial sector. Indeed, the stress given to light industry after 1978 has already been modified. It might be argued that the modification of 1981 was a temporary step necessitated by dislocations caused by the

---

18.   Li Kehua, Wenhuibao (Hong Kong), 5, 6, 7 July 1983, JPRS., 84310, 13 September 1983, p. 31.

too rapid switch in priority. More probably we are seeing a return to the more normal pattern of a command economy dictated by its internal systemic logic. The capital-output ratio in light industry might be higher but this cannot be seen, so long as the relationships of means to ends are seen only in quantitative terms.

One of the weaknesses of the command economy which the post-1978 reforms sought to redress, it will be remembered, was the excessive concentration on capital construction. The national investment plans in the past were poorly implemented and extremely difficult to control. This was because enterprises had an interest in enlarging their claims for capital construction funding in order to increase their claims in future years. This is a phenomenon of bureaucratic organisation everywhere; if one may get away with over-spending one year one has an increased chance of a higher spending target the next. If over-spending takes the form of investment in new capacity, then planners oriented to extensive development will be inclined to excuse it in the hope of increased future growth. In the past, the relative visibility of capital construction, compared with technological improvement, led to a situation where existing equipment became more and more obsolete. The preceding chapter noted the determination to rectify that situation; and at the beginning of the reform, there did seem to be some recognition that the excessive stress on capital construction was due to systemic causes. By 1984, however, the central command system was seen not as the cause of investment bias but as the only means by which the bias might be remedied. Instead of thoroughgoing administrative reform, it was simply proposed that the control function of the State Council be strengthened; 'from now on...and according to the level of the growth rate of the national income (we must) decide on a rational investment rate'.(19) But can bureaucracy control bureaucratism?

Chapter Three argued that capital construction investment is getting out of control because of enlarged enterprise autonomy. In fact, under a command economy capital construction investment has <u>always</u> tended to get out of control. All that a limited amount of enterprise autonomy has done is to change the kind of projects into which that investment pours. In the past, capital construction above the planned level took place in large-scale projects in which administrative units had the political muscle to compel the planners to accept <u>de facto</u> situations. Now, as a result of the mushrooming growth of extra-budgeted funds, there has been the rapid development of small-scale capital construction projects initiated by enterprises

---

19.   Xinhua, 14 June 1983, <u>JPRS</u>., 83816, 5 July 1983, pp. 33-4; Liu Huiyong, <u>Jingji Yanjiu</u>, 6, 1983, <u>JPRS</u>., 84013, 1 August 1983, pp. 19-25; <u>Jingji Ribao</u>, <u>JPRS</u>., 84136, 17 August 1983, pp. 31-3.

themselves. This has been at the expense of priority projects which have sometimes been fleeced of their necessary funds.(20)

China's planners now demand that China's limited investment funding should be concentrated on key projects. This means that investment funding going to localities and to individual enterprises should be cut back. Administrative departments are required to practice strict financial discipline and banks, acting like financial departments rather than banks, are to make sure that credit priority goes to key projects rather than those which bankers' logic suggests would offer a better return. At all costs, one has to prevent the growth of a myriad of small projects, each competing for scarce raw materials, energy and transportation facilities. Managers are urged to realise the relationship between what are called 'partial' and 'basic' interests (or between on the one hand, the interests of localities and enterprises and on the other, the interests of the nation). Cadres are urged to bear in mind that, although many key projects require a relatively large amount of investment funding coupled with a long lead-time before they go into production, in the end they take priority over small projects requiring less capital and with shorter lead times.

In the initial reform proposals of 1978, the preference for key projects was also stressed, though at that time the argument was made in relation to scarce foreign exchange. This preference has now been generalised in the desire to build on the existing industrial foundation for the national good. If funds are dispersed, it is argued, the Chinese national economy would be denied its 'impressive financial strength', and an industrial 'fist' necessary to punch through to the goals of modernisation, will not be formed. This 'fist' will be made by concentrating on existing medium and large cities; eventually the benefits will flow through to economic zones based on those cities according to 'economically-rational principles'.(21)

The above official policy suggests that China's planners have not considered adequately the old arguments about the problems associated with 'trickle down' theories of development. The point which needs to be underlined here, however, is that to deal with what is considered to be financial indiscipline, the government has strengthened the old command structure which caused so many problems in the past. Fleecing funds from key projects, tax evasion, delay in remitting funds to the state, squeezing costs and exhorbitant hikes in the price of land sold to the state are to be dealt with not by a reform of the system which causes all those problems but by a reassertion of administrative control. If recentralised control is successful, how will one prevent the

---

20. Zhejiang Ribao, 5 July 1983, JPRS., 84356, 19 September 1983, pp. 33-4.
21. Tao Zengji, GMRB., 29 May 1983, JPRS., 84356, 19 September 1983, pp. 61-5.

recurrence of the old problem where those in charge of key projects 'think themselves important and squander money without restriction'? Once again, central allocation will provide an avenue for enterprises and localities to inflate claims for scarce funds. What is required is much more than exhortations to observe the difference between 'basic' and 'partial' interests, better land-use regulations and 'educating the broad masses of the people'. The old problems will no doubt recur during the Sixth Five Year Plan which focusses on developing priority construction projects as the <u>sine qua non</u> of economic revitalisation in the 1980s.(22)

The Decentralised Control of Circulating Funds.

It has been argued that to transfer the funding of enterprises from industrial ministries to the banks would be simply to reproduce the same system under other names. There would, however, be two differences. The People's Bank has the power to issue currency, and banks, in general, have the power to charge interest rates. Considering this, some critical economists have argued that a single system of bank-funding could actually create a worse situation than that which exists. As is the case now, capital construction would put a squeeze on the available finance, but in the new situation banks would respond by expanding the money supply and create inflation. In such a situation, the critical economists doubted the ability of banks to control capital construction by manipulating interest rates. This view led them to advocate that the funding of capital construction and the provision of circulating funds be separated.

The veteran political economist Sun Yefang once argued that the continued role of the state was crucial in controlling 'expanded reproduction' whilst 'simple reproduction' should be handled by the enterprises themselves.(23) As the government bent all efforts to bring the burgeoning capital construction (expanded reproduction) under control, Sun's point was stressed once again. More broadly, it seemed that if the major reforms had been delayed because of the need to preserve the existing price structure in the name of stability, at least some reforms could be pursued in the provision of circulating funds. Relative autonomy in the provision of circulating funds, after all, could help enterprise management achieve one of the major goals of economic reform - the mobilisation of enthusiasm at enterprise level.

The critical economists, it seems, wish to combine the current stress of the central planners on scientific management and central

---

22. <u>Jingji Ribao</u>, 9 June 1983, <u>JPRS.</u>, 83865, 11 July 1983, pp. 8-12; <u>Jingji Ribao</u>, 10 June 1983, <u>ibid.</u>, pp. 13-14.
23. Sun Yefang, (1963),Sun, 1979, pp. 239-45. See the discussion by Liu Guoguang, Liu (ed.), 1980, p. 7.

control with the basic idea (now attenuated) of enterprise autonomy celebrated in the reform proposals of 1978. They wish to go further than the current policy of streamlining the central command structure by insisting that the control function and credit provision function should remain with the banks but that circulating funds should be disbursed by a separate administrative network.(24)

One cannot but be sceptical about the belief that such administrative changes will actually promote enterprise autonomy. The reform cannot be expected to overcome 'multi-headed management', with authority out of line with responsibility and resultant wrangling. But even if that problem were overcome, enterprise profit is so dependent upon the administrative pricing structure that the handling of circulating funds at enterprise level will not make much difference in terms of efficiency. Those enterprises with a favourable price structure will continue to make large profits regardless of efficiency and vice versa. Enthusiasm at enterprise level will not be improved when the manifest injustice of the pricing system is underlined.

It is felt officially that enterprise autonomy in the use of circulating funds will be enhanced by the system generalised in 1983, of replacing the delivery of profits to the state by a corporation income tax. Chapter Three noted that this policy was probably adopted as a response to declining state revenue consequent upon limited enterprise autonomy. It is promoted, however, with the official claim that it is designed to increase enterprise initiative to raise profits and augment those circulating funds required to develop production, pay bonuses and provide for collective welfare. It is claimed that the pilot projects which employed the scheme have shown increases in output and profits; these result from the incentive given to improved administration and management. It is estimated that if an enterprise shows no increase in the funding of fixed assets but increases output, then it might expect about one third of the value of the increase to revert to its own use. If output or output value remain the same but costs are reduced, an enterprise might expect to retain up to one half of the increased profit. In some cases, where an enterprise has been able to reduce its use of fixed assets and circulating capital, it might even retain the full amount of its increased profit. Conversely, if

---

24.   Lin Anjun, Zhongguo Jinrong, 7, 1983, JPRS., 84310, 13 September 1983, pp. 10-16.

production falls or costs rise, the enterprise will have to bear the losses.(25) But even if it be granted that,

> as compared with profit retention and the sole responsibility for profits and losses, contract substitution of tax payment for profit delivery is better able to reflect a spirit of encouragement to advanced enterprises and to motivate backward ones,

one has to conclude that 'as a result of unfair prices, some enterprises can increase profits greatly without effort, while others will find it hard to increase earnings with great effort'.(26)

We are back to the old problem of prices. One takes no solace in the assurance that the pricing structure will be 'moderated through balances and adjustments' so long as subsidies grow, so long as there is different pricing in different regions and between enterprises in the same industry and so long as commercial enterprises are better able to maintain profits than industrial enterprises. Moreover, when implemented, the tax-payment system has resulted in enterprises which run at a planned loss receiving more income than those which run at a profit. One needs some evidence that this problem will be solved by increased scientific knowledge of economic procedures.

The preceding chapter argued that the adoption of corporation income tax calls into question the Stalinist orthodoxy that there is something qualitatively different between the state and collective sectors of the economy - a point elaborated on in the very definition of 'undeveloped socialism'. But it does more than that. It is claimed that it provides an indirect method of imposing discipline on enterprises. A Weberian cannot but remark that the adoption of the system implies that increased policing duties will be exercised by tax-collecting agencies. They will clearly require much greater powers of inspection than they now possess, much greater staff and much greater bureau-cratic back-up. They will impose not indirect discipline but <u>direct</u> discipline. A move toward excessive rigidity will probably result. Government organs will be granted greater powers of inspection. When bureaucratic means are chosen to deal with bureaucratism, flexible economic policy can not be expected.

---

25.   Zheng Wei and Cai Yan, <u>Jiefang Ribao</u>, 12 July 1983, <u>JPRS.</u>, 84244, 1 September 1983, pp. 63-4; <u>Jingji Ribao</u>, 15 July 1983, <u>JPRS.</u>, 84244, 1 September 1983, pp. 75-6; Yao Guogang, <u>Jingji Ribao</u>, 27 May 1983, <u>JPRS.</u>, 84356, 19 September 1983, pp. 66-7; Sui Zong, <u>Jingji Ribao</u>, 11 July 1983, <u>JPRS.</u>, 84356, 19 September 1983, pp. 74-6; Luo Wenjia, <u>Nanfang Ribao</u>, 30 May 1983, <u>JPRS.</u>, 84356, 19 September 1983, pp. 77-80.
26.   <u>Shehui Kexue</u>, 3, 1983, <u>JPRS.</u>, 83816, 5 July 1983, p. 21.

The Use of Foreign Exchange.

The argument so far has been that measures undertaken to promote productivity have been undermined by the rationality of the existing system. Formal rationality, it will be remembered, is seen as the choice of means appropriate to ends within a set of rules. This chapter has argued that the ends of productivity may not be served by the existing means (administered prices set according to rules oriented to stability). Irrationality, therefore, may only be avoided by re-defining the ends of economic activity according to the old formula. If productivity is really to be pursued, then the rules must be changed to allow for new more 'economic' means to be employed. Alas, few of the old rules have changed.

One aspect in which the rules have changed is the use of foreign capital. Since 1978, the foreign funds used in importing new technology have mostly been repaid. Joint ventures set up after feasibility studies, moreover, have successfully promoted the national economy without posing any threat to national economic sovereignty. It seems that the 1978 policy of limiting indebtedness to the capacity to repay and concentrating overseas investment in enterprises with a fast return on capital has been maintained.(27) China need not fear the debt-trap in which some socialist societies in Eastern Europe are caught.

The importance of the above change in the rules cannot be under-estimated. Prior to 1978, considerable fears were expressed concerning national sovereignty. Now the fear is that investment opportunities for foreign firms might not be attractive enough. Thus, the concern in the early reform period to develop the industrially-backward areas has been replaced by a concern to attract investment to those areas which promise foreign firms the greatest return.(28)

Foreign loans and direct foreign investment, however, can only be expected to have a limited effect on the huge Chinese economy. They cannot be expected to solve the enormous problems of backward technology and dilapidated equipment. If the goal of the Sixth Five Year Plan to ensure that 30 per cent of the total volume of imports consists of modern technology is to be achieved, then exports must dramatically increase. But what should the import-export mix be? In the first quarter of 1983, the value of primary products exported amounted to ¥4.13 billion and the value of industrial products exported

27. Chen Jiaqin, Caimao Jingji, 5, 1983, JPRS., 84244, 1 September 1983, pp. 118-26.
28. Wenhuibao, (Hong Kong), 17 May 1983, JPRS., 84310, 13 September 1983, pp. 37-8.

was ¥4.66 billion. The value of primary products imported amounted to ¥2.8 billion and the value of industrial goods imported amounted to ¥6.1 billion. Clearly, China's primary exports are being used to subsidise the import of industrial products. This pattern will intensify if China's leaders are able to realise the intention of cutting down on food (mainly grain) imports.(29)

Such a policy is necessary if China is dramatically to increase its technological imports. But one must conclude that agriculture's subsidising industrial imports is but another form of hidden 'super-tax' which the 1978 reforms in the 'price scissors' aimed to rectify. To put it bluntly, China's plans for technological imports depend once again on the violation of the much vaunted 'law of value'.

Despite all the talk about adhering to the 'law of value', the use of agriculture to pay for technological imports has Stalinist antecedents. Yet one new feature is profoundly unorthodox. This is the proposal to export labour to capitalist countries. Labour is held to be a most valuable resource. But of all the policies pursued by the present Chinese government, it is surely the least Marxist.

Agricultural Policies.

The continued extraction of a 'super-tax' from the countryside is rational in terms of the need to pay for technology necessary for improving industrial productivity. It is less rational when one considers raising the level of agricultural output. Here, one has seen the sharpest break from the old system of administered prices. Free markets are thriving and though seen as only a 'supplement' to the planned economy, they are a pretty powerful one. Increased income for many peasants has led to an increase in investment in agriculture. Looked at nationally, however, failure to reform the pricing structure overall has still meant that excessive investment has flowed into the industrial sector and that the intensification of the agricultural sector has taken on a form different from that intended in 1978.

At the time of the 1978 reforms, intensification of the agricultural labour process was to be promoted through a substantial increase in investment funding in relevant science and technology.(30) But, with any substantial flow of investment funds into the agricultural sector having been blocked by failure to reform the pricing structure, greater reliance was then placed on the 'correctness' of basic-level policy. This boiled down to advocacy of what we now know as the

29. Wen Sijia, Wenhuibao, (Hong Kong), 22-3 June 1983, JPRS., 84244, 1 September 1983, pp. 146-9.
30. Xinhua Ribao, 1 April 1982, JPRS., 81128, 25 June 1982, pp. 9-13.

'economic responsibility system'.(31) By 1981, sideline production was no longer felt to be the temporary measure promoted in 1978 as a means of supplementing household income until the effects of scientific and technological investment became effective in intensifying rural production.   It was recognised that a viable agricultural policy would not eventuate from benefits 'trickling-down' from the industrial to the agricultural sector. The result has been a focus on sideline production as an incentive-led means to the intensification of the rural labour process. A general programme of de-collectivisation has been the outcome.

At the start of the reform period, the central government regarded the policy of contracting to households with considerable alarm. It now boasts about the success of the resultant agricultural 'economic responsibility system' developed since 1981. The policy of contracting directly to the household is seen to be in accord with the principle of 'payment according to labour'. It is said to promote a more specialised division of labour as a means of tapping the enthusiasm of the peasant worker.(32) The household responsibility system is credited with being efficient. But is it? Here we are back to the definitional problem discussed earlier. In the economists' logic of measuring output in relation to inputs, it is efficient. If, however, we take the sociological definition of efficiency - the attainment of a goal with the least possible detriment to other goals - then some aspects of the efficiency are in doubt. Take, for example, the much-publicised impact on population. With land apportioned on the basis of family size and available labour power (the most significant input), there is an incentive to produce more children (especially male children who will remain part of the family labour force). This contradicts China's 'one child family' policy, designed to correct a situation where gains in agricultural output had been consumed by the growing population. This is a 'scissors crisis' of a new type. The householder is caught between the twin blades of an incentive to increase labour power and the draconian measures adopted by the state to limit population.(33) The peasant, driven into a utilitarian calculus, will hardly develop a socialist morality.

A system, moreover, which encourages 'some to get rich first' leads to a rather curious situation. De-collectivisation is promoted in order to develop the productive forces. Those units which are most reluctant to de-collectivise are wealthy suburban communes which already have a relatively developed infrastructure and which are able to generate considerable cash income from light industrial undertakings. These units have done well under the old system and will do even better under the new system provided that it is someone else

---

31.   See Watson, 1983.
32.   See Su Xing, 1982(b).
33.   See O'Leary, 1983.

who de-collectivises.   Being near the towns they will profit considerably from the new ease with which contracts might be signed with industrial enterprises.   Their members, moreover, have the advantage of urban access without being subject to the acute urban housing shortage.   In as much as they generate individual income, there is a ready free market in the towns.   The rural units in the deep countryside however have none of these advantages.   At the extreme are villages living on the edge of subsistence which have hardly any surplus at all with which to get rich.   The irony of all this, it seems, is that socialism is the prerogative of the rich units which will get richer under collective conditions, whilst the poor fail to generate funds sufficient to make any improvement in the productive forces and lack the collective facilities to provide for elementary schooling and the provision of basic skills.   In the end, such disparities might undermine the stability which, as we have seen, is one of the basic goals against which rationality is measured.

Though it is clear that in the short-term from an overall perspective, agriculture is more efficient than hitherto, it is much less under central control.   Autonomy at various levels is much more real than in the industrial sector.   Central planners are preoccupied with such questions.   At a macro-economic level, planners are concerned over how to carry out the injunction to cut down on the need for grain imports when peasants are encouraged to diversify and concentrate on those crops which will yield the best return in cash.   At a more prosaic level, central planners are beset with a myriad of routine control problems such as how to collect tax at rural markets.(34)

Conclusion.

This chapter has argued that the economic 'soft shoe shuffle', adopted by the Chinese Communist Party since 1978, can be seen as a response to damaged Party legitimacy.   In the wake of the programme for economic reform sanctioned by the Central Committee's Third Plenum of late 1978, the C.C.P. planners have followed the path trodden by Soviet and Eastern European 'socialists'.   They have shifted their substantive (value) rational goal from attaining a classless society to promoting 'socialist modernisation'.   Like their Soviet and Eastern European counterparts, they have allowed their re-definition of a functionally orientating substantive goal to be reduced to value-free purposive (means-ends) rationality.   They have then been caught in the trap of a further, even less theoretically dignified reduction whereby means and ends are seen in terms of each other.

One may, of course, criticise Weberian functionalism from a Marxist theoretical position.   Nevertheless, criticism is possible even

---

34.   Xining, Qinghai Provincial Service, 22 August 1983, JPRS., 84310, 13 September 1983, p. 17.

within the Weberian functionalist paradigm. If one accepts that one can not neatly separate substantive and purposive rationality, then we should expect that the functional orientation of the C.C.P. which reduces purposive to functional rationality will not provide grounds for the repair of Party legitimacy. In short, we may well have reason to question the current and future health of C.C.P. legitimacy. Having made the 'strategic decision' to accord a primary focus to economic efficiency, the means have come ends in themselves. Moreover, China's planners have failed sufficiently to change the rules necessary to ensure that appropriate means may be found to realise the goal of efficiency.

Fears that the same kind of instability which had occurred in Eastern Europe would also occur in China meant that only some of the reform proposals of 1978 were carried through. Attempts were made to enlarge enterprise autonomy without a change in the pricing structure which would allow that autonomy to contribute to efficiency. Considerations of the 'law of value' led to a dramatic rise in the price of grain. Urban instability was then bought off by increasing state subsidies which made the law of value seem ridiculous. Increased subsidies demanded increases in state revenue at a time when limited enterprise autonomy reduced the flow of funds to the state. Attempts were then made to augment state revenue by changing the system of profit delivery to corporation income tax. This required further bureaucracy which might be expected to generate further difficulties.

Though many of the reform economists saw major problems in the economy as systemic, policy makers tended to see their function as improving the existing system rather than fundamentally restructuring it. Thus, initial moves to change the method whereby capital construction was funded led not to a decrease in capital construction investment but simply to a change in the nature of projects chosen for investment. There was a massive increase in such funding whilst priority projects remained starved of capital. Fears that control might be lost led eventually to much more modest proposals for enterprise funding and to cautious moves to reform the provision of circulating funds - moves which, in an unreformed price structure, will probably not contribute substantially to efficiency.

The rules which were significantly changed were those governing foreign economic relations and the agricultural sector. Considering the size of the Chinese economy, the former could not produce decisive efforts. If China really wanted dramatically to increase imports of technology it could only do so by continuing the policy of imposing a 'super tax' on the countryside. Reforms in agriculture were indeed far-reaching but, it has been suggested, efficiency in terms of the relationship between inputs and outputs might have been purchased at the cost of inefficiency in terms of long-term goals.

Considering the agricultural sector one has to conclude that if undeveloped socialism is characterised by multiple forms of ownership, then it is here for a long time. Looked at from the perspective of agriculture, 'undeveloped socialism' seems almost like a synonym for a mixed economy. Looked at from the perspective of industry, 'undeveloped socialism' seems like the continuance of the command economy in a hostile underdeveloped environment. Looked at from the perspective of Chinese acadaemia 'undeveloped socialism' is the name given to a package of policies which are still deemed worthwhile but which Chinese planners find destabilising.

Chapter 5

THE SOCIALIST TRANSITION AND THE SOCIALIST MODE OF PRODUCTION

Greg McCarthy

The focus of this chapter is on the theory of the socialist transition as it applies to China. The discussion of this theory will be divided into two distinct but inter-related sections. The first part will concentrate upon the theoretical arguments which underpin the current 'economic reform' period in China. This period may be characterised as a juncture of experimentation and change.(1) The economic reform period may be divided into two phases. The first phase was one in which the experiments still remained within the traditional structures of Chinese socialism. The theoretical arguments supporting this first phase are to be found in the book, China's Socialist Economy, written by the prominent theorist, Xue Muqiao.(2) The second phase of the economic reform period was given political approval at the Sixth Plenum of the Chinese Communist Party Central Committee in June 1981, and is notable for rapid economic changes in agriculture. The first part of the chapter will examine the views of Xue, as they apply to the first phase of the reform period, and then will analyse the theoretical arguments which support the current period of accelerated change.(3)

The second part of the chapter extends the criticisms made of the theory underlying the whole economic reform period. The argument moves from a critique of the orthodox view of socialism and the socialist transition to the presentation of a different approach to conceptualising post-revolutionary societies. It is argued that the most appropriate method of analysis for understanding the socialist transition is that provided by Marx which utilises the theoretical construct - mode of production. This methodology is summarised by Skocpol in the introduction to her book States and Social Revolutions in the following manner,

Once successful, a revolution marks the transition from the previous mode of production and form of class

---

1. Examples of debates on the experiments are Zhao Renwei and Xiang Qiyuan, Xue Muqiao (ed.), 1982, pp.947-56; Lin, 1981; Feuchtwang and Hussain (eds.), 1983.
2. Xue Muqiao, 1981.
3. For arguments supporting phase two of the economic reform period, see Wan Li, RMRB., 23 December 1982, SWB/FE/7228/C1-18.

dominance to a new mode of production, in which new social relations of production, new political and ideological forms, and, in general, the hegemony of the newly triumphant revolutionary class, create appropriate conditions for the further development of society.(4)

It will be argued that the above analysis is highly fruitful for comprehending the revolutionary development of China and for evaluating current experiments.

Problems of the Current Orthodoxy.

Xue Muqiao's book was written within the orthodox framework enunciated by Stalin, primarily in his 1952 monograph, Economic Problems of Socialism in the U.S.S.R.. Xue, following the example of Mao, creatively applied Stalin's 'principles' to the Chinese economy.(5) China was characterised as an 'immature socialist system' - referred to in earlier chapters as 'undeveloped socialism';(6) The transition from this stage to mature socialism (advanced socialism) was seen as requiring a protracted period of time. As Chapter Three noted, China was regarded as socialist principally because ownership of the means of production was public and not private. This was undeveloped socialism because public ownership was not unitary, but was divided between 'ownership of the whole people' and 'collective ownership'.(7)

Ownership designated the character of the regime. Its transition, however, was conceived in terms of the development of the productive forces. The theoretical couplet - public ownership and the advancement of the productive forces - became the determining element in the socialist transition. Following the argument discussed in earlier chapters, Xue noted that the basic law of economic growth was that 'the relations of production must conform to the level of the productive forces'(8); moreover, the relations of production could never surpass the level of the productive forces.(9) Xue, like Stalin, saw the primacy of the productive forces and the necessary conformity of the relations of production to the level of the productive forces as universal laws.

But, he added, there are specific principles which guide the socialist transition. The most apparent of these is that the principle of

---

4.   Skocpol, 1979, p.8.
5.   See Mao, 1977(b).
6.   Xue Muqiao, 1981, p.14.
7.   Ibid., p.16.
8.   Ibid., p.5.
9.   Ibid.

labour is 'to each according to work'(10)   Xue believed that this principle would exist even in advanced socialism. It would remain until the productive forces reached such a level that there was general abundance. At this stage of the transition, Xue felt that the principle of 'to each according to need' would come into being. Thus, the principles of labour were also determined by the level of the productive forces.

Xue noted that these laws of economic growth were proven in practice. He argued that past attempts to transcend such laws, as in the Cultural Revolution, had dire consequences for the development of China.(11) Xue here echoed the new Party history which asserted that the Cultural Revolution was responsible for,

> the most severe setbacks and heaviest losses suffered by the Party, the state and the people since the founding of the People's Republic.(12)

Needless to say, the findings of the new Party history are open to the criticism of rewriting history to serve current practice.(13) The point here is that the primacy of the productive forces was used as a yardstick to measure the past.   'Practice' was 'true' whenever it advanced the forces of production.

One may object that to take the productive forces as primary might be to equate socialism simply with modernisation. Bettelheim has argued that the 'primacy' thesis causes an ideological displacement to occur.(14) Socialism is no longer evaluated in class terms, as the 'dictatorship of the proletariat', but becomes identified with the all-round advancement of the productive forces.(15)   Moreover, the couplet of forces of production and public ownership is also misleading since the relations of production cannot simply be reduced to property relations (ownership).(16) The relations of production involve not only ownership but also the whole system of social production including the control exercised within it and the form in which the surplus is extracted from the productive labourers.

For Xue, the relations of production were determined by ownership which, he argued, corresponded to the level of the

---

10.   Ibid., p.17.
11.   Ibid., p.311.
12.   CCP.CC., 27 June 1981, BR., 27, 6 July 1981, p.20.
13.   Brugger, 1984(b).
14.   Bettelheim, 1971, p.22.
15.   Corrigan, Ramsay and Sayer, 1978, p.153.
16.   Ibid., pp.148-54. Some Western scholars uphold the primacy of the productive forces. The most prominent is Cohen, 1978. See the critical reviews by Elster, 1980, and Ruben, 1981.

productive forces. Moreover, he noted that the forces of production in China were 'backward'. It was to be expected, therefore, that the relations of production would also be at a low level. Agriculture was singled out for special attention in this regard. The formula of 'mutual correspondence' allowed for a distinction to be drawn between industry and agriculture. State industry was established by 1956, as the dominant economic sector and was completely consolidated in 1967, with the abolition of dividend payments to capitalists. Industry was now able to advance through planned state investments.(17) The labourers were united with the means of production which they owned.

But in agriculture, Xue argued, the productive forces were at a very low level and were unevenly developed. The form of ownership was not that of the state (ownership by the 'whole people'), but of the collective exercised through communes, brigades and teams. For Xue, the team represented the basic level of ownership and the base accounting level in agriculture.(18) That is, three levels of public ownership had been established by the late 1950s, but the functioning organ for land ownership, labour management and income distribution was the team. The labourers were not primarily paid a wage, but received work-points and were paid collectively. According to Xue, the work-point system was fundamentally the same as that which operated in industry.

Xue believed that in order to advance the productive forces, it was necessary to channel investments through the corresponding forms of ownership and to allow for individual incentives. For example, in agriculture, he expressed the point of view that 'substantial state assistance' was essential to create the conditions for developing production.(19) That is, Xue saw an increased state role in channelling investments to agriculture through the collectives as a means of advancing the productive forces.

In this respect, Xue's position reflected the first phase of the economic reform period. As was noted in the preceding chapter, it was thought in this period that agricultural production could be stimulated by increased investment and mechanisation. Modernisation was to be achieved via a new investment strategy. It became apparent by the Sixth Plenum in June 1981, however, that this strategy was to be abandoned. Agricultural 'self reliance' was emphasised alongside the new policy of advancing productivity through the contract responsibility system. That is, it was not to be collectives but households which were to become the focus of improving productivity. The emphasis was on increasing the productivity of land by allowing the peasants to lease the land in return for contracted quotas to the

17. Xue Muqiao, 1981, p.13.
18. Ibid., p.5.
19. Ibid., p.101.

collective and allowing the peasants to be able to market any surplus above the quota.

The concern for productivity increases in Chinese agriculture is genuine and understandable.(20)   The Chinese agricultural economy suffers from a number of underlying economic problems. For example, Barker, Sisler and Rose calculated that,

> The growth in grain production over the past two decades has been slightly above the rate of growth of population and close to the average of the performance of other developing countries.(21)

Moreover, in terms of agricultural productivity, Barker and Sinha, commented that,

> Despite the favorable growth record, the efficiency of agricultural production, measured by growth in output relative to growth in inputs, has been declining...it is unclear whether the net effect of collectivisation on agricultural efficiency has been positive or negative.(22)

The need for change in agricultural policy was evident to all; but the form this change would take was open to debate. As noted, Xue argued for an increase in state investment to raise the level of the productive forces, and this was to be channelled through the collectives.   His perspective here is consistent with his stress on 'mutual correspondence' between forces and relations of production. Nevertheless, it was possible to utilise this theoretical couplet to justify the emphasis upon household contract farming as the means of raising the level of the productive forces. The policies after the Sixth Plenum reflected the view that households were an integral part of production and would remain so, so long as Chinese agriculture was 'backward'.

For example, Wan Li observed that Chinese agriculture had stagnated for a 'long time', that the rural economy was dominated by subsistence and semi-subsistence farming; thus the new policies would arouse 'the enthusiasm and initiative of the peasants'. When the productive forces have developed, then 'production relations and superstructure also need to be readjusted and changed'. Nevertheless, he added,

---

20. The point here is that the economic reforms are not merely ideological but have a real basis.   For the debate, see Christensen, 1983, and Zhao Renwei and Xiang Qiyuan, Xue (ed.), 1982, pp.947-56.
21. Barker, Sisler and Rose, 1982, p.179.
22. Barker and Sinha, 1982, p.200.

Prudence is necessary when approaching the reform of the commune institutions. We should not require each level to reform from top to bottom by prescribing a time limit for fulfilment. Until suitable new organisational forms can replace production brigades and teams, we should not recklessly change existing forms and bring about a disorderly situation.(23)

Here Wan Li articulated the policy of the new period of economic reform. The level of correspondence between productive forces and ownership was lower than that allowed for in the commune, brigade or team structures. The old form of 'three level' ownership was to undergo fundamental change and, consistent with the demands of undeveloped socialism, a new correspondence was to be found at the household level. Wan Li advanced the point of view that the changing agricultural system was developing into a new mode of production, geared to 'socialised commodity production',

This mode of production conforms to the cultural, technological and management levels of the vast number of agricultural producers in our country and provides conditions for Chinese peasants to bring their wisdom and intelligence into play. It is also conducive to the utilisation of large numbers of small-sized and simple production tools and facilities. By using fewer investment funds and by absorbing more of the labour force, it can achieve quick returns and great benefits....Consumption of energy can also be reduced so as to avoid the drawbacks of the so-called 'petroleum agriculture'. The co-existence of the individual economy and the collective economy based on taking households or household groups into the units of labour and production and operation, therefore, may be suitable for most areas in our country and may be in conformity with the characteristics of most areas' agriculture,...In short, the mode of production of small size, which is gradually developing towards specialisation, may be a good way to develop a socialist agriculture of Chinese style.(24)

Wan Li's position was supported by Du Runsheng who also argued for a three-tiered system of agricultural production. The most important tier was the household economy. Accompanying this was the possibility for voluntary combinations of households to utilise the means of production. Finally, there were the collectives which

---

23.   Wan Li, <u>RMRB.</u>, 23 December 1982, SWB/FE/7228/C8; wording changed for stylistic reasons.
24.   <u>Ibid.</u>, C/9; wording changed for stylistic reasons.

retained certain governmental functions but had lost their control over the labour process.   With legerdemain, Du Runsheng used Marxist theory to support the household economy as the basic unit of production. He claimed that,

> a principle of Marxism is that every change in the relations of ownership is an inevitable outcome of the development of new productive forces which can no longer fit in with the old relations of ownership.(25)

When the productive forces had 'fully developed', then the household undertakings would advance to a higher socialist stage.

Du Runsheng noted that the household economy was not the same as previous family farming,

> Today's household undertakings are very different in nature.   Since land is owned by the public, they are restricted by the collective economy in many ways. They represent a level of management in the co-operative economy, and constitute an organic component part of the entire socialist economy.

But, Du Runsheng did add a note of caution,

> It is feared that the household contracting system will promote the conservative idea of private possession among the peasants. This fear is not without grounds. However, we must be able to see the other side of the matter, which also happens to be the prevailing aspect. Today's peasants are different from those of the past. They are now new-type labourers under the socialist co-operative system.(26)

The second phase of the economic reform period, sanctioned by the Sixth Plenum, departed from the first phase in that the structure of agriculture underwent fundamental change. The policies, argued for by Xue Muqiao in China's Socialist Economy, were no longer applied to Chinese agriculture.   Yet, the underlying theoretical justification for the policies remained the same. Wan Li and Du Runsheng both argued for 'mutual correspondence' and for the primacy of the productive forces. They also asserted that agriculture was still socialist since the land remained publically-owned and was no longer in the private possession of peasant households.

Stalinist orthodoxy was used here as ideological justification for policy. But the talmudic wisdom of Stalin could not hide the critical

---

25.   Du Runsheng, RMRB., 7 March 1983, SWB/FE/7288/B11/6.
26.   Ibid., B/11/7-8.

changes that were occurring in agriculture. The orthodoxy, as expressed by the Chinese theorists, was incapable of conceptualising the character of the changes since it ignored the form of surplus extraction. Though the alterations in the form of surplus extraction were noted, they were not incorporated into an evaluation of the 'socialist economy'. The relations of surplus extraction were subsumed under property relations and therefore, were not considered crucial to the argument about socialism in China.(27)But it was impossible for these theorists completely to ignore the form of surplus production and appropriation that existed within China. Xue initially argued that because the means of production were public, then exploitation had been basically eliminated.(28) Later in his book, he expressed the orthodox view that labour during the transition had a dual character. The labourer produced 'value' which was partly consumed by society for its needs and partly possessed by the labourer in the form of consumption goods. The labourer worked both for society and for himself.(29) Thus, while 'value' was created, and a part of it appropriated by society, this was not exploitative since society operated in the interests of the worker. That is, there was no exploitation since the surplus was appropriated through public property. The surplus, moreover, also assisted in the reproduction of that property and provided for the state welfare fund.

The above position was traditional in that it discussed the process of surplus extraction in terms of the way it was used. But, it looked at the use of the surplus uncritically and did not discuss the control exercised over the production and appropriation of the surplus. The important question of control over the surplus remained untheorised in the orthodox view of socialism. Given that the issue of control was ignored, it is not surprising that the question of the class relations associated with it was also not raised.

Wan Li and Du Runsheng compounded the weakness of Xue's position by understating the changes that were occurring in the process of surplus extraction in agriculture. They both admitted that the shift to the household responsibility system broke with the collective work-point structure of remuneration for labour. For Xue, the work-point system was analogous to rewards in industry. But now its subordination to the household economy constituted a major change in the production and appropriation of the agricultural surplus. Wan Li argued that the state would still be able to control the household system through legal and administrative means,

---

27. For arguments on legal property rights and actual 'possession', see Bettelheim, 1976(a).
28. Xue Muqiao, 1981, p.14.
29. Ibid., pp.68-9.

The existence of the individual economy is not a terrible thing, because the state can appropriately manage it by utilising legislative and administrative means. It can control or readjust its production, operation and income - by utilising such economic levers as pricing and taxation (including progressive taxation), so that it will become an organic component of the socialist economic system.(30)

Du Runsheng asserted that the contract responsibility system was an 'impure form' of the 'dual nature' of labour and still accorded with the principle of 'to each according to work',

Under the present contracting system with payment linked to output, the method of distribution according to contract is practised. 'After ensuring the state's needs and giving a sufficient amount to the collective, the remaining portion is ours.' Here, the 'remaining portion' also includes rewards for private investment. As far as its form is concerned, we can not say that it is distribution according to work in the purest form. However, since it provides that those who do more work and put in more can get more, and since what is put in is still the materialised form of one's labour, we can not say that it runs counter to the principle of distribution according to work.(31)

Thus, neither Du Runsheng nor Wan Li theorised the change in the nature of surplus extraction; they simply looked for ideological support, using Marxism as defined by Stalin, to justify current policies. The consistency in their and Xue Muqiao's use of theory is to be found in the use of orthodoxy, as a methodological device to incorporate change, rather than in their explanation of shifts in practice. There was no unity in theory and practice, and this is not surprising, since all three accepted the point of view that 'practice is the test of truth'. But, concealed within this phrase is the notion that the test of truth is not socialism but modernisation - the advancement of the productive forces. In conclusion, the theory of socialism adopted by the C.C.P. is not useful for explaining current changes or the historical development of China. It it necessary, therefore, to reject this orthodoxy and to return to pre-Stalinist notions of historical transition. It is to this task that part two of this chapter is directed.

The discussion in the second section of the chapter centres upon the theoretical construct - mode of production. It is argued that the socialist transition in China can best be understood by using this aspect

30.   Wan Li, RMRB., 23 December 1982, SWB/FE/7228/C/7-8; wording changed for stylistic reasons.
31.   Du Runsheng, RMRB., 7 March 1983, SWB/FE/7288/B11/11.

of Marxian methodology. Associated with the use of a mode of production to explain Chinese revolutionary history will be an emphasis upon the relations of production. The reason for this is that it is through the relations of production, conceived of in terms of the social process of surplus production and appropriation, that one may conceptualise class within China.(32)

Towards a Different Theory of Socialist Transition.

The order of the argument in part two will be as follows. There will be a discussion of the historical establishment and consolidation of the socialist mode of production in China. The stabilisation of the socialist mode implied the end of the socialist transition, without the possibility of moving directly to communism; that is without the fundamental displacement of the socialist mode of production. The consolidation of the socialist mode was the crucial element in shaping post-1949 Chinese history. It was the unfolding of the contradictions inherent in this mode of production which set the parameters for policy decisions. The perspective offered, therefore, is dynamic and does not rely upon a linear analysis as does the account based on the primacy of the productive forces.

The exposition will begin with a reflection on presuppositions and explanations of the socialist transition. The aim of this section is to establish a theoretical position with regard to modes of production and the socialist transition; this position will then be applied to China. Once the examination of the transition from one mode of production to another in post-revolutionary China has been undertaken, then it will be possible to return to the current policies in China. A number of concluding points will be made with regard to the future development of the socialist mode in that country.

The concept of a transition implies a process which has a definite beginning and an identifiable end. As has been noted, in Marxist theory the notion of a transition has been seen within the context of modes of production. This was especially the case with the transition most familiar to Marx, that from feudalism to capitalism. Nevertheless, when Marx discussed the transition to communism, he argued that the material basis for communism was inherent in the dynamic of capitalist development(33), and that the chief imperative was that the proletariat capture state power and neutralise the political power of the bourgeoisie.(34)

Previous chapters have dwelt on Marx's famous comment in the 'Critique of the Gotha Programme',

---

32.   This notion of class is more fully theorised in the seminal work of De Ste. Croix, 1981. See also Dupre and Rey, 1973; Rey, 1973.
33.   Marx, (1867), Marx I, 1954, pp.458-9.
34.   Marx, (1864), Marx and Engels, <u>SW</u>., II, 1970, p.17.

Between capitalist and communist society lies the period of the revolutionary transformation of one into the other. Corresponding to this is also a political transformation period in which the state can be nothing but the revolutionary dictatorship of the proletariat.(35)

Marx's concept of the 'dictatorship of the proletariat' was an expression of the historical form of the state during the period of revolutionary transformation to classless communism. In 'The Civil War in France', Marx indicated that the proletarian state was 'to serve as a lever for uprooting the economical foundations upon which rests the existence of classes, and therefore of class rule'.(36) The dictatorship of the proletariat was regarded by Marx as a form of political transition from the capitalist state to stateless communism. That is, in a classless society there would be no state.(37)

Thus, when Marx discussed the transition to communism, he shifted the debate away from the mode of production to class struggle and the role of the proletarian state. Marx argued that it was the role of the 'dictatorship of the proletariat' to destroy the 'foundations' of classes; but the problem, unseen by Marx, was that in the process of 'uprooting' the basis of classes, the 'proletarian state' might establish its own foundations. While the 'proletarian state' might destroy the basis for capitalism, that is the capitalist mode of production, it does not necessarily follow that the state will 'wither away'. Marx did not contemplate the possibility that in using the proletarian state to undermine the capitalist mode of production, the power of the state would be consolidated and the state would become an integral part of a new mode of production.

In this light, the transition from capitalism to communism may be considered as, firstly, the negation of the capitalist mode of production. The state plays a crucial role in this action. The transition, however, goes much further than the negation of capitalism and, in this process, the state becomes integrated into a whole new system of production, as was abundantly clear in the discussion in the preceding chapter. But what previous chapters have not seen is that the latter involves not only the negation of capitalism, but the creation

---

35.   Marx, (1875), Marx and Engels, SW., III, 1970, p.26; italics in original.
36.   Marx, (1871), Marx and Engels, SW., II, 1970, p.223.
37.   Ideas for this section on Marx's views of communism are adapted from Barbalet, 1977.

of a different and unique mode of production.(38) This mode of production can be considered as socialist. This notion of a socialist mode of production relates specifically to the integrated process of negation and construction. It, therefore, breaks fundamentally with Marx's conceptualisation of the transition to communism.

The theory outlined above has major implications for the transition to classless communism. The establishment of the socialist mode of production acts as a barrier to developing communism. The socialist mode contains its own contradiction between the technical and social relations of production. Furthermore, the antagonisms in the social relations of production, especially over the extraction of a surplus, are the basis for the class structure in the social formation. That is, a class is a group of persons identified by its position in the whole system of social production, defined primarily by its relationship to the means and labour of production and to other classes. Moreover, class is conceptualised in terms of the appropriation of part of the product of the labour of others (exploitation). Class domination involves the control over the surplus produced by the labour of others. That is, class and mode of production are integrally related. The socialist mode of production, and the classes associated with it, shape the development of the country in terms of their own logic. That is, just as the capitalist mode effects the countries in which it has developed, so the socialist mode effects those countries in which it has become established.

The consolidation of the socialist mode of production within a country does not establish the basis for the transition to communism. In socialist countries, the transition to communism needs to be conceptualised in terms of the displacement of this mode of production and the class and state structures associated with it. In other words, it is not possible to contemplate the transition to communism as simply an extension of this mode of production. The development of the productive forces of the socialist mode can not lead to communism, since the expansion of the productive forces will not transform the mode of production. The development of the productive forces may, as Marx argued with respect to capitalism, intensify the inherent contradictions within the mode of production, but it can not lead directly to a classless, stateless society. A much more revolutionary transformation is required; it is vital to change the form of surplus extraction, before a transition to communism may become

---

38. The view here extends the comments of Brugger when he speaks of the 'negation of some, but never all of the capitalist mode' and provides a means of conceptualising the socialist mode. See Brugger, 1981(b), p.328.

possible.(39)   This transformation requires the displacement of the socialist mode of production and the overthrow of those classes which dominate it during its expansion and reproduction.   Whereas Marx argued that socialism would be a classless society, current societies which call themselves socialist, have a discrete class structure based on the socialist mode of production.

Mode of Production and Socialist Transition in China.

Prior to the Communists' 'political' victory,(40) the old modes of production in China were undergoing extensive change, due primarily to the influence of foreign penetration.   This was most apparent in the cities and the areas surrounding them.(41)   It is generally accepted that these regions were dominated by capitalism.   But, in contrast, there is considerable debate in the literature on the nature of production in the rest of the rural regions.   The usual view is that production in those areas was quite different from that in the cities.   Concomitant with this argument is the assertion that the character of production in most of the countryside was geographically quite isolated from the influences of urban capitalism and imperialism.   Agriculture is often described in terms of residual categories, that is as 'traditional' or 'feudal'.(42)

But the notion of a dual economy in China before the revolution has been challenged by recent evidence.   The study conducted by Myers

---

39.   See Marx, III, 1959, pp.782-813.   Following Marx there has been much interest in the transition.   Recently the debate on the transition to capitalism has been considered in two phases with two distinct geographical and theoretical foci.   The first focus was on Britain and France.   A pioneer here was Dobb (1946), 1975.   This stimulated an interchange of views, reproduced in Hilton, 1976.   The second focus was on the question of development and underdevelopment, looking outside Europe and most interestingly to India.   See Foster-Carter, 1978, and McEachern, 1976.   Contributions containing useful parallels for the socialist transition are Mayer, 1981 and Mayer, 1982.
40.   On the notion of a narrow 'political' versus a broad 'socialist' revolution, see Claudin, 1975.
41.   Feuerwerker, 1968.
42.   For a short review of the deficiencies associated with the residual categories of 'feudal' or 'traditional' China, see Brugger, 1981(a), p.17.   In this brief introduction, it is not possible to canvass all the debates on whether a 'state mode of production' was evident in this period or whether the 'Asiatic mode' predominated.   On the latter, see Anderson, 1975, pp.462-549. Melotti, 1977, pp.105-13, accepts that the Asiatic mode was evident and came under the pressure of Western penetration.   For a critique, see Dirlik, 1982.

into the peasant economy, reveals the widespread character of commodity relations in the countryside.(43)   There is also evidence which shows the commercialisation of credit and financial arrangements in the twentieth century.(44)   Land tenure was changing and as Riskin notes, many observers in the 1930s believed that 'the socio-economic institutions in the countryside were growing even more exploitative and burdensome to the peasants...'(45).

The character of the mode of production in Chinese agriculture is neatly encapsulated in the following,

> The dominant form of rural production in China, which the Chinese Communist Party inherited, was simple commodity production. Ground rent was capitalised and a significant volume of peasant production was for sale on the market. This is clearly a form of capitalism. What may be described as 'feudal' about the situation were simply the hierarchical, patriarchal and communal values which sustained the dominant ideology.(46)

In summary, by 1949 the whole of Chinese production was dominated by capitalism. Nevertheless, as was the case in other Asian countries (e.g. India), the method of its domination varied and its growth and potency was uneven. This unevenness was especially the case in China because of its sheer size and regional diversity. Moreover, the capitalist mode of production in China did not mirror European capitalism in any simple manner.(47)   The mode was integrated into a society which had different values and different historical structures (e.g. patron-client relationships). The introduction of capitalism sharpened class antagonisms and helped to undermine a politically bankrupt ruling class.

For its part, the C.C.P. was concerned to define the 'main enemies' in the revolutionary struggle as 'imperialism' and 'feudalism'.(48)   The C.C.P.'s strategy was to appeal to feelings of revolutionary nationalism and to end 'feudal exploitation'. The Party saw the transformation of China occuring in two distinct but related stages; the first involved the struggle against imperialism and feudalism, and this was to be followed by the transition from capitalism to communism via the phase of socialism.

---

43.   Myers, 1970.
44.   Feuerwerker, 1968; Donnithorne, 1967, pp.31-6.
45.   Riskin, 1975.
46.   Brugger, 1984(b) pp.174-5.
47.   See Dirlik, 1982.
48.   Mao Zedong, (1939), Mao, <u>SW</u>., II, 1965, p.315.

The victory of the C.C.P. over the Nationalist Government in 1949, gave the Party the state power with which it could carry out its programme throughout China. The first moves made by the Party were to stablise a war-ravaged economy. Once relative stability had been attained, the C.C.P. turned its attention towards confiscating imperialist property and to changing the pattern of control over enterprises formally owned by the Nationalist Government; the latter the Party called 'bureaucratic capital'. These resources provided a solid foundation for the nationalisation of industry. The Party, however, pursued a gradualist programme utilising both economic and political pressure to transmit urban industrial property into state hands.

The dominant position of the state in the economy, which had been inherited from the previous government, helped the Party carry out its policies. State owned enterprises constituted approximately two-thirds of total industrial capital. The previous National Government had controlled 90 per cent of the country's iron and steel output, 33 per cent of its coal, 67 per cent of its electrical power, 45 per cent of its cement, and all petroleum and non-ferrous metals. In addition, state-capital controlled the major banks, transportation, communications and airlines. It has been estimated that, 'by the end of 1949, the new régime's state industrial enterprises accounted for 41.3 per cent of China's industrial output'.(49)

With foreign capitalists' property confiscated and the position of state ownership secured, the C.C.P. could then turn its attention to transforming the private property of the Chinese bourgeoisie. The Party used an all-round approach to defeat industrial capitalism. For example, it constructed its taxation policies in such a manner that industrial profits paid a significantly increased share. An ideological assault was launched against unfair profit-making practices in the Five Anti campaign. The Party adopted a series of measures to obtain control over banking and used the centralised People's Bank to exert pressure on private industry. Furthermore, the C.C.P. made a distinction between those who had supported the previous regime, the 'bureaucratic capitalists', and those who had not, the 'national capitalists'; the Party moved directly against the former while adopting a gradualist approach with regard to the latter.

The State corporations moved into the retail areas and were able effectively to dominate retail sales throughout the country. Private enterprise felt itself to be continually enclosed and restricted by the state. The state used its investment policies to attract private capital into joint state-private enterprises. By 1954, 33 per cent of the total value of industrial output came from such enterprises. By 1955, this

---

49.   Breth, 1977, p.231.

had been extended to approximately 50 per cent of the total value of industrial output.(50)

In 1956, increased political and economic pressure was applied to transform the social forms of production throughout China, and private capital soon felt this compulsion. As previous chapters have argued, the year 1956 was a turning point; the various forms of private ownership were transformed into two basic types - state ownership proper and joint private-state concerns.(51) Mao argued that the latter were no longer capitalist but had a 'socialist character'.(52) Within the joint enterprises, the former owners were originally allotted a portion of the profit which was not permitted to exceed a quarter of total net earnings. But, from 1956 onward, the former owners were to be paid interest on their shares at fixed rates which were generally set at five per cent per annum. This new policy was termed 'buying off' and implied a peaceful transformation from private to state ownership. The aim of the policy was that, by 1962, the state would own these enterprises outright. But in the end, it was the Cultural Revolution which ensured that this aim was achieved.

The important point is that by 1956, the character of private property had been fundamentally altered. Private capital became subordinate to the state. This had implications ·for the class structure. As Breth notes,

> The businessmen, seeing the general trend of events, seemed resigned to accept their fate. At the end of that year, the joint state-private industrial enterprises constituted 99 per cent of all private industrial establishments, and 99.6 per cent of the total value of industrial output.(53)

It is clear that by the end of 1956, the balance between private capital and the state had shifted towards the latter.

The state had control over industry, either directly or through its investment policies and joint ownership. The nature of profit had changed. The capitalists no longer obtained surplus in the form of labour power embodied in commodities. Instead, the joint owners received a state payment for the value of their property. The state now controlled the products of labour which it appropriated and distributed. The form of surplus product was thereby transformed. In addition, the supply of labour was allocated by the government through labour bureaux, and this undermined the old competitive labour

---

50.   Ibid., p.27.
51.   Eckstein, 1977, pp.75-6.
52.   Mao Zedong, (1953), Mao, SW., V, 1977, p.101.
53.   Breth, 1977, p.28.

market.(54)   Furthermore, the extension of state ownership promoted an expansion of government intervention and planning.   In the initial period, the administration of labour and capital was over-centralised and rigid.   From 1957 onward, there were attempts to make planning decentralised and flexible, complementing the general policy move towards regional self-reliance and regional responsibility.

The changes in private property and the form of surplus stimulated the transformation of the technical relations of production in Chinese industry.   The period between 1949 and 1956 was one in which the Chinese adopted a Soviet model to negate capitalism and introduce 'socialist' production.   For example, the government established a standardised wage system which planned the wage differentials for tasks performed.(55)   Prior to 1956, the state experimented with incentive and bonus schemes with the aim of integrating personal production and remuneration.   This was in accordance with Soviet practice which favoured sharp wage differentials and piece-rates.   The Chinese, however, tended to be cautious in their application of an incentive system (e.g. piece-rates were never so widely used as in Russia and even at their peak in China, piece-rates covered only 42 per cent of industry).   They soon became disenchanted with the Soviet system.   The most significant difficulty concerning wages policy, during the First Five Year Plan, was the growing gap between urban and rural incomes.   Substantially higher urban wages acted as an enticement for rural labourers to move to the cities, thus aggravating the urban employment problem.(56)

In 1957, a policy shift was initiated which restrained wages.   In the same year, the principles of a new 'rational low-wage policy' were announced.   The basis of this policy was that increases in wage levels were tied to, but restricted to less than, upward movements in productivity.(57)   Complementing this policy was strict control over labour mobility, especially the movement of labour into the cities. From 1957-58 onward, the level of real wages declined in comparison to the previous period where wages had been used as an instrument to stimulate work effort.   Productivity was promoted through an appeal to political commitment.

Thus, by 1957 the state controlled the majority of industrial enterprises and the products produced by them and was able, through its wage policy, to ensure that a surplus was extracted above the cost of reproducing the labourers.   The strict control over the mobility of labour and its direct allocation into industry reinforced the dominance of the state in the relations of production.

---

54.   See Howe, 1971.
55.   Howe, 1973, pp.28-54.
56.   Ibid., pp.63-115 and 142.
57.   Donnithorne, 1967, p.205; Brugger, 1976, p.265.

The capitalist relations of production were even further suppressed by the government's decision to use Party cadres to regulate and stimulate production. The relationships between planners, enterprise managers and direct producers were monitored by Party committees. The tensions which existed in these new technical relations of production were now mediated by Party cadres. The Soviet system of 'one person management' was replaced by committees incorporating Party representatives and technical experts, including managers. The Soviet management model, introduced into China, allowed the enterprise a degree of autonomy over the size of the wage fund, bonuses and productivity.(58) Nevertheless, this autonomy was circumscribed by strict controls over enterprise inputs and outputs. However insufficient they might have been according to the orthodoxy of the 1980s, the 1957-58 reforms did give enterprises in China more discretion over production. Quantitative targets were reduced from twelve to four; these were, output of main commodities, total profit, average size of the workforce and total wage. These targets were most important in terms of the surplus produced. The role of the Party in the enterprises was to oversee this quantitative element of production and to emphasise quantitative goals.

The end result was that the contradictions in the technical relations of production - those between enterprises, direct producers and state planners - were mediated by the Party. This allowed for more flexibility and the decentralisation of planning. The Party became integrated into the technical relations which helped stabilise the socialist mode in industry.

The surplus extracted from Chinese industrial enterprises was embodied in the products of labour. This represented both the absolute and relative methods of obtaining surplus from production. In the period between 1952 and 1957, according to Hoffman, the expansion of industry was due to the dual effects of the increase in labourers and the rise in productivity. He writes that, 'about 45 per cent of...industrial growth was due to increases in productivity, and 54 per cent was due to increased numbers of workers.'(59) But, as Hoffman adds, the highest rates of productivity occurred in the priority, heavy industrial plants. He notes that,

> From 1952 to 1957 in the coal, iron, steel, cement and cotton textile industries, official statistics show respective increases in output per worker of 46, 138, 93, 74, and 8 per cent....The significant lower rate of increase

---

58. Brugger, 1976, pp.146-83.
59. Hoffman, 1974, p.56.

in productivity for cotton textiles is consistent with the priorities of the FFYP.(60)

Howe takes this perspective further, and argues that increased labour productivity accounted for an estimated 40 to 50 per cent of China's industrial growth.(61) Wang Haibo and Wu Jiajun estimate that, between 1952 and 1979, the number of industrial workers increased from 12.46 million to 53.4 million. They add that the rate of fixed assets per worker was ¥2,101.9 in 1952 and ¥10,577.3 in 1979, an increase of more than 400 per cent.(62)   Chapter Three has already noted that, according to official 1983 figures, labour productivity rose from ¥3,016 in 1949 to ¥12,133 in 1982, a 300 per cent increase.(63)

The success of the new mode of production in industry placed enormous pressure on the transformation of agriculture.   This was especially the case as the increase in industrial productivity went hand in hand with capital intensity.(64)   It was essential that agricultural productivity grew and that it was able to absorb labour.   This dual necessity may seen paradoxical, as it is often the case that the raising of productivity levels entails the displacement of labour.   But Chinese agriculture was suffering from a shortage of skilled labourers and an inefficient use of labour.   In addition, there was a general lack of capital.   Mass mobilisation was seen as a means of overcoming these problems   while   containing   unemployment   and   underemployment. Moreover, it was vital for the whole mode of production that rural productivity rose and labour was absorbed in the agricultural sphere. The reason for this was that unless rural productivity expanded, the urban-rural gap would grow, thus creating a structural imbalance in the socialist mode of production.   This distortion, as in the Soviet Union, would lead to a drain on the surplus (especially the industrial surplus) and create instability.   Given that the bulk of the population lived in the rural areas, it was even more important that a balance be found between industry and agriculture: hence all the talk about the 'law of planned and proportionate development'.   Before looking at how this was achieved, the investigation needs to examine the transformation of the mode of production in agriculture.

The   capitalist   mode   of   production   in   pre-1949   Chinese agriculture, was unevenly developed and highly complex.   The complexity of capitalist relations (e.g. tenancy arrangements, share

60.   Ibid., p.60.
61.   Howe, 1978, pp.95-6.   Howe calculates that between 1952 and 1960   producer   goods   advanced   at   25.3   per   cent,   whereas consumer goods rose by only 8.3 per cent.
62.   Wang Haibo and Wu Jiajun, Xue (ed.), 1982, p.444.
63.   State Statistical Bureau, Abstract, 1983, JPRS., 84111, 12 August 1983, pp.100-101.
64.   Howe, 1971, p.109.

cropping, rental contracts etc.) was underestimated by the C.C.P. This was compounded by the Party's insistence on the 'feudal' character of rural exploitation. The Communist Party exaggerated the role of the landlords and misjudged the growing strength of the rich and middle peasants. Initially, the C.C.P. believed that landlords and rich peasants comprised about 10 per cent of the population and owned more than 70 per cent of the total arable land.(65) Nevertheless, as in industry, the Party was cautious in its strategic practice and moved very gradually. This enabled it to overcome many of the weaknesses in its theory. The first major campaign in the transformation was land reform. This was specifically aimed at the landlords and their 'feudal' forms of exploitation and excluded the rich peasants and the 'capitalist' methods of landlord exploitation. The C.C.P. was convinced that an attack on 'feudal' exploitation would have profound implications for the transition.

Two problems emerged as the land reform programme developed. The first difficulty was to restrain the poor peasants when they sought to extend the assult on to the rich peasants' property. The second problem emerged on the completion of land reform. The results of the transformation were not so far reaching as had been expected. One reason for this disappointment was that the Party had exaggerated the landlords' holdings. According to Schran, on average, the landlords and rich peasants owned around 46 per cent of the land (not 70 per cent) and they constituted about 12 per cent of rural families.(66)

The land reform redistributed approximately 40 per cent of the land in China to about 60 per cent of the peasantry. Schran estimates that more than two-thirds of this land came from the landlords and less than one third from the rich peasants.(67) In terms of land redistribution the land reform was marginal. As Shue notes: 'land reform made a relatively few people poorer, and a great many people somewhat better off. But it made no one rich.'(68) Moreover, Domes calculates that the difference between the holdings of the rich, middle

---

65. Chao, 1977; Schran, 1969, p.14.
66. Schran, 1969, p.18. See also Shue, 1980, pp.47-66. Shue compares land holdings in Hunan with the Central South region. The tables 4-10 on these pages reveal the diversity of landlord ownership within Hunan and between the two regions. Shue argues that the Party's original estimation of landlord holdings were based on Hunan and did not account for regional diversity (p.57). See also Lippitt, 1974; Modern China, 1, 1978.
67. Schran, 1969, p.35.
68. Shue, 1980, p.90.

and poor peasants was often only marginal, between one half and one acre.(69) Many holdings were too small for subsistence farming.

Yet there was still a marked division in the countryside, as Donnithorne notes,

> the rich and middle peasants still had greater than average holdings, as well as more and better equipment and animals. They, too, were more likely to be literate than their poor fellows:...(70)

Furthermore, many of the better-off peasants were convinced that they had now merely to consolidate their advantages and prosper. But, the Communist Party saw land reform as simply 'the initial battle of a protracted war'(71)

Land reform had seen the economic and political power of the landlords destroyed, not only in the village but throughout the whole community. The first step in the rural transformation was the demise of the landlords. But, the C.C.P. did not move directly towards a 'second revolution' against the rich peasants and capitalist exploitation; it consolidated its gains. The Party utilised a gradualist programme to absorb the rural surplus and to promote further transformation.

There were three key elements in the advancement of the transition after land reform. The first was progressive taxation, which was especially severe upon tenancy arrangements, thereby attacking a major aspect of rural capitalist exploitation. Secondly, the state began to expand its wholesale and retail trading outlets through the state trading companies, thereby undermining private trade. Lastly, the peasants were encouraged to form mutual aid teams. These were particularly popular with poor peasants, as the means of production available to such peasants were often inadequate for efficient farming.

As the state became more prominent in the market, the conflict between it and the private traders intensified. The private traders dealt primarily with the 'better-off' peasants. The poor peasants tended to sign advance purchase contracts with the government, thereby obtaining pre-harvest credit (when it was most needed) in

---

69.   Domes, 1980, pp.10-11.
70.   Donnithorne, 1967, p.37.
71.   Shue, 1980, p.96. Shue neatly summarises the C.C.P. strategy: 'by 1949-50, the emphasis was definitely on minimising the number of automatic class enemies, and on absorbing as many potentially revolutionary elements in the villages as possible, even if at the time they were recruited their opinions could not be called progressive.'(p.18)

return for post-harvest quotas delivered to the state trading co-operatives. The 'better-off' peasants were prepared to speculate on the market for high grain prices. By engaging in this practice, they undermined the state system for grain pricing and supplies. In 1953, conflict came to a head. The state administration was under pressure from cities for grain and the situation was exacerbated by speculation in grain prices. It became apparent that the government was subsidising the private grain trade. The amount of grain sold by the state in 1953, was 38.42 per cent greater than that purchased by it.(72)

The state moved swiftly and decisively against this private trade. All grain sales were monopolised by the state, thereby forcing all peasants to sell their surpluses to the government at fixed prices. These were set at the prevailing market price and were thus only disadvantageous to the speculators, that is those peasants who had acted against the state's grain trade. The rich peasants, in particular, were hardest hit by the domination of the state in the grain market; but their power was to be even more curtailed by the growth of the Agricultural Producer Co-operatives.

Using economic and political incentives, the Party promoted co-operativisation. The early A.P.Cs, which grew from the mutual aid teams, were unstable. These were known as lower stage co-operatives, as the income share accruing to the members, after state and investment obligations had been met was based primarily upon private property. The ratio was fixed at 70 per cent for land contributed by the peasant family to the co-op and 30 per cent on the basis of work performed.(73)

The most significant element in the A.P.Cs' instability was the ability of the rich and 'better-off' peasants to compete effectively against them. By 1955, Mao was greatly concerned over this threat to the transformation process and decided, therefore, to increase the momentum of co-operativisation. Loans were granted to the poor peasants to join A.P.Cs, and political and economic pressure was applied to the middle peasants to make them also enter the co-ops. It was crucial that the peasants with the greater means of production should join the co-ops as this would raise their level of productivity to a point where the private peasant economy could no longer compete effectively against them. Moreover, as the co-operative movement grew, the strength of the private sector would be sapped. That is, the rich peasants would find themselves without labour to employ in their fields.

By late 1956, the turning point had been reached. The A.P.Cs were now firmly established and able to compete against the private

---

72.   <u>Ibid</u>., p.21.
73.   Domes, 1980, p.13.

producers. By the end of 1956, 87.8 per cent of peasants had joined the A.P.Cs, and in 1957 this figure rose to 93.5 per cent.(74) The rich peasants had also been drawn into the co-ops and the balance had now shifted fundamentally towards the state. The A.P.Cs were established on a higher level than their predecessors with private property overshadowed by the labour performed by the peasants. That is, the co-operatives paid the peasant primarily in kind, on the basis of labour, and property was no longer the foundation for wealth or status.

As Brugger notes, the higher level A.P.Cs resembled the Soviet kolkhoz in that,

> all land, draught animals, major production materials, etc. were turned over to the collective and individual peasants retained a plot of land, a few animals and some tools. Provision was still made for share funds determined according to property and labour status but payment was now exclusively according to work, not according to resources originally pooled. Nevertheless compensation was made for loss of property.(75)

With the consolidation of the A.P.Cs, the old capitalist relations of production were displaced by the new co-operative ownership and the new process of surplus extraction. The A.P.Cs needed, however, to be further integrated into the newly-formed technical relations of production. There was considerable confusion in the technical relations over the autonomy of different levels and the power and control to be exercised along the surplus chain. Initially, the co-operatives were given the key position in organising and supervising labour and land. But there was pressure at the point of production, expressed through the teams, for more responsibility over labour allocation and remuneration. Moreover, the A.P.Cs found it difficult fully to co-ordinate the land and were often too small to use the fields efficiently. Thus, while the new form of surplus product was established, the technical relations were in a state of disharmony. Furthermore, the A.P.C.s were still inefficient compared with industry, and the gap between the two sectors continued to grow. Mao decided to resolve these micro and macro contradictions by further transforming agriculture. The Great Leap Forward was introduced and one of its basic policy directions was to control agricultural production through communisation. The communes were constructed from a number of A.P.Cs, and they extended even further the revolution in the relations of production.

Combining A.P.Cs increased land holding per agricultural unit, thereby allowing the communes to plan land use more effectively. But

---

74.   Eckstein, 1977, p.71.
75.   Brugger, 1981(a), p.124.

the most significant effect of the commune movement was in increasing the labour supply; this was brought about primarily through the transfer of women from 'traditional' (family) roles into the fields. In some areas, this had a profound effect on the peasant family.(76) Furthermore, private plots were communised and the teams began to move from field to field in a manner which resembled the work practices of the state construction industry. Commune management was given more responsibility and became an over-arching organ of government agricultural administration. Thus, the communes became much more than mere economic units transmitting directives downward and ensuring that the surplus was channelled upward to the state. They were now political institutions which had power to decide upon many issues including health, education and investment policies.

The technical relations of production were extended far beyond the kolkhoz boundaries. Some 'radicals' saw the communes as embodiments of Marx's vision in the Paris Commune. According to such people, the state would soon 'wither away'. But, it became apparent that there were still contradictions in the technical relations of production. The teams demanded more authority over production and work-points. With the demise of the family economy, the peasant farmers wanted to ensure that they had increased control over their labour and its organisation. Initially, this pressure was resisted by commune management. Thus, tension grew over the size of the surplus and between the levels of authority within the labour process. Moreover, the commune was itself somewhat confused as to its relationship with the state planners. In their study of the Yangyi Commune, the Crooks noted that the commune retained a high surplus because the cadres considered the commune's interests above those of the state.(77) Brugger has indicated, however, that other communes were enthusiastic supporters of state quotas and tended to over-estimate their capacity, always raising their quotas. Eventually, this also undermined the orderly state planning of commune production.(78)

The conflicts over authority within the rural relations of production and the failure to raise the level of agricultural productivity were criticised within the Communist Party. The divisions in the C.C.P. were accentuated by a series of climatic disasters which led to widespread food shortages. Mao's influence over policy direction declined; there was a retreat away from the policies of the Great Leap and a modified Soviet model was introduced. The power of hierarchical authority was emphasised and this was accompanied by the promotion of individual incentives to increase productivity at the point of production.

---

76. Schurmann, 1966, p.472.
77. Crook and Crook, 1966, p.100.
78. Brugger, 1981(a), p.195.

In agriculture, these new policies had different effects at the various levels of production. The decentralised planning system was granted stronger powers, but the communes were denuded of authority, especially over investment decisions. The team became the unit of labour co-ordination and responsibility. It was the team which carried out state planning policies with regard to production and extraction of the agricultural surplus. The communes became a link from the planners to the producers. Private plots and individual production were re-introduced. For many peasants, the private plots supplemented their income from the collective and became an area for competition for their attention.

The retreat thus reinforced the team and disadvantaged the commune. Regional self-reliance and decentralisation, however, gave more power to the local state and Party institutions. Production revived and the threat of famine was averted. There was a sense in which the retreat had left the agricultural relations of production in a state of incompleteness. The retreat from the communes had not led to a complete rebuilding of the A.P.C. structure; but the communes were frustrated by the lack of investment power to increase production through increased mechanisation. Productivity levels were thus restrained by the fact that the organisation of labour was chiefly performed by the team. Conflicts still remained within the relations of production and it was not until the Cultural Revolution that efforts were made to restore the communes to a position of authority (especially over heavy machinery).

After the Great Leap Forward, the C.C.P., no longer heavily influenced by Mao, decided to stabilise the relations of production. Self-reliance and decentralisation were retained and they were complemented by the decision to allow agriculture to retain a higher level of its surplus increment. It was felt that, with this approach, industry would grow alongside the agricultural market and that the drain upon the industrial surplus would be minimised. Thus, the relative degree of autonomy over production in agriculture was complemented by the increase in the teams' control over their surplus. That is, the teams were units with greater autonomy than their industrial counterparts and they were now provided with an added incentive to expand their production. Nevertheless, the state would still obtain its share of the agricultural surplus. It was hoped that this would increase agricultural productivity and also allow industry to retain its surplus for expansion.

Paine argues that the aim of this strategy was,

> by providing a collective material incentive at the grass
> roots level, to achieve a higher agricultural output and
> marketed surplus than would otherwise have been the case,
> and to encourage a good part of such an additional surplus
> to be utilised for rural production of agricultural inputs on

a small-scale basis. The important point is that, to the extent that this policy succeeded, it attracted fewer resources away from investment in producer goods for industry than would otherwise have occurred.(79)

Moreover, Paine believes that this programme was quite successful and state industry became overwhelmingly dominant in the production of state revenues. She notes that,

State revenues have accrued increasingly from profits and taxes and state industrial enterprises - these amounted to 90% of state revenues in 1974 as against 34% in the early post-liberation years.(80)

Recent figures support Paine's argument that there has been an obvious divergence between industry and agriculture, both in terms of productivity and in the availability of surplus to the state. According to Wang Haibo and Wu Jiajun,

During 1950-79, the total output value of industry increased by an annual average of 13.3%, while the output value of agriculture increased only by 4.5% yearly.(81)

In his article on 'Agricultural Employment and Technology', Rawski calculates that between 1957 and 1975, agriculture absorbed nearly 100 million new workers.(82) He estimates that during this period, the average product of labour in Chinese agriculture did not decrease. Moreover, the average number of days worked rose considerably, from 159 annual work days per worker in 1957, to 207 in 1975.(83) He concludes that,

When productivity is measured in terms of output value per man-day the results are equally clear. Output per man-day declined sharply between 1957 and 1975, with the fall ranging from 15 to 36 per cent, depending upon which assumptions are chosen with regard to the labor intensity of cultivation and fertilization preparation.(84)

Rawski herein identifies a critical weakness in Chinese agriculture between 1957 and 1975. While labour absorption and the hours worked rose, the efficiency of labor declined.

---

79.   Paine, 1976, p.285.
80.   Ibid., p.299.
81.   Wang Haibo and Wu Jiajun, Xue (ed.), 1982, p.445.
82.   Rawski, 1982, p.121.
83.   Ibid., p.130.
84.   Ibid., pp.131-2.

In summary, from 1949 to 1960, the transformation of the capitalist mode into the socialist mode was embodied in a continual revolutionary process. Capitalist property and surplus extraction were negated and socialist ownership, accompanied by a new form of surplus product, was introduced. Yet, it was necessary for these fundamental elements of the mode of production to become integrated into a coherent and stable set of technical relations. The Great Leap Forward played an important role in the latter process by undermining the possibility of capitalism and extending the socialist relations of production. But the Leap extended the transformation to a point of instability. The retreat reinforced the socialist mode and those classes associated with its reproduction.

The Socialist Mode After 1960.

Since its consolidation, the socialist mode of production has shaped the development of China's economic, political and social structures. The contradictions contained in the socialist mode have provoked sharp divisions in the C.C.P. and have stimulated debates over the basis of class struggle in China. Party policies have attempted, in different ways, to mediate the inner contradictions of the mode of production. The Cultural Revolution promoted worker participation, Party and Army intervention in the economy and restrictions upon material incentives as means of moderating the contradictions. The early 1960s and post 'Gang of Four' policies have turned towards material rewards and financial incentives to raise productivity and surplus extracted from the direct producers.

The policies under Deng Xiaoping emphasise individualism and material incentives. Deng has argued that 'state ownership' ensures the socialist transition towards communism and that the productive forces will be the final arbiter of the transition.(85) He has added that the appropriate criterion for remuneration is the principle of 'payment according to work'. As previous chapters have discussed, his views are 'orthodox', as defined by Stalin. But state ownership, as has been demonstrated, is only one aspect of the transition. Deng ignores the changes in the surplus form and disguises the surplus extraction process behind the claims that this represents 'bourgeois right'. It is, however, not a return to capitalism as some commentators imply.(86)

Undoubtedly, Deng's policies will widen the income gap within China.(87) But egalitarianism is not an essential characteristic of the socialist mode of production nor of the present stage of Chinese development. Deng's policies have, of course, political ramifications

---

85. See Watson, 1978; Watson, 1980.
86. See Bettelheim, 1978, p.115.
87. See O'Leary and Watson, 1982-3; O'Leary and Watson, 1980; O'Leary, 1979.

and imply a shift away from regulated incomes and those policies which emphasised political incentives.(88) The emphasis upon individualism is relatively compatible with the socialist mode of production. But the present policies are threatening the old form of surplus extraction which may have effects upon the property relations of the socialist mode. Deng's policies reflect the fact that China is not in a transition to communism. The development of the productive forces cannot lead in any linear fashion to communism. Deng's strategy will intensify the contradictions within the relations of production which will in turn increase class antagonisms.

In the past, these class conflicts have been expressed through the Party; but that also has undergone a change and now reflects the view that the crucial issue is raising the level of production, that is the four modernisations.(89) The collective bureaucratic class, which controls the surplus extraction, appropriation and distribution process, will benefit by an increase in production. Its power, however, is threatened by the shifting of responsibility for productivity and remuneration to the lower levels. The transfer of responsibility to the direct producers is felt most strongly in agriculture because this sector is already based upon a higher degree of autonomy in the relations of production. Though the contract responsibility system is undermining the collective economy, the outcome is still uncertain. The conflicts in the agricultural relations of production are still unfolding; but the tendency is towards a major transformation of the collectives, with control over land and labour passing from the teams, brigades and communes to the contracted households. The surplus will be controlled through the contract system and no longer through collective work-points. The bureaucratic class still obtains part of the surplus of the agricultural labourers and it directs what is to be produced; but it seems likely that tensions will arise between the bureaucratic class's control over what is produced and how much it appropriates, and the household producers, who will be keen to retain as much control over their produce and how it is produced.

On a broader scale, the household system has the potentiality to clash with the socialist mode of production. This particularly will be the case if state industry can not obtain steady planned supplies and if the prices of agricultural products rise too high. That is, there is a danger that agricultural relations of production, operating through the market, will force a rise in the prices of agricultural goods; of critical importance here is the price of grain, since its rise will increase pressure on wage levels which will disturb the planned relations of industry. The previous chapter has already noted that increased subsidisation has been a temporary and costly means of dealing with that clash. As the clash develops, so will the inner class contradictions

88. O'Leary, 1979, p.18.
89. See Young, 1980.

between fractions of the bureaucratic class and within the working class (e.g. between permanent, temporary and unemployed workers) and within the peasantry.

In conclusion, China is not in a state of transition to communism, but has established a socialist mode of production. It is conceivable that this mode of production could be displaced, but this does not appear to be the case at present. The property relations still remain dominated by state ownership, and the surplus extraction form, characteristic of the socialist mode, is still firmly entrenched; although in the countryside this is changing rapidly. When these elements are fundamentally transformed, it will be time to conceptualise a new transition to a different mode of production, maybe to communism.

Chapter 6

THE LAW OF VALUE DEBATE - A TRIBUTE TO THE LATE SUN YEFANG*

Steve Reglar

In 1983, Sun Yefang, China's most controversial political economist, died. From as early as the mid-1950s, Sun had been a major protagonist in debates over how China should modify the Stalinist conception of economic organisation. Long the butt of the ultra-left in China, called China's Liberman,(1) and subject to public derision as an advocate of 'capitalist restoration' during the Cultural Revolution,(2) Sun finally gained in his declining years the veneration he so richly deserved. His book Theoretical Questions of the Socialist Economy, containing much material written before the outbreak of the Cultural Revolution, was finally published in 1979.(3) In the atmosphere generated by the reforms of the Third Plenum of late 1978, Sun's ideas have gained a new currency. Following his death, Sun was acclaimed as one of the nation's foremost economists. This chapter will examine Sun's contribution to a crucial series of debates which have taken place since 1978. It will contrast Sun's views with those of other prominent political economists. In particular, the views of He Jianzhang, Ma Jiaju, Liu Guoguang, Zhao Renwei and Jiang Yiwei will be examined. These people have put forward views and have advocated policies which contrast strongly with those of Sun, and many of their programmes entail a more dramatic break with the policies of the past.

While the overall assessment of Sun in this chapter will be positive, his work is not above reproach. Sun's arguments for maintaining that the law of value should regulate production during

---

*   A version of this chapter was presented at the conference 'New Directions in the Social Sciences and Humanities in China', Adelaide University, 20-22 May 1984. Thanks are due to the participants at that conference, and also to Vicki Spencer for her comments on an earlier draft.
1. See Sun Yefang, (1964), Sun, 1979, p. 297.
2. See RMRB., 9 August 1966, SCMP., 3765, 22 August 1966, pp. 4-13.
3. Sun Yefang, 1979. 16 of the essays in the book were written before the Cultural Revolution and were circulated as internal (neibu) documents for criticism. Some valuable documents were lost, precisely because it was inexpedient for them to be criticised, (see ibid., pp. 1-6). References to this book in the chapter have been added by the editor.

socialist transition are persuasive. His closely argued definition of the scope of the law of value has profundity. Moreover, Sun put forward a substantial case for tying the law of value to the law of planned and proportionate development. This chapter, thus opposes the position taken by Brugger in Chapter Three which denies the objectivity of these economic laws. The operation of such laws must be recognised and their stipulations adhered to if the least traumatic and most rapid economic advance is to be obtained. Sun's views, therefore, are not esoteric nor ephemeral. As the Introduction to this book noted, the kind of debates in which Sun engaged affects the real world profoundly. It affects directly the life chances and the social and political organisation of the Chinese people. It has practical importance as well as being of intrinsic interest in the more abstract field of political economy and socialist theory.

This chapter will reject those positions which see the debate in terms of planning and market. There are many different types of planning in operation around the world and in most circumstances an economy is neither fully planned nor fully integrated by the market. It is difficult to envisage just what the term fully planned economy might mean. As for a price-regulating market, in the sense defined by Polanyi, one must observe that very few economic transactions in the world are market regulated. Polanyi, in fact, argued that market regulation was characteristic of only a brief period of history.(4) For his part, Marx regarded the concentration, by political economists of his day, on market activities and price behaviour as examples of 'vulgar economy'. Such economists were guilty of concentrating on phenomenal forms rather than the underlying relationships which he thought 'economic science' should address. The same argument applies to analyses which concentrate on the plan. The focus should not be on whether planning exists or not but on what considerations make up the plan and what relationships it embodies or reflects. Plans, after all, take many forms, ranging through Stalinist command planning to indicative or guidance planning (to use the Chinese idiom).(5) Raising questions about the substance and form of planning entails an examination of more basic social and economic relationships. As with examining the relationships underlying the market, this necessitates analysis of commodity production and exchange; it entails an examination of value theory.

The above were Sun Yefang's great achievements. Nevertheless, this chapter will argue that there were some deficiencies in Sun's approach, particularly the belief that a socialist system or mode of production was in existence. The analysis will build on that of previous chapters which reject that way of thinking. In so doing, it will mount

---

4.   Polanyi, (1944), 1957, pp. 68-76.
5.   See Liu Suinian, 1982, pp. 49-50.

an argument diametrically opposed to that of McCarthy in Chapter Five.

The Historical Context.

To understand the importance of Sun Yefang and the intricacies of his approach, it is necessary to outline certain salient features of Marx's methodology, incorporated in Capital - a work read and re-read by Sun in his seven years in perdition. Marx's analysis did not involve the construction of an ideal type - 'the synthesis of a great many diffuse, discrete, more or less present and occasionally absent phenomena which are arranged according to... one sidedly emphasised viewpoints into a unified analytical construct'.(6) As Chapter One pointed out, Marx argued that his analysis in Capital did not start from concepts, such as exchange value and use value, but from an analysis of the commodity. Hence his analysis was based on a historically-given reality. Marx was at pains to show how capitalist commodity production emerged on the basis of pre-existing commodity production. The capitalist mode of production was not just a construct theoretically separated from other modes of production; it was a historical development of earlier modes. Marx's starting point was historical reality, as was quite clear in his recognition that Adam Smith's account of laissez faire was intended as a programme rather than a historical description. Marx's approach to capitalism was to be echoed by Sun Yefang in his treatment of socialism.

Marx's concern with history, therefore, made him scornful of political economists who regarded economic categories as 'eternal'. Instead of seeing economic categories as abstractions expressing 'real, transitory, historic social relations', such political economists, 'thanks to a mystic transposition', saw real relations as embodiments of abstractions.(7) For Marx, the study of political economy took place in the real world; it concentrated on 'real active' human beings on the basis of 'their real life processes'. From an analysis of reality, Marx and Engels set out to demonstrate 'the development of the ideological reflexes and echoes of this life process'. But this methodology was not devoid of premises. It began with 'real premises' and did not 'abandon them for a moment'. Its premises derived from human beings 'not in any fantastic isolation and fixity, but in their actual, empirically perceptible process of development under definite conditions'.(8)

In the most general terms, Marx's mode of production might be seen as the set of social relations within which human production took place. The relationships which human beings entered into were

---

6. Weber, (1904), 1949, p. 90.
7. Marx, (1846), Marx and Engels, SW., II, 1970, p. 522.
8. Marx and Engels, (1845-6), CW., V, 1976, p. 37.

'indispensible and independent of their will'. Such relations corresponded to 'a definite stage of development of their material
productive forces'. It was the totality of those relationships which
constituted 'the economic structure'.(9) The mode of production had
two distinct but inter-related levels - the mode of appropriation of
nature and the mode of appropriation of the product. It was in the
appropriation of nature that humans combined in a definite set of
relationships stemming from the historical development of production
techniques, organisation of the labour process, division of labour,
cultural characteristics and patterns of authority. The appropriation of
nature, Marx saw as resulting from social relationships. There were no
abstract human beings in a 'state of nature'.

The mode of appropriation of the products of the appropriation of
nature varied in each mode of production. Under slavery and
feudalism, the surplus product was appropriated directly, whilst under
capitalism it was appropriated indirectly. This was because surplus
labour was expropriated in the form of surplus value, produced under
conditions whereby human labour power was exchanged for
commodities, and was itself bought and sold as a commodity. Such was
the defining feature of capitalism as a mode of production. That said,
the two modes of appropriation were not reducible one to the other.
Laws of motion applicable to the capitalist mode of production
stemmed from the interaction between these two relatively
autonomous levels. The relationships of exchange in capitalism came
into being because there was a common substance underlying that
exchange - namely value which was an expression of the labour
embodied in commodities. Exchange occurred because of developments
in the mode of appropriating nature, the creation of social labour
through the development of the social division of labour, the historical
development of the labour process and the development of technology.
Hence, to be the universal expression of value, labour had to be
abstract labour and not concrete labour. To say that the capitalist
mode of production is defined by the existence of labour-power as a
commodity is not to dissolve the difference between the two levels of
appropriation. The existence of labour power as a commodity occurred
because of the interaction of the two levels which had developed and
would continue to develop relatively autonomously.

Investigations of the capitalist mode of production, therefore,
rested on an analysis of value which was the 'secret' of why commodity
exchange existed. Hence Marx argued that,

> In bourgeois society the commodity form of the product of
> labour - or the value form of the commodity - is the
> economic cell form. To the superficial observer, the
> analysis of these forms seems to turn upon minutiae. It

---

9.   Marx, (1859), Marx and Engels, SW., I, 1970, p. 503.

does in fact deal with minutiae· but they are of the same order as those dealt with in microscopic anatomy.(10)

The whole anatomy of capitalism, to extend Marx's analogy to one from a later historical period, relied on an analysis of the equivalent of D.N.A., which gave a particular anatomy a particular life. Of course, the way one recognised the essential life force was through the force of abstraction. That abstraction was value theory!

Out of the creation of value, wrought by the interaction of the modes of appropriating nature and product, stemmed other levels of activity. The extraction of surplus product in the form of surplus value was at the heart of the basic contradiction in capitalism, that between those who monopolised the possession of the means of production and those who could only exist by selling their labour power. This was manifested as a class contradiction between the bourgeoisie and the proletariat. Because of the existence of social labour and commodity exchange, that contradiction emerged not as thousands of relationships between individuals but in contradictory interests and oppositional practices at the level of historically and structurally determined collectivities.

For Marx, it was out of those class contradictions that the state emerged. The state was necessary to enshrine the relationships of appropriation in law. Thus, the proletariat won the right to alienate its labour and the bourgeoisie won the right of property. Put simply, bourgeois legal forms mirrored the basic commodity exchanges in the capitalist mode of production.

Particular forms of distribution emerged from the historical configuration of, on the one hand, the relationships between the modes of appropriation of nature and of product and, on the other, of the state of class struggle and class practices in general. Distribution, moreover, relied on the structure of investment which itself depended upon the organic composition of capital in different departments of production, the stability of money as well as the forces of supply and demand. Distribution, therefore, was a sphere different from exchange. In so far as it emerged from relationships of appropriating nature and the appropriation of the products of that process, distribution was dependent upon them. Nevertheless, distribution also exerted a relationship back on to the production process, by providing the conditions under which investment might move from one department to another and by conditioning simple and expanded reproduction within a department. Distribution, moreover, had a relatively autonomous relationship with the level of class struggle; it might both condition class struggle and be conditioned by it. It was for that reason that Marx argued that a reciprocal relationship existed between

10. Marx, (1867), I, 1954, p. 8.

distribution and production. The sphere of distribution was relatively autonomous; it should not be seen as completely independent nor completely dependent, nor for that matter completely determining. As Marx put it,

> If you proceed from production you necessarily concern yourself with the real conditions of production and of the productive activity of men. But if you proceed from consumption, you can set your mind at rest by merely declaring that consumption is not at present 'human', and by postulating 'human consumption', education for true consumption, and so on. You can be content with such phrases, without bothering at all about the real living conditions and the activity of men.(11)

Marx did not primarily criticise capitalism because of its distributive practices. Indeed, he argued that earlier socialists were wrong in concentrating their critique on the fields of circulation and distribution. Exploitation under capitalism did not lie in the activities of merchants 'buying cheap and selling dear' nor in usurious practices. Nor, indeed, did profit stem from 'robbery' on the part of the capitalist. In his rebuttal of Wagner's attribution of this idea to him, Marx said,

> In fact, in my presentation, profit is not 'merely a deduction or "robbery" on the labourer'. On the contrary, I present the capitalist as the necessary functionary of capitalist production and show very extensively that he does not only 'deduct' or 'rob', but forces the production of surplus value, therefore the deducting only helps to produce; furthermore, I show in detail that even if in the exchange of commodities only equivalents were exchanged, the capitalist - as soon as he pays the labourer the real value of his labour power - would secure with full rights, i.e. the rights corresponding to that mode of production, surplus value.(12)

Distributive justice then, was a right which corresponded to a particular mode of production. The workers sold their labour-power as a commodity for its value to the capitalist class for the length of the working day. The fact that the capitalist class gained surplus value from this transaction was not robbery. The exchange which had taken place was one of equivalents. The capitalist had purchased labour-power at its price; what was done with the fruits of that labour-power bore no relationship to this prior exchange. As Marx said, this was particular good fortune for the capitalist but no injustice for the

---

11. Marx and Engels, (1845-6), CW., V, 1976, p. 518.
12. Marx, (1879-80), Carver (ed.), 1975, p. 186; emphasis in original.

worker.(13)   Indeed, capitalists would simply go out of business if surplus value were not extracted.

And so we come to the law of value.   This was the key to understanding the contradictions of the capitalist mode.   Marx's comments on its place deserve to be quoted at length,

> Even if there were no chapter on 'value' in my book, the analysis of the real relations which I give would contain the proof and demonstration of the real value relation. All that palaver about the necessity of proving the concept of value comes from complete ignorance both of the subject dealt with and of scientific method. Every child knows that a nation which ceased to work, I will not say for a year, but even for a few weeks, would perish. Every child knows, too, that the masses of products corresponding to the different needs require different and quantitatively determined masses of the total labour of society. That this <u>necessity</u> of the <u>distribution</u> of social labour in definite proportions cannot possibly be done away with by a <u>particular form</u> of social production but can only change the <u>mode</u> of its <u>appearance,</u> is self-evident. No natural laws can be done away with.   What can change in historically different circumstances is only the <u>form</u> in which these laws assert themselves.   And the form in which this proportional distribution of labour asserts itself, in a state of society where the interconnection of social labour is manifested in the <u>private exchange</u> of the individual products of labour, is precisely the <u>exchange value</u> of these products. Science consists precisely in demonstrating <u>how</u> the law of value asserts itself. So that if one wanted at the very beginning to 'explain' all the phenomena which seemingly contradict that law, one would have to present the science <u>before</u> science.(14)

An appreciation of the above position was the strength of Sun Yefang. A number of important propositions followed from it. It highlighted Marx's insistence that a 'scientific' understanding of economics required the use of abstractions which elucidated underlying real relations. But such abstractions had an ontological basis. Marx took it as given that societies had to appropriate nature, otherwise they would starve. But the quantitative proportions in which the social division of labour was allocated had two aspects. There was a need for the total labour of society to be allocated between different products; but there was also the fact that different goods required different quantities of

---

13. Marx, (1867), I, 1954, p. 194.
14. Marx, (1868), Marx and Engels, <u>SW</u>., II, 1970, pp. 418-9; emphasis in original.

labour. Though the distribution of labour always occurred, the pattern of distribution varied at different times in history. Thus, the laws governing the distribution of labour could change from epoch to epoch. Under capitalism, the laws governing the distribution of labour for the appropriation of nature had to correspond to changes in the way products were appropriated and exchanged. Hence, factor proportions had to follow the dictates of exchange value.

The problem for Marx, therefore, was to determine what constituted value and how the law of value operated. He rejected the approaches of Ricardo and Proudhon and also, one may say with hindsight, the approach of Weber whose ideal types took, as given, categories which should emerge later in the analysis (i.e. 'presenting the science before science'). Marx argued that as use values were not constant in different historical societies(15) and could not determine the exchange values of essentially useless articles with high exchange values or the converse, values had to be determined by something else. The only common factor involved in all exchanges was, of course, the embodiment of human labour. Such was the basis of the law of value.

I have argued, so far, that for Marx, a relative autonomy existed between the mode of appropriating nature and the mode of appropriating the products of that process. Secondly, while production had ontological priority, once distribution occurred, it existed in a reciprocal relationship with production and exchange. A logic of internal relations existed between all spheres of activity within the mode of production. Thirdly, the relationship between those spheres was contradictory; thus a mode of production should not be seen as a 'system'. Its laws of motion existed precisely because there were contradictions in the totality. Because all spheres were interconnected and contradictory, an examination had to consider all aspects of the totality.

The law of value then, was a law pervading all aspects and levels of the capitalist mode of production. But what happened when one moved towards socialism? Chapter Three discussed Marxist-Leninist views on the existence of the law of value under such conditions. The earliest of these was summed up in Trotsky's famous dictum of 1920, 'socialist organisation of production begins with the liquidation of the market...production shall be geared to society's needs by means of a unified economic plan'.(16) The law of value and commodity exchange were denied.(17) Such was also the position of Bukharin when, in his ultra-left days, he wrote his Economics of the Transformation

---

15. Marx, (1879-80), Carver (ed.), 1975, pp. 189-209.
16. Trotsky, (1920), cited in Smolinsky, 1967, p. 113.
17. Leontiev, n.d., pp. 67-91.

Period.(18) Transfers of products from one factory to another within a single organisation were like a person moving money around from one pocket to another; such activity made no difference to a person's wealth; transfers in the economy were simply book-keeping exercises. By the 1930s, anyone who argued otherwise had a precarious future.

It was quite clear, however, that it was very difficult to keep the books. In 1920, Trotsky put forward his ideal for the planning and integrative roles of the Supreme Council of the National Economy,

> This presupposes...that (the Supreme Council) disposes of an ideal apparatus of accounting and resource allocation...that it has at its disposal an ideal keyboard such that, by pushing a button, you can transfer a certain amount of coal, firewood, labour, to a place where the need for it arises. Of course, we do not have an ideal keyboard of this kind in any agency as yet.(19)

As Chapter Three noted, not only was there no keyboard, there was no intention to develop any mathematical economics which might challenge the beautiful simplicity of the administrative vision. Ignorance of statistics was a positive asset in planning; statistics were apparently anti-Marxist.(20) Ad hoc planning was the order of the day.

In 1952, a chink of light was opened by Stalin in his Economic Problems of Socialism in the U.S.S.R.(21) Reviving the position put forward thirty-two years before by Obolensky,(22) Stalin, it will be remembered, established a theory of commodity exchange between two types of ownership (by 'the whole people' and by collectives). The law of value operated between these two sectors and was supposedly to be governed by the exchange of equal values - though clearly under Stalin this was never the case.

Stalin's limited concessions to the law of value were eagerly seized upon by Chinese economists who had recently started planning which utilised the law of value. By the mid-1950s, in parallel with the Soviet thaw following the publication of Khrushchev's 'secret speech' to the Twentieth Congress of the C.P.S.U., many aspects of Stalinist planning came under scrutiny. One by one, aspects of Stalinist orthodoxy were challenged. Lin Lifu used a Marxian perspective to

---

18. Bukharin, (1920), 1971.
19. Trotsky, (1920), cited in Smolinsky, 1969, p. 114.
20. Smolinsky, 1967, p. 123.
21. Stalin, (1952), 1972.
22. L. Obolensky was probably N. Osinsky (whose original name was V.V. Obolensky). He was manager of the State Bank after the October Revolution and later the first chairman of the Supreme Council for National Economy. See Szamuely, 1974, p. 34.

question the rapid collectivisation of agriculture. Ma Yinchu argued for more balanced, equilibrium-based, growth and raised the thorny question of the economic effects of population pressure. Chen Chenhan even went so far as to advocate the incorporation of aspects of non-Marxist Western social science.(23) The atmosphere of the time was reminiscent more of Lenin's N.E.P. than of Stalin's five year plans, which is not surprising when, as Brugger noted, there was some confusion as to exactly which Soviet model ought to have been followed.(24)

One economist who preferred such N.E.P. policies was Gu Zhun. Gu, together with Ying Chengwang, pleaded that the law of value should be observed under socialism to facilitate economic and financial accounting and to keep management up to scratch. Enterprises should have full financial autonomy and should be responsible for their own profits and losses.(25) There was, it was argued, no incongruence between planning and the law of value. Indeed, some economists even went so far as to advocate Yugoslav-style decentralisation, though arguing from different premises. For a time, it seemed, some of the proposals had official blessing. This was clear in Chen Yun's unusual speech to the Eighth Party Congress which has been discussed in Chapter Two.(26)

Yet China did have its voluntarists who, for a while, were quite influential. Such voluntarists differed little from the Soviet teleological school of the 1920s. In a piece of 'mountain-top-ism', which rivals Trotsky's pronouncements discussed earlier, Chen Boda declared that the era of commodity production was at an end and that the law of value was redundant.(27) Such a statement was too much even for the C.C.P. during the Great Leap Forward, and Chen's emulation of King Canute was rejected.

Far from being a supporter of the economic ideas of Chen Boda, Mao Zedong argued that Stalin's formulation of the law of value was inadequate. Mao was unwilling to accept Stalin's exclusion of the means of production from the operation of the law of value. Stalin had done this as a rationalisation of his distrust of the peasants.(28) Overall,. Mao saw a positive role for the law of value. In 1959, he declared that it was 'a great school; only if we use it, teach our

---

23. See Lin, 1981.
24. Brugger, 1976; especially pp. 76-7.
25. Lin, 1981, p. 18.
26. Chen Yun, C.C.P., 1956, II, pp. 157-76.
27. See Lin, 1981, p. 19. Sun heartily endorsed Mao's criticism of this in 1959; see Sun Yefang, (1978), Sun, 1979, p. 347.
28. Mao Zedong, (1959), Mao, 1974, p. 191.

millions of cadres and masses about it, can we build socialism and communism'.(29)

In the same year, Mao, following a consistent trend in his thought since his speech 'On the Ten Major Relations' in 1956, argued that planning priorities should be reversed.(30) Instead of stressing heavy industry followed by light industry and agriculture, agriculture should now be given priority, followed by light industry, heavy industry, communications and commerce. Mao returned to the position of Chen Yun,

> Comrade Chen Yun said 'we should arrange the markets before we go into capital construction'. Many comrades disagreed. But now we realise that Comrade Chen Yun was right. We have to solve the problems of clothing, food, housing, utilities and travel first, for they concern the stable life of 650 million people...This will be advantageous to reconstruction, and the state will be able to accumulate its resources.(31)

Mao saw a positive role for the law of value in facilitating the reversal of the Stalinist order of planning priority. Previous chapters have noted, however, that the order of priority was not so easily reversed, and this gave rise to major imbalances in the economy.

Sun Yefang's Criticism of Stalin.

Previous chapters have considered just how far Mao did move away from Stalin. Suffice it to say here that Mao failed to draw out the implications of his affirmation of the commodity status of the means of production. Mao reflected the orthodoxy of most Chinese political economists who followed Stalin in seeing the operation of the law of value in terms of commodity exchange between two spheres of ownership. Sun Yefang, on the other hand, rejected the very basis of that theory.(32)

Sun argued that Stalin's conception was akin to saying that commodity production and exchange was born when two primitive communes met to exchange goods. This was inadequate. Arguing on firm Marxist grounds, Sun maintained that commodity production occurred only when a whole series of conditions were met. Stalin's principal error was his separation of ownership from other aspects of

---

29. Quoted in Lin, 1981, p. 19. See Sun's comments on this; Sun Yefang, (1964-5), Sun, 1979, pp. 306-13.
30. See Reglar, 1980.
31. Mao Zedong, (1959), Mao, 1974, p. 183.
32. Sun Yefang, 1980.

the relations of production.   Ownership, Sun believed, could not be separated from production, exchange, distribution and consumption. Thus, in treating ownership as a disjunctive entity, Stalin produced an analysis of property similar to that of Proudhon.   Sun found Marx's comments on Proudhon's theory of property most instructive,

> The last category in M. Proudhon's system is constituted by property.   In the real world, on the other hand, the division of labour and all M. Proudhon's other categories are social relations forming in their entirety what is today known as property;   outside these relations bourgeois property is nothing but a metaphysical or legal illusion.   The property of a different epoch, feudal property, develops in a series of entirely   different   social   relations.   M. Proudhon,   by establishing property as an independent relation, commits more than a mistake in method; he clearly shows that he has not grasped the bond which holds together all forms of bourgeois production, that he has not understood the historical and transitory character of the forms of production in a particular epoch.(33)

Following Marx, Sun argued that property developed as a discrete entity particular to each historical epoch, since it was the product of a completely new set of social relationships.   Hence, Marx insisted that the definition of bourgeois property had to be derived from the whole sphere of bourgeois social relations of production.(34)   Such relations of production stemmed from the productive associations within which people appropriated nature, and included relations of exchange and distribution.   Hence, in Sun's view, 'to define any kind of ownership, the first step is an analysis of how the human and material factors are combined in production, how people exchange their products and how the products are distributed'.(35)   As Sun saw it, to divorce property from the other relations of production resulted in distorted policies. Stalin's formulations, therefore, led to many of the ills of China's development strategy.   It was the focus on property which led to the excessively rapid formation of communes and misguided attempts to elevate the level of public ownership.   A concentration on new, higher forms of ownership caused neglect of other relations of production, and the real basis of production specified by the law of value was forgotten.   Such policies were voluntarist!(36)

Stalin erred also, Sun felt, in denying the role of exchange in that sector defined as owned by 'the whole people'.   Thus, circulation was

---

33.   Marx, (1846), Marx and Engels, SW., I, 1970, pp. 521-2;   italics in original;   the quote in Sun is a little different, (1980, p. 159).
34.   Marx, (1847), cited in Sun Yefang, 1980, p. 159.
35.   Ibid., p. 160.
36.   Ibid., pp. 159-60.

replaced by state allocation, and exchange was replaced by rationing. While Sun agreed with Stalin (and not Mao) in denying the commodity nature of the means of production, he did not see that denial as invalidating the role of the law of value. This was because there still occurred an 'exchange of products' which ought to represent an exchange of equal values. Stalin's major error was in not ensuring that the exchange of commodities between different sectors of ownership did, in reality, involve equal values. On the contrary, the state exacted a tribute from the collectives. The uneven relationship between urban and rural areas was a direct consequence of a violation of the law of value. Neglecting the law of value led to distributive injustice!(37)

Sun argued that Stalin's conception of the origin of the law of value was fundamentally misconceived. For Sun, the law of value was a feature of all large-scale production. Under socialism, it continued because the basic production of value was still the average amount of socially necessary labour time taken to produce a product. Though commodity production had ceased in the state-owned sector, the production cost of products to meet social use value still had to be measured in terms of socially necessary labour time.(38) It was in this light that Sun interpreted Engels' famous statement,

> Value is the relation of production costs to utility. The first application of value is the decision as to whether a thing ought to be produced at all; i.e. as to whether utility counterbalances production costs. Only then can one talk of the application of value to exchange. The production cost of two items being equal, the deciding factor determining their comparative value will be utility.(39)

Nevertheless, a major problem in the writings of Marx and Engels, Sun discovered after scrupulous and detailed exegesis, was their occasional glossing over the distinction between exchange value and value in general.(40) 'Negating the influence of value', he felt referred to exchange value not value in general. The lack of clarity in Marx and Engels had led to much confusion in Marxism-Leninism.

Exchange value, reflecting relations of commodity production under the individual economy of capitalism, Sun argued, was what

37. Ibid.
38. Ibid., p. 156.
39. Engels, (1843), Marx and Engels, CW., III, 1975, p. 426; cited in Sun Yefang, 1980, p. 164; Sun's wording is slightly different; see also Lin, 1981, p. 14.
40. Sun Yefang, 1980, p. 162. Sun uses the word 'value'; I have used the words 'value in general' to avoid confusion. For further discussion, see also Lin, 1981, p. 14; Meek, (1956), pp. 256-84; Rosdolsky, 1977, pp. 428-36.

would become redundant after the social reorganisation of production. This was because prices in competitive capitalism were shaped by the influence of supply and demand.   Hence, the amount of socially necessary labour time embodied in a commodity was not manifested in a direct way.   The manifestation was averaged through a myriad of exchanges.   Furthermore, the price of commodities was expressed in terms of another commodity - money - subject to speculation, profiteering, inflation and deflation.   Communism would remove the above conditions and would abolish exchange value.   But value in general would continue to be important.   Indeed, under communism, value (socially necessary labour time) could be reflected directly.   But of course, Sun felt such a situation was still a very long way off due in part to the inadequacies of statistical and accounting provisions.(41)

The distinction between exchange value and value in general is central to the disagreement between this chapter and Chapter Three. In that chapter, Brugger advances the well-known objection that one must have a solution to the transformation problem if the law of value is to have any impact on policy. In saying this, Brugger collapses value in general into exchange value - an error pointed out with much force by Sun Yefang. Thus, for Brugger, the law of value is consigned merely to a pricing mechanism and is seen to be dependent on market relations. This suggests a determining role for distribution rather than Marx's reciprocal relationship between product and exchange on the one hand and distribution on the other.

Brugger's second objection, made elsewhere,(42) is that the money wages workers in China receive are set by the state.   Since wages are part of the costs of production and are the price of labour power, the price of products does not reflect the law of value. This is because, it is claimed, a market relationship must exist between purchaser and seller of labour power so that labour power, like any other commodity, can reflect its value. The problem here is two-fold. Not only is the market, which governs distribution, accorded dominant rather than reciprocal status but, once again, the law of value is seen only as governing exchange value.   In neither case does Brugger's analysis of the law of value start from the point of view of production; nor does he recognise the logic of internal relations which tied together Marx's conception of the capitalist mode of production.

The Practical Implications of Sun's Position.

Summing up Sun Yefang's contribution to economics, an influential article by Sun Shangqing and others, outlined five major areas in which Sun's views on the operation of the law of value had

---

41. Sun Yefang, 1980, p. 163.
42. Brugger, 1984(b).

effect.(43)   These were: maximising efficiency in the productive process, the improvement of planning, the role of circulation, profit as a measure of competence at enterprise level and using the cost of production as a basis for pricing.

Chapter Four noted the tendency, in conventional policy, to maximise the number of goods produced. This led to neglect of the costs of production of particular goods and to confusing consumption in particular cases with consumption in general. Little heed was paid to whether the value of products could be realised in the circulation process. Sun countered this by seeking to calculate costs in terms of the law of value;   the prime objective was efficiency at the point of production. In attempting to achieve exchange of equal values, Sun also emphasised the realisation of value in circulation;   this would reduce waste. Here Sun re-invoked a crucial element of Marx's labour theory of value - the distinction between <u>concrete</u> labour and <u>abstract</u> labour - a distinction neglected by many Soviet and Chinese economists.   For Marx, the concrete labour of private individuals became social labour through the exchange of values, the conversion of commodities into money and the further conversion of money into other commodities. Abstract labour presupposed a particular form of production, social organisation and division of labour; it presupposed, moreover, an exchange process resting on the exchange of equal values. Abstract labour, therefore, was realised through the process of exchange.(44)   Thus, Sun insisted it was just as important to examine the exchange and distribution process as it was to examine production. Each aspect was inextricably linked, one to the other.

The second aspect of Sun's contribution, noted by Sun Shangqing and others, was his insistence that planning should be based on the law of value. This has been touched on above. Sun not only attacked those who denied its role but also those who sought to manipulate it through planning.   For Sun, the <u>law</u> was exactly that - a law of objective reality. It was 'not like the slave girl at Grand View Garden in the classical novel, <u>A Dream of Red Mansions</u>, who can be "ordered", "utilised" and dismissed at will'.(45) For the law to be observed, much decision-making had to be decentralised to the level of the enterprise. Planning should concentrate on targets 'belonging to the category of abstract labour and value'. Specific targets 'belonging to the category of concrete labour and use value', however, should be handled by lower level agencies.   Above all, decision-making about the design and

---

43. Sun Shangqing et. al., <u>Jingji Yanjiu</u>, 1, 1983, abridged in <u>BR</u>., 24, 13 June 1983, pp. 16-9.
44. See Rubin, 1975, pp. 131-58 and Meek, (1956), pp. 165-86, as opposed to Sweezy, 1976.
45. Sun Yefang, 1980, p. 155.

variety of products should be left to the lower levels. Integration between the lower level units should be achieved through contracts.(46)

Sun's third contribution was his attack on the tendency to confuse the circulation of commodities with their distribution. Though distribution was part of the circulation process, it was not identicial with it. Distribution referred simply to the allocation of commodities. Circulation, however, referred to the way goods and resources flowed through the economy and brought about expanded reproduction. Circulation was dependent upon the way mass production was socialised and in turn shaped the way resources might be allocated efficiently. It shaped also the development of the division of labour in the future. Central planners might feel that they had some freedom in deciding patterns of distribution. When it came to circulation, in a developing economy which consisted of a number of independent accounting units, their freedom had to be seen as bounded by objective laws.

Treating the question of circulation as though it were simply one of distribution denied that a complex division of labour existed between and within enterprises. Instead of efficient circulation, one had simply arbitrary allocation and rationing; the result was imbalance between production, supply and sales. The roots of that confusion went right back to Bogdanov's textbook of 1919 in which the illusion of a non-circulating natural, self-sufficient economy, epitomising socialised production, had been put forward. Stalin, in neglecting exchange in his limited definition of relations of production, continued the confusion; here there was a link between Stalin and Bogdanov additional to the epistemological one noted in Chapter One. The result of all this was the phenomenon discussed in Chapter Four - the attempt to use pricing as an arbitrary tool to redistribute the national income, in particular between industry and agriculture.(47)

One may see here why, in the Cultural Revolution, Sun was denounced along with Liu Shaoqi. In the early 1960s, Liu had argued that an exchange of equal values should exist between industry and agriculture, between state-owned and collectively-owned enterprises and between heavy and light industry. Without that, the economy lost equilibrium.(48) Indeed, Sun showed that the subjective manipulation of prices had several times resulted in such a situation and that, in such cases, both simple and expanded reproduction had been severely hampered.

Furthermore, the use of pricing as a rationing device could lead to one enterprise's problems being transferred to another, with a consequent decline in overall performance. When profit became a

46. Sun Shangqing et. al., BR., 24, 13 June, 1983, p. 17.
47. Ibid., pp. 17-8.
48. Sun Yefang, 1980, p. 167.

criterion for enterprise success, individual enterprises increased production and provided more surplus labour for the state. But China's present price system was 'a distorting mirror' which misrepresented the average amount of socially necessary labour; prices did not reflect the law of value. Thus, enterprises sought to increase profit merely by intensifying circulation and distributed bonuses without regard for other enterprises. Here we have a classic problem of composition; what held good for individual enterprises ultimately harmed the whole network.(49)

To solve such problems, Sun urged more attention be paid to the schemas for simple and expanded reproduction outlined by Marx in Volume II of Capital and that they be utilised in planning and organisation. Proper circulation was required to bring about equilibrium between raw material and manufacturing needs and the demand for products. Material replenishment and equipment replacement, moreover, required that the means of production also be subject to circulation. In sum, there was a need for planned co-ordination between production, supply and sales, to be achieved by the exchange of equal values specified by the law of value.(50)

A related problem was that noted in Chapter Four. A different-iation between simple and expanded reproduction should be maintained at enterprise level. Given Sun's arguments about equilibrium, funds for the renewal of fixed assets (depreciation funds) should be kept separate from funds for new investment. Priority, moreover, should be given to the former if one was to avoid the appalling deterioration of equipment discussed in Chapter Three. Too often, in the past, attempts to do this had been frustrated by those who claimed that the distinction between simple and expanded reproduction was simply an abstraction. Such thinking had led Wen Ping to observe,

> In actual practice, a construction project is listed under the capital construction plan when there are sufficient funds for capital construction, and is squeezed out and becomes a technical renovation project when funds for capital construction run short.(51)

For Sun, such malpractice in accounting, whilst prevalent, should not be used as a justification for glossing over the distinction between simple and expanded reproduction. Observations such as that of Wen

---

49. Ibid.
50. Sun Shangqing et.al., BR., 24, 13 June 1983, p. 18.
51. Wen Ping, RMRB., 25 July 1980, p. 5, cited in Sun Yefang, 1982, p. 232.

Ping suggested the need for reforms in financial management not an abandonment of basic theory.(52)

Sun, therefore, stressed the importance of simple reproduction at the enterprise level. The depreciation rate for fixed assets should be raised. By encouraging technical transformation of older enterprises, the tempo of development would be speeded up. Such technical trans-formation of existing enterprises would save at least one third of the cost of building new ones, half the construction time and would use only 60 per cent of the materials and energy otherwise committed.(53) Clearly, Sun's stress on the distinction between simple and expanded reproduction had concrete relevance for the real world.

Sun's response to the above problem illustrates his understanding of Marxian economic methodology. He set great store by Marx's oft-quoted statement that 'in the analysis of economic forms...neither microscopes nor chemical reagents are of use. The force of abstraction must replace both'.(54)   Hence, the study of socialist economics should be undertaken through the collection of ample data, the analysis of economic phenomena and the delineation of essential elements.   Those essential elements, one must reiterate, were expressed as objective economic laws.

Sun Yefang's stress on the law of value clearly informed his discussion of the other objective economic laws which operated in a socialist economy. One of the most important of these was, of course, the law of planned and proportionate development. For Sun, as for Marx, it was a law and not, as Chapter Three claims, merely a truism. Marx's arguments, outlined above and elaborated on by Sun Yefang, were much more complex than Brugger allows. The law may not simply be reduced to the statement 'porridge should neither be too sweet nor too salty'. Marx argued that proportionate development was not a constant for all time. Both the mode of appropriating nature and the mode of appropriating products developed over time. Thus, proport-ionate development had different meanings at different stages of history. Proportionate development under capitalism reflected the level of the development of the productive forces, the development of specific relations of production and the reciprocal relationship between these and the patterns of distribution. Marx saw proportionate development as a kind of equilibrium point, which the contradictory nature of the capitalist mode of production was always breaking down. Under capitalism, proportionate development was a datum point which was never achieved in actuality. This was due to divisions between the capitalist class and the proletariat as well as between fractions of the capitalist class, not to mention the other classes in

---

52. Sun Yefang, 1982, p. 233.
53. Sun Yefang, BR., 9, 28 February 1983, p. 23.
54. Marx, (1867), I, 1954, p. 8.

capitalist society. Proportionate development, under capitalism, moreover, was geared to the maximum accumulation of capital. Proportionate development was geared towards other goals in other societies where other modes of production existed.

Whilst disagreeing with Brugger on the above points, I fully agree that proportionate development in a socialist transitional society should be geared towards a goal different from that in private and monopoly capitalism. Sun Yefang was aware of that, and recent Chinese debates which have accompanied the debate on the law of value have centred on that issue. The aim of socialist production is said to differ from that of capitalism. Stalin's formula that the aim of socialist production should be to meet 'the constantly rising material and cultural requirements of the whole people through the continuous expansion and perfection of socialist production on the basis of higher techniques' has been taken as a starting point. Nevertheless, it is widely accepted that in reality, the principle governing Stalinist organisation was production for its own sake - the position for which Stalin himself criticised Yaroshenko in 1952.

But if one is going to talk about the aim of socialist production, one must explore what is meant by need. Whilst early attempts to discuss need amongst academics after 1978 seemed to be heading in a promising direction, recent developments such as the denigration of Marx's discussion of alienation have betrayed that promise. Clearly, problems arise in working out a theory of need to accompany the law of planned and proportionate development due to the logic of internal relations governing productive activity, but such remains a necessity. Marx was quite clear on that point,

> Society...has to distribute its time in a purposeful way, in order to achieve a production adequate to its overall needs ...Thus economy of time, along with planned distribution of labour time among the various branches of production, remains the first economic law on the basis of communal production. It becomes law, there, to an even higher degree. However, this is essentially different from a measurement of exchange values (labour or products) by labour time.(55)

Marx argued, therefore, that planned and proportionate development would continue to exist even though it would be geared to achieving new aims; moreover, it would no longer arise from exchange value, but on the basis of direct calculation of labour time which had lost its qualitative differences (i.e. it was no longer abstract labour)(56). Clearly, the law of planned and proportionate development was vital to

---

55. Marx, (1858), 1977, p. 173.
56. Ibid.

Marx's and Sun's conception of communal production. Moreover, under socialism, it would be a qualitatively different law expressing different relationships from former epochs.

But did Sun Yefang realise he had subordinated the law of planned and proportionate development and other objective economic laws to the law of value? Sun admitted that he had done so once. But this had been an extraporaneous statement made at a meeting to criticise his views,

> In fact, my critics forced me to sharpen my tone and blurt things out so as to make those 'leftist' gentlemen aware that they should be a little more honest in the face of objective laws. I oppose ranking laws, saying that one is major and another minor or that one is primary and another secondary. Capital does not rank laws. It talks most clearly about each law in the development of capitalist society through analyses of the process of production, the process of circulation and the overall process of social production. In researching socialist relations of production, we also should take as our topic objective economic processess as they develop historically. We should start from concrete facts and reveal the essence of problems.(57)

Sun's approach to the law of value, therefore, was to see it in the context of a totality. Despite Sun's protestations, the law of value formed the essential core of his approach.(58) Whilst value could not exist without quantity, it also involved quality; this was clear in Marx's conception of socially necessary labour. That conception, moreover, involved the contradiction between concrete and abstract labour and between individual labour and social labour. It involved comparing cost and effects. Herein, Sun argued, lay 'the dual nature of labour and of products'.(59)   Likewise, simple and expanded reproduction were components of an inter-dependent totality, as were laws governing value, circulation, exchange and distribution. The methodology was clear; because all were inter-related, only by recognising the place of each in the productive process and at the same time seeing how each concept might be separated analytically might one come to grips with the laws of movement of the economy. Thus, simple reproduction was always a component of expanded reproduction. It was,

> an actual factor embodied in the latter. The starting point of enlarged reproduction is founded on the scale of simple

---

57. Sun Yefang, 1980, p. 170;   editor's translation from Zhongguo Shehui Kexue, 4, 1980, p. 36.
58. For this to be quite clear, see Sun Yefang (1978), Sun, 1979, pp. 371-6.
59. Sun Yefang, 1980, p. 171.

reproduction. It is, therefore, possible to make a separate analysis of simple reproduction itself.(60)

This approach to totality is a beautiful example of the Marxist methodology described in the Introduction to this book and at the beginning of this chapter - a methodology which many of Sun's leftist critics failed to understand.

Sun's fourth contribution to the economics of socialist transition was his stress on the role of profit as a measure of the competence of enterprise management. Profit provided a qualitative as opposed to a merely quantitative measure. The use of output quotas, he argued, was akin to making an ox move by lifting its legs whereas the use of profit was more like 'pulling the ox's nose'.(61) This was because overall balance in the economy had to rest on value in general rather than use value. It was not only impossible for central planners to work out the myriad balances in the economy, it was also undesirable. The impossibility of the task has been suggested by Nove who pointed out that in the Soviet Union one could identify 12 million different products, produced by 50,000 industrial enterprises and thousands of collective or state farms; these were despatched, and circulated by thousands of transport enterprises, wholesale and retail agencies.(62) But even if it were possible adequately to control the production and circulation of all those commodities, such could only be achieved at the expense of the democratic control of production by the direct producers. Aware of that problem, Sun noted with some approbation the Yugoslav attempts at democratisation.(63)

Sun's discussion of profit takes us back to the earlier discussion of efficiency. A stress on profit minimised costs and such led to an increase in society's surplus labour. Given constant and rational prices, cost reduction was the main element in profitability - the true test of competence. Socialist profit differed from capitalist profit, or for that matter (at least in 1964) from Liberman's 'revisionist' profit.(64)

As Chapter Four stressed, the effectiveness of profit as a measure of competence depends upon prices being rational. Sun's fifth contribution, therefore, was his insistence that planned prices reflect the costs of production. More precisely, the price of goods should reflect the average cost of production in the particular branch of

60. Sun Yefang, 1982, p. 233.
61. Sun Shangqing et.al., BR., 24, 13 June 1983, p. 18.
62. Nove, 1983, p. 33.
63. Sun Yefang, 1980, p. 169.
64. Sun Shangqing et.al., BR., 24, 13 June 1983, p. 18. See Sun Yefang, (1978), Sun, 1979, pp. 354-5. See also Sun's arguments distancing himself from Liberman; Sun Yefang (1964), Sun, 1979, pp. 297-8.

industry plus an allowance for profit based usually on the average profit level for that particular industry. Such a practice would promote the efficient use of resources and labour productivity in accordance with the law of value.(65)   Enterprises with a higher organic composition of capital would find it easier to realise a surplus; thus the policy would encourage enterprises to adopt new technology. From the point of view of the entire economy, this practice would facilitate both simple and expanded reproduction and would secure equilibrium between different departments of production, between different sectors and between different regions.

Sun's approach to pricing, therefore, was much more subtle than that of many Chinese and Western economists who have argued simply that prices should be the result of supply and demand. Such was the way the prominent political economist Xue Muqiao explained the law of value. Xue, however, qualified his views by observing that prices would only <u>tend</u> to reflect the operation of the law of value.(66)   Sun's approach was very different. Following Marx, Sun did not see supply and demand acting alone in controlling prices;   other factors such as the organic composition of capital, the distribution of investment between different departments of production, the stability of currency and the level of wages in response to all the above, all influenced prices.   Sun would have been most unhappy with the suggestion in Chapter Four that efficiency simply follows price.

Consideration of the reasoning in the writings of Marx and Sun Yefang have led me to question arguments which talk simply about prices responding to scarcity.   Scarcity, after all, is historically relative.   There are many reasons why prices in China do not reflect scarcity.   One is that a violation of the law of planned and proportionate development has favoured heavy industry (Marx's department I) at the expense of light industry (department II). This has created a shortage of consumption goods. If hardship is to be avoided the prices of consumption goods need to be controlled. Price control is not just a matter of preserving social order. Another reason is that depreciation rates have been set too low. Unless depreciation rates are realistic and unless measures are taken to ensure that depreciation funds are used for equipment renovation, one can not expect prices to reflect scarcity.   Prices will continue to reflect costs inflated by expensive capital construction.   This is a point remarked on time and again by Sun Yefang. Planners have failed to understand the relationship between simple and expanded reproduction.

One is tempted here to go much further than Sun in considering the price structure. In my opinion, a major error has been the belief that the substitution of capital for labour develops consistently;   as

---

65. Sun Shangqing et.al., <u>BR</u>., 24, 13 June 1983, p. 19.
66. Xue Muqiao, 1981, pp. 135-41.

profit rates increase, a regular pattern of substitution will result. In actuality, different mixes of labour and capital can be rationally employed at different levels of profit. It may be, for example, that a given combination of labour and capital provides the best rate of profit at low levels and at high levels but not at medium levels. Capital should not be always treated as an incremental variable. In response to this attack from the Cambridge school of neo-Ricardian economics, the 'orthodox' reply was to suggest that capital resembled 'putty', to which Joan Robinson remarked that 'ectoplasm' would be more apt.(67) The problem for planners is that, in reality, capital is not putty; it has a concreteness which makes it hard to shift techniques. Planners have to deal with concepts which are tangible. Hence their concern to base prices on actual costs is quite rational; it is not just a question of bureaucratic inflexibility. But here I am straying far from the concerns of Sun Yefang!

A Major Weakness in Sun's Position - The Socialist Mode of Production.

It will be immediately apparent from the above that there was an inconsistency between Sun's criticism of Stalin's treatment of property and his treatment of commodity exchange. Sun rightly criticised Stalin for divorcing property from the other relations of production. Yet, later in the same essay, Sun maintained that commodity exchange did not take place within the state-owned system because articles did not change ownership. Sun was doing just what he had criticised Stalin for. Sun, for example, merely asserted that products of the defence industry were not commodities, without looking at the relationships involved in product transfer.(68) But if the products of the defence industry were not commodities and if value was created, exchanged and realised, then what were they? What, after all, was the difference between commodity exchange and product exchange? Sun, moreover, skipped lightly over the major problem discussed by Western Marxists as to whether the defence industry contributed to production or was merely a consumer of surplus.(69)

At the root of the above inconsistency was Sun's continued adherence to the Stalinist view that socialism was a distinct mode of production. Marx never accorded socialism such a status. For Marx, the 'lower stage of communism' (socialism) was a period of transition in which nascent communist relations of production emerged and capitalist relations were progressively overcome. A mode of production, moreover, generated classes on the basis of clashes of objective interests arising out of contradictions between the relations of production and the productive forces. What were the classes in Sun's

---

67. Cited in Dobb, 1973, p. 251.
68. Sun Yefang, 1980, p. 161.
69. Baran and Sweezy, 1966; Poulantzas, 1975.

socialist mode of production and what were the contradictory interests and conflicting oppositional practices from which they arose? This is the same question one might ask McCarthy after reading the preceding chapter. Sun logically could not invoke Stalin's 1936 formula of two friendly classes and one stratum (urban workers, kolkhoz workers and intellectuals). Apart from the non-Marxist absurdity of defining classes in terms other than antagonism, Stalin's classes derived precisely from his disjunctive conception of property which Sun was at great pains to debunk. In short, Sun needed to explain how socialist relations of production were different and how they affected the objective interests of the direct producers. Sun failed to do this and Chapter Five of this book merely touched on the subject.

Chinese Criticisms of Sun: The Move to the Right.

For Sun, one of the characteristics of China's socialist mode of production was that China's currency, the Renminbi, was no longer a universal equivalent as was money in a capitalist economy; it had become a 'measure of value and a certificate of labour'.(70)   No justification was given for this assertion and predictably it has come under challenge. One critic, Li Chonghuai, argued that the Renminbi was just like any other form of paper money not backed by gold.(71) It fulfilled the function of measuring value certainly; but it was still a 'universal equivalent'. Thus, the regulation of Renminbi had to exist in the same relationship to the value of commodities as did Western money. Li endorsed Xue Muqiao's claim that the commodity price index was the standard for examining currency value. Reviewing monetary policy since 1949, Li argued that the ratio between the quantity of money in circulation and the volume of retail sales should be higher that the hitherto considered optimum of 1:8.5 or 1:8.(72) The reasons given are informative,

1.   The development of the rural economy requires a large turnover of cash.
2.   The development of industry, commerce, communications and services requires a considerable increase of money.
3.   Some means of production which were allocated in the past by means of transferring accounts have been put

---

70.   Sun Yefang, 1980, p. 157.
71.   Li Chonghuai, 1982, p. 28.
72.   Ibid., p. 34.

into the market, thus greatly increasing the demand for money.(73)

Considering the above, Sun Yefang's assertions concerning the role of money do not withstand scrutiny. One tends to agree with Li Chonghuai and Xue Muqiao(74) as to the status of the Renminbi as a universal equivalent. This was the position also taken by Lavigne's study of Soviet money which suggested that its role was similar to that in a capitalist economy; credit created by the State Bank, moreover, was similar to that created by capitalist banks.(75)

If the above criticism of Sun is correct, then money in a socialist economy is itself still a commodity. We are back to the earlier discussion of Sun's confusion about exactly what commodities were. Is it possible to deny that commodities exist in certain key areas of the economy and still maintain that the law of value operates within them? Can one divorce the law of value from commodity production? Sun's critics on the 'left' always denied that one could. In recent years, however, such criticisms have come from the 'right'. One such critic, Ma Jiaju, noted that Sun really talked about two laws of value - one relating to commodity production and the other to a product economy.(76) Such was misleading. Ma argued that enterprises in the state-owned sector really did carry out exchange 'only according to commodity production and circulation and that their products can only be produced and exchanged as commodities'.(77) This was because of the pattern of the social division of labour at the current stage of history. Value had to take the form of exchange value.(78) Sun's error was to confuse the concept of value with the substance of value. He was not studying what had conventionally been taken as the law of value, namely the law of value of commodities.(79) It was one thing, Ma claimed, to allocate social labour for the production of various goods to fulfil social needs according to rational proportions. It was quite a different matter to allow the time of necessary social labour in production to determine the value of a commodity. A linkage might exist, as in competitive capitalism, only when the supply of a given commodity was in equilibrium with demand for it; only then could the commodity be sold at its value. But to say that a linkage could exist is not to say that it always did. In Ma's view, it would still be necessary in communist society to measure the social labour involved in producing a particular product and to weigh this up against the

73. Ibid., p. 35.
74. Xue Muqiao, 1981, p. 125.
75. Lavigne, 1978.
76. See Ma Jiaju, 1980, p. 222; Sun Yefang, (1964), Sun, 1979, p. 300.
77. Ma Jiaju, 1980, p. 223.
78. Ma Jiaju, Jingji Yanjiu, 5, 1979, Chinese Economic Studies, 4, 1980, pp. 64-70.
79. Ma Jiaju, 1980, p. 223.

expected use value of the product in meeting social needs. But this should not be seen as an example of the operation of the law of value, since value given by average necessary social labour would not be transformed into exchange value. Socially necessary labour time might be the substance of value, but it was not equivalent to the concept of value.(80) Sun's confusion on this point, Ma and others felt, rested on a misinterpretation of certain passages in the works of Marx and Engels.(81)

According to Ma, Sun's theoretical shortcomings had important policy ramifications. Whilst Sun proposed many reforms based on profitability and enterprise autonomy, he neglected the question of material interest. Whilst stressing enterprise profit, Sun argued that such profit should be absorbed by the state. Thus, this 'correct criterion' for judging performance did not provide an adequate incentive for enterprises to perform. Political and ideological education had not provided sufficient incentive in the past; thus any reform now must squarely address the question of material incentive. Sun had indeed designed numerous 'reasonable mechanisms for socialist economic operations'. But 'he overlooks the internal economic impetus for setting the entire economic machine in motion. The result is a well assembled clock with the mainspring left out'.(82)

Sun's neglect of material interest, Ma felt, derived from his denial of commodity production and exchange in the state sector - in his denial of the importance of the market. Thus, Sun simplified the process by which the law of value operated in socialist planning. He laid too great an emphasis on the cost side of the equation and not enough on the side of demand. Such criticism is ironical when one considers Sun's Cultural Revolution tag as 'China's Liberman'. Ma Jiaju's criticisms from the 'right' should be considered by those Western commentators who see Sun as the standard bearer of market socialism.

The belief that commodity relations exist within the state sector is now quite prevalent in China as is the view that technically bringing exploitation to an end by a change in ownership does not involve the end of clashes of interest. This latter view evokes memories of the 'leftist' Shanghai school of political economy - a school which earned Sun Yefang's bitterest scorn.(83) But nowadays, Marx's discussion of 'bourgeois right' is used for very different purposes. Liu Guoguang and Zhao Renwei, for example, seemed to agree with the Shanghai school that conflicting interests emerged from the distributive system which

---

80. Ma Jiaju, _Jingji Yanjiu_, 5, 1979, <u>Chinese Economic Studies</u>, 4, 1980, pp. 70-83.
81. <u>Ibid</u>., pp. 64-70. See also Dong Dasheng, _Jingji Yanjiu_, 5, 1979, <u>Chinese Economic Studies</u>, 4, 1980, pp. 84-8.
82. Ma Jiaju, 1980, p. 224.
83. Sun Yefang, (1977), Sun, 1979, pp. 333-45.

granted equal pay for equal work; as different people had different
capabilities, they gained different rewards, and these differences found
expression in unequal performances at the enterprise level. But that is
where the similarity ends! Instead of 'restricting bourgeois right', Liu
and Zhao argued that different performance should be reflected in the
reward structures; the efficient should gain and the inefficient should
be punished.   It was precisely this nexus of material gain which
provided   the   'direct   contributing   factor'   for   the   presence   of
commodities and the market under socialism. As the conditions were
not yet present in China to implement the principle of exchange of
equal labour, and hence the exchange of equal value, labour as a direct
social act could not be reflected except through a planned market.(84)
In calling for increased market integration, Liu and Zhao went much
further than Sun Yefang. In fact, they implied that Sun's advocacy of
using the law of value as the basis of planning was not yet feasible.

Stress on the all-pervasive nature of commodity production and
the need for material incentives represented a more radical departure
from Stalin than even Sun was prepared to make. This was even more
clearly expressed by Fan Jigang who argued that the products of
society, without exception, were commodities.(85) Such was true both
for the means of production and the means of consumption, regardless
of whether they were produced under state or collective ownership.
Fan not only rejected the Stalinist view that commodity production
stemmed from two distinct spheres of ownership but even went against
the position of Liu Guoguang and Zhao Renwei outlined above. It was
not the principle of distribution according to work which determined
the existence of commodities.   It was the continued existence of
'qualitative   differences   in   labour'   which   determined   commodity
production and the different economic interests which developed within
the same system of ownership. Distribution of the products of society
did not determine the social relations of production. On the contrary,
Marx maintained that the structure of distribution was wholly
determined by the structure of production; the particular way of
participating   in   production   determined   the   specific   form   of
distribution.

Fan's insistence on the all-pervasiveness of commodities under
socialism inevitably led him to a criticism of Sun Yefang. He rejected
ideas such as Sun's that the categories of value and socially necessary
labour time would continue to exist even under communism when
commodity production and exchange ceased.   Here Fan invoked Ma
Jiaju's criticism that Sun confused the concept of value with the
substance of value. But Fan's reasoning was different. As Fan saw it,
Sun's thesis collapsed the concept of socially necessary labour time into

---

84. Liu Guoguang and Zhao Renwei, Jingji Yanjiu, 5, 1979, Chinese
     Economic Studies, 4, 1980, pp. 3-31.
85. Fan Jigang, 1980.

actual individual labour time. It also separated 'commodity' from 'value', which Fan regarded as the form and content of one and the same thing. Labour time, Fan argued, was the basis of value, but value was not reducible to labour time. This was because value represented a broader conception of labour time; it was a social average, historically relative, and therefore, inaccurate measure of actual individual labour time. Social labour and the existence of value were based on qualitative differences between labour inputs which had developed since the beginning of commodity production. Only when such qualitative differences disappeared would it be possible to measure labour time directly without reference to the phenomena it engendered in commodity producing societies. Thus, Fan claimed commodity production and value would disappear simultaneously.(86)

Moving even further away from Sun Yefang, Zhang Chaozun, Xiang Qiyuan and Huang Zhenqi, whilst affirming the importance of property, placed even more emphasis on the nature of the division of labour in determining the existence of commodity production.(87) Whilst presenting an account of property as the product of an entire ensemble of relations, similar to that of Sun, they came to a different conclusion. Since different enterprises within the state-owned sector had a degree of autonomy and conflict of interests, they should be considered as 'relatively independent commodity producers'. From a completely opposite ideological perspective, these writers had come to much the same conclusion as Bettelheim who argued that the existence of economic calculation between enterprises meant that such enterprises should be considered as the sites of 'separate capitals'.(88) Clearly, it was ideologically too dangerous to argue in these terms; though the position boiled down to the same thing.

From a position similar to Fan's, Zhang et.al. argued that clashes of interest emerged on the basis of an uneven development of the productive forces, differing managerial competence at the enterprise level, payment according to work and the resulting creation of socially necessary labour instead of direct calculation according to labour. The result was a social division of labour which both determined and was determined by the need for commodity exchange and circulation. Since property was the product of all those relations, one needed to recognise

---

86. Ibid., p. 223.
87. Zhang Chaozun, Xiang Qiyuan and Huang Zhenqi, Jingji Yanjiu, 4, 1979, Chinese Economic Studies, 3, 1980, pp. 58-68.
88. Bettelheim, 1976(a).

different levels of real property within sectors legally granted the same property status.(89)

We have moved a long way from Stalin! The last plank in Stalin's 1952 thesis has been broken. The analysis of Zhao and others completely did away with the notion of two levels of ownership. We have also moved a long way from Sun Yefang. Indirectly, the above thesis challenged Sun's partial endorsement of Stalin's views about product circulation and exchange in the state sector. The policy implications are even more profound. Zhang et.al. began to question the need for close state direction of economic life. The autonomy of enterprises arose out of the operation of objective laws. That autonomy, therefore, should be recognised if the law of value was to enjoy greater freedom and effectiveness.

One of the most prominent advocates of enlarged enterprise autonomy has been Jiang Yiwei who argued that government organisations at central or local levels should be separated from economic organisations.(90) Government should be responsible for overall supervision but should not engage in direct economic management. The units of government were geographical whereas those of the economy were not necessarily so. Thus, arguments about geographical centralisation or decentralisation missed the point. Decision-making in the economy could not be decided according to administrative divisions. The enterprise was basic, and combination of enterprises should be decided according to economic rather than geographical criteria. Like some of the theorists discussed earlier, Jiang believed in the all-pervasive nature of the commodity system; this demanded the relative independence of enterprises even in the state sector. Enterprise autonomy was not just a question of expanding powers of purchase and sales. It was, above all, a question of 'independent management and development'. It was necessary, moreover, if socialist economic democracy was to be fully realised.

The control exercised by the state over relatively independent enterprises, Jiang felt, should primarily be legislative and fiscal (using economic levers). As a major purchaser, the state, moreover, could control the general direction of the economy through contracts and subsidies. Although this represented a considerable diminution of state power, Jiang argued that it did not endanger socialist objectives. Socialism, he asserted, was the combination of public ownership with the abolition of exploitation and with distribution according to work. All other principles were derivative. With public ownership, labour power had ceased to be a commodity; for that reason commodity production would not bring about exploitation. Socialism, moreover,

---

89. Zhang Chaozun et.al., <u>Jingji Yanjiu</u>, 4, 1979, <u>Chinese Economic Studies</u>, 3, 1980, pp. 58-68.
90. Jiang Yiwei, 1980.

was a network of many economic units not a monolithic entity. If socialism was to be 'an association of free and equal producers', then an impersonal monolith actually impeded its realisation.   Here, Jiang clearly challenged the Stalinist notion that collective ownership was less socialist than that of the state.

For these reasons, Jiang believed that as long as an enterprise fulfilled its obligations to the state, there was nothing to be feared in its pursuing profit.   When a socialist enterprise made a profit, it benefited not only its own staff but the economy as a whole. But that freedom to make a profit had to be accompanied by workers and managers assuming full responsibility for any losses. Since the state ceded control over the means of production to a particular enterprise, it ought to be able to demand some responsibilities from that enterprise, so long as this was within the rights and obligations enshrined by law.

While Jiang admitted that a certain degree of income and material disparity might occur as a result of his advocacy, he argued that egalitarianism was distinct from socialism. Socialism was bounded by the principle of distribution according to work - a principle which recognised that disparities had to exist. The state, however, should act to ensure that vast disparities did not become entrenched; it could do this by using legislative or indirect economic powers. For Jiang, enterprise-based reform was the embodiment of the economic principles and economic organisation of the Paris Commune. It was an association of free and equal producers in large-scale industry and manufacture which was based not only on 'the association of workers in each factory', but also 'the combination of all those associations in one great union'.(91)

The shifting of the debate away from the concerns of Sun towards an 'enterprise-based economy' has led to many new ideas about the role of planning. He Jianzhang, for example, argued that though. planning was necessary to overcome the anarchic spontaneity of capitalism, mandatory planning should be restricted.(92) Clearly, however, it had to be maintained with regard to major materials in short supply but which were crucial to people's needs and the national economy. In such cases, the law of planned and proportionate development had to take precedence over the law of value. Such was also the case in areas where the level of development of the productive forces was low. But long-term divergencies of values and prices should be avoided since they contributed to imbalances. As He saw it, mandatory plans were emergency or stop-gap measures to be phased out as economic

---

91. Engels, (1891), Marx and Engels, SW., II, 1970, p. 186, cited in ibid., p. 69.
92. He Jianzhang, Jingji Yanjiu, 5, 1979, Chinese Economic Studies, 4, 1980, pp. 32-62; He, 1982.

conditions improved. People should have no illusions that the previous stress on mandatory planning was a carry-over of the mentality of the small-scale, self sufficient patriarchal economy. The small producer was always hostile to the development of a commodity economy and often rationalised this hostility by support for utopian socialism. Such had been the basis of support for Proudhon and Dühring whom Marx and Engels had given short shrift. One had to recognise the influence of small-scale patriarchal thinking on both the early Soviet and Chinese attempts to build socialism. Now, one should implement Lenin's call to learn business techniques and carry on 'trade in a civilised way'. Only that way might one prevent alternating cycles of decentralisation (to deal with imbalances caused by the patriarchal economy) and recentralisation (as patriarchal thinking reasserted itself).

Lenin's statement to the effect that 'any plan is nothing more than a yardstick'(93) was invoked to justify the introduction of guidance planning. Initially this ought to apply to products of lesser importance, but the sphere of its operation should be steadily enlarged. Under this system, enterprises would receive targets which were for reference only. Prices, moreover, would be allowed to fluctuate within given boundaries. Commercial departments would place orders with industrial departments for a given number of products, the quality of which would be determined jointly by guidance plans and market demand. The virtue of this guidance planning was its indirect nature.

The introduction of indicative planning implied that the main area of planning shifted to the enterprise. New ideas about the relationship between the state and the enterprise have already been discussed in Chapter Four. Enterprise planning, it will be remembered, was to be guided not only by contracted obligations to the state but also by market forces. For contracts to be effective and legally enforceable, the state should recognise the rights and interests of enterprises. If market orientation was to be effective and enterprise initiative maintained, enterprises should be given greater power over the disbursement of funds, the power to sell fixed assets, power over wage and bonus determination (within state norms) and the right to transfer 'surplus workers' to other enterprises. The enterprise should be given greater power over price determination, so that prices might more accurately reflect supply and demand.

He Jianzhang also advocated that different kinds of company be set up to facilitate the further intensification of the division of labour, to improve specialisation, to enhance technological progress and to increase both the quantity and quality of goods, whilst improving productivity and reducing costs. These companies could take the form of syndicates or trusts such as might be found in Yugoslavia or

---

93. Lenin, (1921), CW., XXXII, 1965, p. 323, cited in ibid., p. 58.

Romania.   Even   the   pattern   of   organisation   of   monopoly   capitalism might be studied.

Conclusion.

He Jianzhang and Jiang Yiwei's programmes represent a signi-ficant departure from orthodox Marxism-Leninism, particularly as interpreted by Stalin.   They also diverge considerably from the prescriptions outlined by Sun Yefang.   The programmes demonstrate the degree to which contemporary Chinese political economists are prepared to question the canons of received orthodoxy in political economic thought, as well as to put forward policies which would change the face of 'socialist' organisation in China.   By restricting the role of the state in direct economic decision-making, He and Jiang are calling for a greater separation of state and civil society.   They are challenging a statism which has been accepted as part of the Marxist project ever since Kautsky.   A different concept of what constitutes democracy has been articulated in these programmes.   Other questions of enormous political consequence have also arisen.   The re-evaluation of what constitutes the aim of socialist production, what is entailed in transforming the system of ownership, the conditions under which commodity production and exchange exist, and the principles of distributive justice strike to the very core of political life.   Whether such underlying issues will continue to be openly discussed is a matter of some doubt.   Recent campaigns to eradicate 'spiritual pollution' and to infuscate Marx's theory of alienation may prove to be ineluctable. Nevertheless, the debates have raised issues of such widespread importance that they deserve to be ranked in importance alongside the great debates of the 1920s in the U.S.S.R.(94)

These issues stem from an analysis of Chinese society which re-invokes the methodology used by Marx himself.   As a pioneer in using Marxian methodology in such conditions, Sun Yefang deserves credit for being the catalyst for an encompassing re-appraisal.   Sun demon-strated that the Marxian method could be usefully applied to discussing problems of socialist transitional society, and hence that Marx's method was not something which could only be confined to arid 'diamat' or 'histomat' textbooks.   Even more important, Sun used Marx to pierce through what was becoming a secular religion.

Sun was able to do this by concentrating on the essential features of political economic life and by evincing the objective laws which govern that life.   He rejected ad hoc approaches as well as funda-mentalism.   His analysis revived Marx's teachings on the role of value theory and on the complex inter-relationships which humans have entered into to appropriate nature and to co-ordinate production.   Sun

---

94.   Compare the current debates with those narrated in Erlich, 1960.

held the practices and theories of Stalinism up to rigorous scrutiny and found them wanting. But, for all his undoubted talent, Sun's account is flawed by his acceptance of the view of socialism as a discrete mode of production. His acceptance of this was a major inconsistency even within his own paradigm.

The issues which have arisen in the debates surrounding Sun's theories raise fundamental questions as to the nature of socialist transitional societies such as China. They are issues in which Marxian categories and methodology have a demonstrable applicability in revealing the essential features of concrete reality. As a person who strove to implement Marx's project and who adhered to his methodology, Sun would have been happy to see the sophistication with which contemporary Chinese poltical economists have approached the problems of mounting a radical critique based on Marx's work. This is probably Sun's monument.

BIBLIOGRAPHY

Alavi, H., Burns, P., Knight, G., Mayer, P. and McEachern, D., Capitalism and Colonial Production, London, Croom Helm, 1982.

Albrow, M., Bureaucracy, London, Pall Mall Press, 1970.

Althusser, L., Lenin and Philosophy and Other Essays, New York, Monthly Review Press, 1971.

Althusser, L., Essays in Self-Criticism, London, New Left Books, 1976.

Althusser, L., For Marx, London, Verso, 1979.

Althusser, L. and Balibar, E., Reading Capital, London, Verso, 1979.

Anderson, P., Lineages of the Absolutist State, London, New Left Books, 1975.

Bahro, R., The Alternative in Eastern Europe, London, New Left Books, 1978.

Balibar, E., 'From Bachelard to Althusser; the Concept of "Epistemological Break"', Economy and Society, Vol. VII, No. 3, 1978, pp. 207-38.

Ballestrem, K., 'Lenin and Bogdanov', Studies in Soviet Thought, Vol. IX, 1969, pp. 283-310.

Baran, P. and Sweezy, P., Monopoly Capital, New York, Monthly Review Press, 1966.

Barbalet, J., The Development of Marx's Social and Political Theory, Ph.D. thesis, University of Adelaide, 1977.

Barker, R. and Sinha, R. with Beth, R. (eds.), The Chinese Agricultural Economy, London, Croom Helm, 1982.

Barker, R. and Sinha, R., 'Epilogue', in ibid., pp. 199-204.

Barker, R., Sisler, D. and Rose, B., 'Prospects for Growth in Grain Production, in ibid., pp. 163-81.

Bauman, Z., 'Officialdom and Class: Bases of Inequality in Socialist Society', in Parkin (ed.), 1974, pp. 129-48.

Bergson, A., 'Towards a New Growth Model', Problems of Communism, Vol. XXII, No. 2, 1973, pp. 1-9.

Bettelheim, C., 'On the Transition Between Capitalism and Socialism', in Sweezy and Bettelheim, 1971, pp. 15-24.

Bettelheim, C., Economic Calculation and Form of Property, London, Routledge and Kegan Paul, 1976(a).

Bettelheim, C., Class Struggles in the U.S.S.R.: Second Period, 1923-1930, Sussex, Harvester, 1976(b).

Bettelheim, C. and Burton, N., China Since Mao, New York, Monthly Review Press, 1978.

Bogdanov, A., 'Proletarian Poetry', The Labour Monthly, No. 4, 1923, pp. 275-85; 357-62.

Bowie, R. and Fairbank, J. (eds.), Communist China, 1955-59: Policy Documents with Analysis, Cambridge Mass., Harvard University Press, 1965.

Boyne, R., 'Breaks and Problematics', Philosophy and Social Criticism, Vol. VI, No. 2, 1979, pp. 203-5.

Breth, R., Mao's China: A Study of Socialist Economic Development, Melbourne, Longman Cheshire, 1977.

Brugger, W., Democracy and Organisation in the Chinese Industrial Enterprise: 1948-53, Cambridge University Press, 1976.

Brugger, B., Contemporary China, London, Croom Helm, 1977.

Brugger, B. (ed.), China: The Impact of the Cultural Revolution, London, Croom Helm, 1978.

Brugger, B. (ed.), China Since the 'Gang of Four', London, Croom Helm, 1980.

Brugger, B. China: Liberation and Transformation, London, Croom Helm, 1981(a).

Brugger, B., 'Soviet and Chinese Views on Revolution and Socialism - Some Thoughts on the Problems of Diachrony and Synchrony', Journal of Contemporary Asia, Vol. XI, No. 3, 1981, pp. 311-32(b).

Brugger, B., 'Alienation Revisited', paper given to the Asian Studies Association of Australia, 5th National Conference, Adelaide University, 13-19 May, 1984(a).

Brugger, B., 'Once Again "Making the Past Serve the Present" - A Critique of the Chinese Communist Party's New Official History', in Maxwell and McFarlane (eds.), 1984, pp. 169-81(b).

Brugger, B., 'Democracy and Organisation in Chinese Industry - New Directions', in Young (ed.), forthcoming.

Brugger, B. and Hannan, K., Modernisation and Revolution, London, Croom Helm, 1983.

Bukharin, N., Economics of the Transformation Period, (1920), New York, Bergman Publishers, 1971.

Callinicos, A., Althusser's Marxism, London, Pluto Press, 1976.

Campbell, R., 'Marx, Kantorovich and Novozhilov; Stoimost versus Reality', in Feiwel (ed.), 1968, pp. 261-77.

Carver, T. (ed.), Karl Marx: Texts on Method, Oxford, Basil Blackwell, 1975.

Castells, M. and de Ipola, E., 'Epistemological Practice and the Social Sciences', Economy and Society, Vol. V, No. 2, 1976, pp. 111-44.

Chao, Kuo-chün, Agrarian Policy of the Chinese Communist Party, 1921-1959, Westport, Conn., Greenwood Press, 1977.

Ch'en, J. (ed.), Mao Papers: Anthology and Bibliography, Englewood Cliffs, N.J., Prentice Hall, 1969.

Cheng Renqian, 'Some Questions on the Reassessment of Rosa Luxemburg', in Su et.al., 1983, pp. 96-123.

Chi Hsin, The Case of the Gang of Four, Hong Kong, Cosmos Books, 1977.

C.C.P., Eighth National Congress of the Communist Party of China, Documents, (1956), BFLP., 1981.

C.C.P., Eighth National Congress of the Communist Party of China, Vol. II, Speeches, PFLP., 1956.

C.C.P., The Ninth National Congress of the Communist Party of China, (Documents), PFLP., 1969.

C.C.P., The Tenth National Congress of the Communist Party of China, Documents, PFLP., 1973.

C.C.P., The Eleventh National Congress of the Communist Party of China, (Documents), PFLP., 1977.

C.C.P., The Twelfth National Congress of the Communist Party of China, BFLP., 1982.

Christensen, P., 'The Shanghai School and Its Rejection', in Feuchtwang and Hussain (eds.), 1983, pp. 74-90.

Christensen, P. and Delman, J., 'A Theory of Transitional Society; Mao Zedong and the Shanghai School', Bulletin of Concerned Asian Scholars, Vol. XIII, No. 2, 1981, pp. 2-15.

Claudin, F., The Communist Movement, From Comintern to Cominform, New York, Monthly Review Press, 1975, 2 vols.

Clausen, S., 'Chinese Economic Debates after Mao and the Crisis of Official Marxism', in Feuchtwang and Hussain (eds.), 1983, pp. 53-74.

Cohen, G., Karl Marx's Theory of History: A Defence, Princeton University Press, 1978.

Collier, A., 'In Defence of Epistemology', in Mepham and Ruben, 1979, pp. 55-106.

C.P.S.U., History of the Communist Party of the Soviet Union (Bolshevik): Short Course, Moscow, Foreign Languages Publishing House, 1939.

C.P.S.U., Programme of the Communist Party of the Soviet Union, 31 October 1961, Moscow, Foreign Languages Publishing House, 1961.

Corrigan, P., Ramsay, H. and Sayer, D., Socialist Construction and Marxist Theory: Bolshevism and its Critique, New York, Monthly Review Press, 1978.

Corrigan, P., Ramsay, H. and Sayer, D., For Mao: Essays in Historical Materialism, London, Macmillan, 1979.

Crook, I. and D., The First Years of the Yangyi Commune, London, Routledge and Kegan Paul, 1966, reprinted 1979.

Cutler, A., Hindess, B., Hirst, P. and Hussain, A., Marx's Capital and Capitalism Today, London, Routledge and Kegan Paul, 2 vols., 1977 and 1978.

Deng Xiaoping, Wenxuan, (Selected Works), 1975-1982, Beijing, Renmin Chubanshe, 1983.

De Ste. Croix, G., The Class Struggle in the Ancient Greek World, London, Duckworth, 1981.

Dirlik, A., 'Chinese Historians and the Marxist Concept of Capitalism', Modern China, Vol. VIII, No. 1, 1982, pp. 105-32.

Dittmer, L., 'The 12th Congress of the Communist Party of China', The China Quarterly, 93, 1983, pp. 108-24.

Dobb, M., Studies in the Development of Capitalism, (1946), revised 2nd ed., London, Routledge and Kegan Paul, 1975.

Dobb, M., Soviet Economic Development Since 1917, New York, International Publications, 1948.

Dobb, M., Theories of Value and Distribution since Adam Smith: Ideology and Economic Theory, Cambridge University Press, 1973.

Domar, E., Essays in the Theory of Economic Growth, New York, Oxford University Press, 1957.

Domes, J., Socialism in the Chinese Countryside, London, Hurst, 1980.

Donnithorne, A., China's Economic System, London, George Allen and Unwin, 1967.

Dupré, G. and Rey, P., 'Reflections on the Pertinence, of a Theory of the History of Exchange', Economy and Society, Vol. II, No. 2, 1973, pp. 131-63; trans. by Hindess, B. from original in Cahiers Internationaux de Sociologie, 46, 1968, pp. 132-62.

Dutton, M., The Crisis of Marxism in China, Brisbane, Griffith University, Griffith Asian Papers, No. 9, 1983.

Eckstein, A., China's Economic Revolution, Cambridge University Press, 1977.

Edgley, R., 'Marx's Revolutionary Science', in Mepham and Ruben (eds.), 1979, pp. 5-26.

Ellman, M., Planning Problems in the U.S.S.R.: The Contribution of Mathematical Economics to their Solution: 1960-1971, Cambridge University Press, 1973.

Ellul, J., The Technological Society, New York, Knopf, 1967.

Elster, J., 'Cohen and Marx's Theory of History', Political Studies, Vol. XXVIII, No. 1, 1980, p. 121-8.

Erlich, A., The Soviet Industrialization Debate, 1924-1928, Cambridge, Mass., Harvard University Press, 1960.

Evans, A., 'Developed Socialism in Soviet Ideology', Soviet Studies, Vol. XXIX, No. 3, 1977, pp. 409-28.

Fan Jigang, 'The Cause of the Emergence and Existence of Commodities', Social Sciences in China, 2, 1980, pp. 213-26.

Feiwel, G. (ed.), New Currents in Soviet-type Economies, Scranton, Pa., International Textbook Co., 1968.

Feuchtwang, S. and Hussain, A. (eds.), The Chinese Economic Reforms, London, Croom Helm, 1983.

Feuerwerker, A., The Chinese Economy: 1912-1949, Ann Arbor, University of Michigan, Michigan Papers in Chinese Studies, No. 1, 1968.

Foster Carter, A., 'The Modes of Production Controversy', New Left Review, 107, 1978, pp. 47-77.

Gardner, J., Chinese Politics and the Succession to Mao, London, Macmillan, 1982.

Geras, N., 'Althusser's Marxism: An Assessment', in New Left Review, (ed.) 1977, pp. 232-72.

Glucksmann, A., 'A Ventriloquist Structuralism', in New Left Review, (ed.) 1977, pp. 282-314.

Goldmann, J., 'Fluctuations and Trend in the Rate of Growth in Some Socialist Countries', in Feiwel (ed.), 1968, pp. 112-22.

Gray, J. and White, G. (eds.), China's New Development Strategy, London, Academic Press, 1982.

Habermas, J., Legitimation Crisis, London, Heinemann, 1976.

Haraszti, M., A Worker in a Worker's State, Harmondsworth, Penguin, 1977.

He Jianzhang, 'More on Planned Economy and Market Regulation', Social Sciences in China, 4, 1982, pp. 46-59.

Hilton, R. (ed.), The Transition from Feudalism to Capitalism, London, New Left Books, 1976.

Hindess, B., Philosophy and Methodology in the Social Sciences, Sussex, Harverster, 1977.

Hindess, B. and Hirst, P., Pre-Capitalist Modes of Production, London, Routledge and Kegan Paul, 1975.

Hindess, B. and Hirst, P., Mode of Production and Social Formation, London, Macmillan, 1977.

Hirst, P., On Law and Ideology, Atlantic Islands, N.J., Humanities Press, 1979(a).

Hirst, P., 'The Necessity of Theory', Economy and Society, Vol. VIII, No. 4, 1979, pp. 417-45(b).

Hoffman, C., The Chinese Worker, Albany, State University of New York Press, 1974.

Howard, M. and King, J. (eds.), The Economics of Marx: Selected Readings of Exposition and Criticism, Harmondsworth, Penguin, 1976.

Howe, C., Employment and Economic Growth in Urban China: 1949-1957, Cambridge University Press, 1971.

Howe, C., Wage Patterns and Wage Policy in Modern China, 1919-1972, Cambridge University Press, 1973.

Howe, C., China's Economy: A Basic Guide, London, Granada Publishing, 1978.

Hua Guofeng, Continue the Revolution Under the Dictatorship of the Proletariat to the End, PFLP., 1977.

Huang Da, 'Some Problems Concerning Pricing', Social Sciences in China, 1, 1981, pp. 136-56.

Hussain, A., 'Marx's Notes on Adolph Wagner: An Introduction', Theoretical Practice, 5, 1972, pp. 18-34.

Ishikawa, S., 'China's Economic Growth Since 1949 - An Assessment', The China Quarterly, 94, 1983, pp. 242-81.

Jasny, N., Soviet Economists of the Twenties: Names to be Remembered, Cambridge University Press, 1972.

Jiang Yiwei, 'The Theory of an Enterprise-Based Economy, Social Sciences in China, 1, 1980, pp. 48-70.

Kerr, C., Dunlop, J., Harbison, F. and Myers, C., Industrialism and Industrial Man, London, Heinemann, 1962.

Konrád, G. and Szelényi, I., The Intellectuals on the Road to Class Power, New York, Harcourt, Brace, Jovanovich, 1979.

Krivitsov, V. and Sidikhmenov, V., A Critique of Mao Tse-tung's Theoretical Conceptions, Moscow, Progress Publishers, 1972.

Lavigne, M., 'The Creation of Money by the State Bank of the U.S.S.R.', Economy and Society, Vol. VII, No. 1, 1978, pp. 29-55.

Lecourt, D., Proletarian Science? The Case of Lysenko, London, New Left Books, 1977.

Lenin, V., Collected Works (CW.), Moscow, Progress Publishers; Vol. V, 1961; Vol. XIV, 1962; Vol. XV, 1963; Vol. XX, 1964; Vol.XXXII, 1965; Vol. XXXIII, 1966; Vol. XXXVIII, 1972.

Leontiev, A., Political Economy: A Beginner's Course, San Francisco, Proletarian Publishers, n.d.

Li Chonghuai, 'On the New Stage in the Development of Monetary Forms', Social Sciences in China, 4, 1982, pp. 14-45.

Lieberthal, K., Central Documents and Politburo Politics in China, Ann Arbor, University of Michigan, Michigan Papers in Chinese Studies, No. 33, 1978.

Lin, C., 'The Reinstatement of Economics in China Today', The China Quarterly, 85, 1981, pp. 1-48.

Lippitt, V., Land Reform and Economic Development in China, White Plans, N.Y., M.E. Sharpe, 1974.

Liu Guoguang (ed.), Guomin Jingji Guanli Tizhi, Gaige de Ruogan Lilun Wenti, Beijing, Zhongguo Shehui Kexue Chubanshe, 1980.

Liu Suinian, 'Economic Planning', in Xu Dixin et.al., 1982, pp. 28-51.

Lukács, G., History and Class Consciousness, (1923), London, Merlin Press, 1971.

Ma Jiaju, 'A Pioneer Work on Economic Reform: Notes on Sun Yefang's Theoretical Questions of the Socialist Economy', Social Sciences in China, 1, 1980, pp. 216-27.

McEachern, D., 'The Mode of Production in India', Journal of Contemporary Asia, Vol. VI, No. 4, 1976, pp. 444-57.

McFarlane, B., 'Political Economy of Class Struggle and Economic Growth in China, 1950-82', World Development, Vol. XI, No. 8, 1983, pp. 659-72; also in Maxwell and McFarlane (eds.) 1984, pp. 21-34.

Macherey, P., A Theory of Literary Production, London, Routledge and Kegan Paul, 1978.

Macherey, P. and Balibar, E., 'Literature as an Ideological Form: Some Marxist Propositions', The Oxford Literary Review, Vol. III, No. 1, 1978, pp. 4-12.

Mao Zedong, Selected Works, BFLP, Vol. 1, 1965; Vol. II, 1965; Vol. III, 1965; Vol. IV, 1961; Vol. V, 1977.

Mao Zedong, Selected Readings, PFLP, 1971.

Mao Zedong, Miscellany of Mao Tse-tung Thought, (1949-68), 2 vols., JPRS., 61269:1 and 2, 20 February 1974.

Mao Zedong, 'On the Origins of Machine Guns and Mortars (etc.)', Chinese Law and Government, Vol. I, No. 4, 1968-9, pp. 73-4.

Mao Zedong, A Critique of Soviet Economics, annotated by R. Levy, trans. M. Roberts with introduction by J. Peck, New York, Monthly Review Press, 1977(a). This is a translation of the same material in Mao, 1974.

Mao Zedong, Mao on Stalin, Edinburgh, Proletarian Publishing, 1977(b).

Marx, K., Capital, Moscow, Progress Publishers, Vol. I (1867), 1954; Vol. II, 1956; Vol. III, 1959.

Marx, K., A Contribution to the Critique of Political Economy, (1857), Moscow, Progress Publishers, 1970.

Marx, K., Grundrisse, (1858), Harmondsworth, Penguin, 1977.

Marx, K., 'Marginal Notes on Adolph Wagner's Lehrbuch der Politischen Ökonomie' (1879-80), Theoretical Practice, 5, 1972, pp. 40-65; another translation may be found in Carver (ed.), 1975, pp. 179-219.

Marx, K. and Engels, F., Collected Works (CW.), London, Lawrence and, Wishart, Vol. III, (1843-44), 1975; Vol. V, (1845-47), 1976.

Marx, K. and Engels, F., Selected Works, 3 vols., Moscow, Progress Publishers, 1970.

Marx, K. and Engels, F., Selected Correspondence, Moscow, Progress Publishers, 3rd. rev. edn., 1975.

Maxwell, N. and McFarlane, B. (eds.), China's Changed Road to Development, Oxford, Pergamon Press, 1984.

Mayer, P., 'The Penetration of Capitalism in a South Indian District: The First 60 Years of Colonial Rule in Tiruchirapalli', unpublished paper, Adelaide University, 1981.

Mayer, P., 'Transformation of Two Provincial Districts', in Alavi et.al., 1982, pp. 77-118.

Meek, R., Studies in the Labour Theory of Value, (1956), New York, Monthly Review Press, n.d.

Meisner, M., Li Ta-chao and the Origins of Chinese Marxism, New York, Atheneum, 1977.

Melotti, U., Marx and the Third World, London, Macmillan, 1977.

Mepham, J. and Ruben, D. (eds.), Issues in Marxist Philosophy, Vol. III, Epistemology, Science, Ideology, Sussex, Harvester, 1979.

Myers, R., The Chinese Peasant Economy: Agricultural Development in Hopei and Shantung, 1890-1949, Cambridge, Mass., Harvard University Press, 1970.

N.P.C., Documents of the First Session of the Fifth National People's Congress of the People's Republic of China, PFLP, 1978.

N.P.C., Main Documents of the Second Session of the Fifth National People's Congress of the People's Republic of China, PFLP, 1979.

Neild, K. and Seed, J., 'Theoretical Poverty or the Poverty of Theory: British Marxist Historiography and the Althusserians', Economy and Society, Vol. VIII, No. 4, 1979, pp. 383-416.

New Left Review (ed.), Western Marxism: A Critical Reader, London, 1977.

Nove, A., The Economics of Feasible Socialism, London, Allen and Unwin, 1983.

O'Leary, G., 'The Impact of Recent Policies on Peasant Income', mimeo. University of Adelaide, 1979.

O'Leary, G., 'New Directions in Chinese Agriculture', paper delivered to 'Chinese Modernisation; the Latest Phase', conference at the Contemporary China Centre, Australian National University, 16-18 February 1983.

O'Leary, G. and Watson, A., 'Current Trends in China's Agricultural Strategy: A Survey of Communes in Hebei and Shandong', The Australian Journal of Chinese Affairs, No. 4, 1980, pp. 119-65.

O'Leary, G. and Watson, A., 'The Production Responsibility System and the Future of Collective Farming', The Australian Journal of Chinese Affairs, No. 8, 1982, pp. 1-34.

O'Leary, G. and Watson, A., 'The Role of the People's Commune in Rural Development in China', Pacific Affairs, Vol. LV, No. 4, 1982-3, pp. 593-612.

Paine, S., 'Balanced Development: Maoist Conception and Chinese Practice', World Development, Vol. IV, No. 4, 1976, pp. 227-304.

Parkin, F. (ed.), The Social Analysis of Class Structure, London, Tavistock Publications, 1974.

Peck, J., 'Introduction', in Mao, 1977(a), pp. 7-29.

P.F.L.P., Three Major Struggles on China's Philosophical Front (1949-64), Beijing, 1973.

Perkins, D. (ed.), China's Modern Economy in Historical Perspective, Stanford University Press, 1975.

Polanyi, K., The Great Transformation, (1944), Boston, Beacon Press, 1957.

Poulantzas, N., Classes in Contemporary Capitalism, London, New Left Books, 1975.

Pravda, A., 'Industrial Workers: Patterns of Dissent, Opposition and Accommodation', in Tokes (ed.), 1979, pp. 209-62.

Rawski, T., 'Agricultural Employment and Technology', in Barker and Sinha (eds.), 1982, pp. 121-36.

Reglar, S., 'The Development of a Chinese Approach to Socialism: Chinese Reforms After the Denunciation of Stalin', Journal of Contemporary Asia, Vol. X, No. 1/2, 1980, pp. 181-214.

Rey, P., Les Alliances de Classes, Paris, Maspero, 1973.

Riskin, C., 'Surplus and Stagnation in Modern China', in Perkins, 1975, pp. 49-84.

Rosdolsky, R., The Making of Marx's Capital, London, Pluto Press, 1977.

Ruben, D., 'Review Article: Cohen, Marx and the Primacy Thesis', British Journal of Political Science, Vol. XI, Pt. II, 1981, pp. 227-34.

Rubin, I., Essays on Marx's Theory of Value (1928), Montreal, Black Rose Books, 1975.

Saich, T., 'New Directions in Politics and Government', in Gray and White (eds.), 1982, pp. 19-36.

Sayer, D., 'Science as Critique: Marx vs Althusser', in Mepham and Ruben, 1979, pp. 27-54.

Schram, S. (ed.), Mao Tse-tung Unrehearsed, Harmondsworth, Penguin, 1974.

Schram, S. 'To Utopia and Back: A Cycle in the History of the Chinese Communist Party', The China Quarterly, 87, 1981, pp. 407-39.

Schran, P., The Development of Chinese Agriculture, 1950-59, Urbana, University of Illinois Press, 1969.

Schurmann, H.F., Ideology and Organization in Communist China, Berkeley, University of California Press, 1966.

Shue, V., Peasant China in Transition: The Dynamics of Development Towards Socialism, Berkeley, University of California Press, 1980.

Sik, O., Plan and Market Under Socialism, White Plans, N.Y., International Arts and Sciences Press, 1967.

Skocpol, T., States and Social Revolutions: A Comparative Analysis of France, Russia and China, Cambridge University Press, 1979.

Smolinsky, 'Planning without Theory', Survey, 64, July 1967, pp. 108-24.

Stalin, J., Works, Moscow, Foreign Languages Publishing House, Vol. I, 1952; Vol. XI, 1954.

Stalin, J., Problems of Leninism, PFLP., 1976.

Stalin, J., Economic Problems of Socialism in the U.S.S.R. (1952), PFLP., 1972.

Starr, J., Continuing the Revolution: The Political Thought of Mao, Princeton University Press, 1979.

Su Shaozhi et.al., Marxism in China, Nottingham, Spokesman, 1973.

Su Shaozhi, 'Developing Marxism under Contemporary Conditions', in ibid., pp. 13-52.

Su Xing, 'China's Planned Economy and the Market', paper presented at conference of the Australasian Association for the Study of the Socialist Countries, Sydney, Macquarie University, 10-11 May 1982(a).

Su Xing, 'The Production Responsibility System in the Chinese Country-side', paper delivered to Asian Studies Association of Australia, 4th National Conference, Melbourne, Monash University, 10-14 May 1982 (b).

Sun Yefang, Shehuizhuyi Jingji de Ruogan Lilun Wenti, Beijing Renmin Chubanshe, 1979.

Sun Yefang, 'What is the Origin of the Law of Value', Social Sciences in China, 3, 1980, pp. 155-71.

Sun Yefang, 'Is There No Distinction between Simple and Expanded Reproduction', Social Sciences in China, 4, 1982, pp. 232-3.

Sweezy, P., 'The Qualitative Value Problem', in Howard and King (eds.), 1976, pp. 140-9.

Sweezy, P. and Bettelheim, C., On the Transition to Socialism, New York, Monthly Review Press, 1971.

Szamuely, L., First Models of the Socialist Economic Systems: Principles and Theories, Budapest, Academiai Kiado, 1974.

Szelényi, I., 'Socialist Opposition in Eastern Europe: Dilemmas and Prospects', in Tokes (ed.), 1979, pp. 187-208.

Thompson, E., The Poverty of Theory and other Essays, London, Merlin Press, 1978.

Tokes, R. (ed), Opposition in Eastern Europe, London, Macmillan, 1979.

Therborn, G., Science, Class and Society, London, New Left Books, 1976.

Wang, G. (ed.), Fundamentals of Political Economy, White Plains, N.Y., M.E. Sharpe, 1977.

Watson, A., 'Worker Self Management and Political Participation in China', paper presented at the Australasian Political Studies Association Conference, Adelaide, August, 1978.

Watson, A., 'Industrial Development and the Four Modernisations', in Brugger (ed.), 1980, pp. 88-134.

Watson, A., 'Economic Co-operation Revisited: The New Economic Associations in the Chinese Countryside', paper delivered at 'Chinese Modernisation: the Latest Phase', Conference at the Contemporary China Centre, Australian National University, 16-18 February, 1983.

Watson, A., 'Agriculture Looks for "Shoes that Fit": The Production Responsibility System and its Implications', World Development, Vol. XI, No. 8, 1983, pp. 705-30; also in Maxwell and McFarlane (eds.), 1984, pp. 83-108.

Weber, M., The Methodology of the Social Sciences, New York, The Free Press, 1949.

Weber, M., Economy and Society, Berkeley, University of California Press, 1968.

Womack, B., 'Chinese Political Economy: Reversing the Polarity', Pacific Affairs, Vol. LIV, No. 1, 1981, pp. 57-81.

Xiong Yingwu and Wang Shaoshun, Sulian Shehuizhuyi Jingji Wenti Yanjiu (rev. edn.), Harbin, Heilongjiang Renmin Chubanshe, 1980.

Xu Dixin et.al., China's Search for Economic Growth, Beijing, New World Press, 1982.

Xu Yi and Chen Baosen, 'On the Necessity and Possibility of Stabilising Prices', Social Sciences in China, 3, 1981, pp. 121-38.

Xue Muqiao, China's Socialist Economy, BFLP, 1981.

Xue Muqiao (ed.), Almanac of China's Economy, 1981 (trans. of Zhongguo Jingji Nianjian), Hong Kong, Eurasia Press, 1982.

Young, G., 'Party Building and the Search for Unity', in Brugger (ed.), 1978, pp. 35-70.

Young, G., 'Non-revolutionary Vanguard: Transformation of the Chinese Communist Party', in Brugger (ed.), 1980, pp. 51-87.

Young, G., (ed.), China: Dilemmas of Modernisation, London, Croom Helm, forthcoming.

Young, G. and Woodward, D., 'From Contradictions Among the People to Class Struggle: The Theories of Uninterrupted and Continuous Revolution', Asian Survey, Vol. XVIII, No. 9, September, 1978, pp. 912-33.

INDEX

accumulation rate, 106-11
agriculture, 6, 9, 15, 35-7, 57, 80, 86-8, 92, 94, 96, 102-7, 110-1, 126-8, 137-42, 154-5, 160-70, 180-3, 186
   responsibility system, 9, 87-8, 92, 95, 138-9, 145-50, 169
alienation, 10-2, 118, 123, 189, 202
Althusser, L., 3, 13, 16-19, 23-6
apriorism, 63-4, 121

Bahro, R., 35
Balibar, E., 24, 28
Ballestrem, K., 40
banking, 94, 96, 124-5, 129, 132-3, 156, 195
Barker, R., 146
base and superstructure, 4, 50-1, 54-5, 64, 68, 75, 146
Bauman, Z., 128
Bazarov, V., 103, 105
Bettelheim, C., 36, 144, 198
Bogdanov, A., 27, 29-32, 34-40, 43, 49, 54-5, 57, 59-60, 186
Bolshevism, 14-7, 29, 32, 35, 60, 117
Breth, R., 157
Brezhnev, L., 99, 117
Bukharin, N., 2, 178
bureaucracy, 7-11, 123-6, 131, 135, 140, 169-70

capital construction, 107-13, 124, 131-3, 140, 187-8
capitalism, restoration of, 6, 9, 50, 84-6, 88-9, 92-7, 101, 117, 119, 168, 171
Chen Boda, 74-5, 180
Chen Chenhan, 180
Chen Yun, 5, 86, 105, 180-1
circulation funds, 133-5, 140
circulation, 65, 93, 120, 176, 182-7, 190-1, 199
class struggle, 4, 7-8, 37-40, 45-52, 54, 56-9, 64, 71-85, 93, 97, 99, 122, 144, 151, 153-4, 168-70, 175, 193-4
command economy, 7, 123, 130-2, 134, 140
commodity, 21-2, 87, 100-2, 119-23, 130, 171-203

communes, 8, 80, 87, 94-5, 138, 145, 147, 164-6, 169, 182
communism, 6, 8, 35, 80, 98-101, 152-4, 165, 169-70, 184, 193, 195-7
Communist Party of China,
   Congresses, 7th, (1945), 90-1
               8th, (1956), 4-5, 52, 67-98, 180
               9th, (1969), 72, 74
               10th, (1973), 72, 74
               11th, (1977), 76
               12th, (1982), 69, 89-91, 97
   Plenums, 3rd of 8th CC., (1957), 69-70
          10th of 8th CC., (1962), 72
          3rd of 11th CC., (1978), 44-5, 48, 68, 77-9, 82, 86, 97, 139, 171
          5th of 11th CC., (1980), 69, 89-91, 97
          6th of 11th CC., (1981), 45, 50-1, 69, 89-91, 97, 142, 145-6, 148
contracts, 117, 123-4, 138-9, 145-6, 150, 161-2, 186, 201
contradictions, 4-5, 37-40, 50-2, 54, 67-77, 79-82, 85, 89-90, 96-8, 151, 153, 159, 175, 178
   basic, 4-5, 67-71, 79, 81, 87, 97, 175
   principal, 4-5, 50, 52, 67-71, 73-6, 79-82, 85, 89, 97, 108, 168-9
Corrigan, P., 14-19, 21-2, 25, 59-60
credit, 111-2, 124-5, 132, 136, 155, 162-3
crime, economic, 93
Crook, I. and.D., 165
Cutler, A., 13, 26, 34

Dai Cheng, 55
democracy, 10, 44-5, 57, 60, 78-9, 82, 123, 199, 202
Deng Liqun, 11
Deng Xiaoping, 74-5, 77-8, 81-2, 90-1, 168-9
development, extensive and intensive, 106-17, 126-31, 137-8

dialectics, 37, 54, 73, 75, 81-2, 95
distribution, 8-9, 35, 169, 175-9, 182-6, 189-90, 197
Dittmer, L., 90
dogmatism, 1, 3, 26-7
Domes, J., 161
Dong Biwu, 84
Donnithorne, A., 162
Du Runsheng, 147-50
Duan Ruofei, 55
Duhring, E., 201

Eastern Europe, 7, 10, 101, 107, 112, 124-5, 127-8, 139-40, 180, 191, 201-2
efficiency, 7, 9, 106-8, 114-5, 117, 126-9, 134, 138-40, 146, 167, 185-6, 191-2
empiricism, 2-3, 5, 13-66
employment, 95-6, 101, 117, 127-8, 158, 160, 165, 167
Engels, F., 70, 118, 173, 183, 196, 201
enterprise autonomy, 10, 44, 65-6, 87-9, 94-5, 102, 106, 111, 113-4, 117, 123-7, 130-4, 140, 159, 180, 185, 196, 198-201
epistemology, 13-66
exchange, 8, 65, 171-203
exports and imports, 124, 136-7, 140
extra-budgeted funds, 111-13, 131

Fan Jigang, 197-8
Fel'dman, G., 103
Feng Wenbin, 87
Feuerbach, L., 11
foreign exchange, 132, 136-7, 140
foreign relations, 15, 64-5, 115
    corrupting influence 93
    economic relations, 87, 94, 108, 115
    imperialism, 154-6
    See also special economic zones
'four principles', 78, 89
functionalism, 4-6, 11, 82, 90, 97, 120-2, 130, 139-40
futurology, 101

'Gang of Four', 1, 11, 44, 51, 72, 74-6, 83, 93, 98, 100, 108, 115, 120, 168
genetic school, 6, 103-7
Geras, N., 17
Gramsci, A., 2
Great Leap Forward, 5, 70-1, 104-5, 109-11, 164-6, 168, 180
Groman, V., 103, 105
Gu Zhun, 180

Habermas, J., 7
He Jianzhang, 171, 200-2
Hegel, G., 7-8
Hindess, B., 13, 26, 34
Hirst, P., 13, 26, 34
Hoffman, C., 159
Howe, C., 160
Hu Qiaomu, 11, 77
Hua Guofeng, 50-1, 75-7, 79, 90
Huang Zhenqi, 198
humanism, 5, 10, 37, 39, 42, 59
Hussain, A., 13, 22, 26, 34

'ideal-type', 4-5, 101, 121-3, 173, 178
industry, 15, 20, 30, 35, 37, 52, 74, 89, 92, 102-18, 122-38, 140-1, 145, 149, 156-60, 167, 169, 171-203
investment, 94-6, 103, 106-15, 124-5, 130-3, 136-7, 145-6, 150, 156, 165-7, 175, 192

Jiang Yiwei, 199-200, 202

Kalecki, M., 107-8, 112
Kautsky, K., 202
Kerr, C., 118
Khrushchev, N., 68, 98, 125, 179
Konrad, G., 8-9

labour, abstract and concrete, 174, 185, 189-20
Lavigne, M., 195
law,
    and legality, 1, 10, 44-6, 57, 82-4, 89, 91-4, 96, 124, 175, 201
    fundamental law of socialism, 117, 126, 189
    natural laws, 3, 28, 45-6, 104
    objective economic laws, 3, 5, 9, 48-9, 56, 65, 77, 86-7, 91, 95, 100-8, 122-3, 143, 172-4, 177, 185, 188-90, 202
    of planned and proportionate development, 5, 102-7, 160, 172, 188-90, 192, 200
    of value, 6, 9, 100-2, 122, 126-9, 140, 171-203
Lecourt, D., 24, 28, 32, 35
Lei Feng, 1
Lei Zhenwu, 46, 58
'leftism', 1-2, 11, 92, 100, 109-15, 190, 195
legitimacy, 6-8, 120-2, 128-9, 139-40
Lenin, V., 12-3, 19-20, 24, 27-32, 34-7, 43, 46-7, 49, 59-60, 89, 125, 180, 201
Li Chonghuai, 194-5
Liberman, E., 171, 191, 196
Lieberthal, K., 75
Lin Biao, 74
Lin Lifu, 179
Lin Zili, 54
Liu Guoguang, 196-7
Liu Huiyong, 109
Liu Shaoqi, 67, 74-5, 89, 186
Lukacs, G., 4-5
Luxemburg, R., 2, 12

Ma Hong, 114
Ma Jiaju, 195-7
Ma Yinchu, 180
McFarlane, B., 107-8, 112
market relations, 1, 6, 8-9, 65-6, 86, 88, 94, 100-1, 105, 110, 123-4, 126-7, 137-9, 155-6, 162-3, 166, 169, 172, 184, 195-7, 201
Marx, K., 2-8, 10, 12-3, 19-27, 29-30, 32-7, 40, 43, 46-7, 49, 60, 70, 80, 84, 99, 101, 118, 123, 142, 151-4, 165, 172-8,

182-3, 185, 187-90, 192-3, 196, 201-3
Marxism,
   as ideology, 1-2, 9-12, 17, 67-97,
      150, 202
   as methodology, 1-6, 12-66, 142, 173-
      7, 188-91, 202-3
   as science, 20-5, 39, 58-9, 63
Mao Zedong, 3-5, 8, 11, 13-7, 19-20, 37-
    47, 49-50, 54-5, 59-61, 67, 69-77, 81-
    2, 85, 89-90, 97-9, 105, 119-20, 125,
    143, 157, 164-6, 180-1, 183
mass line, 39
mathematics, 6, 103-6, 179
mode of production,
   Asiatic, 2
   capitalist, 33-4, 72, 151-5, 160,
      168, 173-8, 188-9
   feudal, 151, 154-5, 161, 174
   socialist, 3-4, 8-9, 142-3, 150-
      70, 172-3, 193-4, 203
   state, 8
models,
   cyclical, 6, 107-18
   linear, 6, 107-9
   mathematical, 6, 103
modernisation, 15, 20, 35-6, 45, 48-50,
    52, 56, 58, 60, 74, 76-8, 85, 121, 126,
    132, 144-5, 150, 169
money, 8, 124-5, 129, 133, 184, 192,
    194-5
Myers, R., 154

National People's Congress,
   1st of 5th, (1978), 76
   2nd of 5th, (1979), 78, 82
   3rd of 5th, (1980), 78
New   Democracy,   see   People's
   Democratic Dictatorship
Nove, A., 191

Obolensky, L., 179
ontological privilege, 3, 5, 13, 23, 27, 29-
    43, 53, 55, 56, 58-60, 122

Paine, S., 166-7
'people, the', 38-9, 43-4, 48, 57-60, 78-9,
    84, 91-2
People's Democratic Dictatorship, 78,
    84, 86, 90
People's Liberation Army, 92, 168
planning, 6-9, 65, 68, 77-8, 85, 89, 93,
    99-141, 145, 157-9, 164, 166, 171-203
Pol Pot, 98
Polanyi, K., 8, 172
population growth, 138, 146, 180
positivism, 20-3, 32-3, 35, 49, 60, 93
practice, 16, 39-41, 44-7, 53-4, 58-9, 62,
    77-8, 143, 150
   theoretical practice, 3, 21-9, 36,
      39-41, 43, 46-7, 60, 63-4
pragmatism, 77-8
Preobrazhensky, N., 2
prices, 7, 101, 110, 122-3, 126-30, 132-7,
    140, 150, 163, 169, 172, 184-7, 191-4,
    201

problematic, 15-9, 22, 25, 59-60
productivity, 107, 114-7, 123-4, 126, 136,
    145-6, 158-60, 166-7, 192
profits, 65-6, 94, 102, 104, 114, 123-4,
    126-7, 130, 134-5, 156-7, 167, 180,
    185-7, 191-3, 196, 199
property, 96, 181-2, 193, 198-9
Proudhon, P.J., 26, 178, 182, 201

Ramsay, H., 14-19, 21-2, 25, 59-60
rationalism, 2-3, 5, 11, 13-9, 23, 25-7,
    34-5
rationality, 6-9, 15, 86, 121-2, 126-8,
    130, 136, 139-40
Rawski, T., 167
'reality', 1-3, 9, 13-66, 99, 117, 173
reductionism, 3, 14-5, 19, 27, 44, 55, 61,
    96, 107, 121, 139
reflection theory, 19, 24-5, 28-9, 42
relative deprivation, 5, 68, 81, 89, 108
reproduction, simple and expanded, 106,
    133, 187-8, 190-2
'revisionism', 72, 84, 191
revolution,
   bourgeois democratic, 90
   continuous, 4, 11, 50-2, 55, 67, 69,
      71-8, 95, 97, 119
   Cultural, 4, 10-11, 60, 64, 72-5, 80,
      84, 110-1, 120, 144, 157, 168,
      171
   scientific and technical, 4, 51-2, 99,
      107
   uninterrupted, 50-1, 69, 73-6, 97
Ricardo, D., 178, 193
'rightism', 11, 78, 93
Riskin, C., 155
Robinson, J., 193
Rose, B., 146

Saich, T., 79
Sayer, D., 14-19, 21-2, 25, 59-60
'Shanghai school', 72, 74, 120, 196
Schran, P., 161
Shue, V., 161
Sinha, R., 146
Sisler, D., 146
Skocpol, T., 142
Smith, A., 123, 173
socialism,
   advanced, 6, 80, 85, 91, 97, 99-104,
      107, 117, 143-4
   advanced, (Soviet), 91, 99, 101, 107,
      117
   as model, (Stalin, 1936), 4, 8, 57, 59,
      67, 79, 99, 102, 119, 194
   as system, 3-6, 48, 51-2, 67-73, 76-
      89, 96-7, 98, 122
   as mode of production, 8-9, 151-70,
      193-4, 203
   as process, 3-4, 8, 11, 72-3, 98,
      101, 118-20, 193
   undeveloped, 5-6, 8, 69, 80-1, 85, 91,
      97-102, 106, 117, 120, 122,
      125, 135, 140, 143
Solidarity, 128

special economic zones, 87, 93, 125
Spinoza, 28
'spiritual pollution', 2, 85, 93, 202
stability, 7, 49-50, 57, 82, 120, 127-8,
    130, 133, 139-40, 168, 192
Stalin, J., 2-4, 6, 8, 10, 13, 15, 19-20, 27,
    29, 31-2, 35-40, 43-4, 47, 49, 52-5,
    57-61, 67-9, 75, 77, 79, 82, 93, 99,
    102-3, 106, 112, 117, 119, 126, 143,
    148, 150, 168, 179-83, 186, 189, 193-
    4, 197, 199, 202
Su Shaozhi, 2, 80-1, 85, 87, 99, 117
subject, knowing, 3, 27-30, 34, 36-9, 42-
    4, 47, 58-9, 61
Sun Shangqing, 184
Sun Yefang, 9, 133, 171-3, 177, 181-200,
    202-3
surplus extraction, 8-9, 149-51, 153, 158-
    70
Szelenyi, I., 8-9

taxation, 102, 129, 132, 134-5, 139-40,
    150, 162, 167
Taylor, F., 35
technology, 15, 29-38, 43, 48-52, 56-8,
    101, 108, 112-8, 124, 131, 136-7, 174,
    187-8, 192, 201
tectology, 30, 34, 37, 39, 42
telos, 6, 9, 98, 103-4, 106, 117-8, 121,
    128
totality, 4-6, 21, 23, 26, 28, 34, 42, 82,
    178, 190-1
Trotsky, L., 8, 178-80

utopianism, 1, 98, 109
utility, 106, 183

voluntarism, 62, 180, 182
wages, 99-102, 123-4, 126, 128, 145, 149,
    158-9, 168, 174-7, 184, 192, 197-8,
    201
Wagner, A., 21-2, 176
Wan Li, 146-50
Wang Guoping, 99, 101, 117
Wang Haibo, 160, 167
Wang Ruoshi, 11
Wang Shuwen, 96
Wang Zhen, 11
Weber, M., 4, 6-8, 121, 123, 178
Wei Jingsheng, 78
Wen Ping, 187-8
Womack, B., 55
Wu Jiajun, 160, 167
Wu Jiang, 51

Xiang Qiyuan, 198
Xu Dixin, 85-6
Xue Muqiao, 94, 142-6, 148-50, 192,
    194-5
Yaroshenko, L., 99, 189
Ye Jianying, 48-9, 52, 56, 79
Ying Chengwang, 180
You Lin, 54

Zhang Chaozun, 198-9
Zhao Guoliang, 54-5
Zhao Renwei, 196-7, 199

Zhou Enlai, 73-4
Zhou Yang, 10-11

For Product Safety Concerns and Information please contact our EU
representative GPSR@taylorandfrancis.com
Taylor & Francis Verlag GmbH, Kaufingerstraße 24, 80331 München, Germany